Princely States, the Muslim League and the Partition of India

PRINCELY STATES, THE MUSLIM LEAGUE AND THE PARTITION OF INDIA

Col. S.C.Dhiman (Retd.)

NEHA PUBLISHERS & DISTRIBUTORS
DELHI

Publisher
NEHA PUBLISHERS & DISTRIBUTORS
4832/24,Prahlad Lane,S-207 Ansari
Road, Daryaganj, Delhi-110002
Ph.: 43570976, 23278261
Email: nehapubdistributors@gmail.com

Edition: 2023

ISBN: 978-93-80318-69-1

Laser Typesetting
JEE-VEE Graphics, Delhi

Price: 1195/-

Printed
Vikas Computers, Delhi

Contents

Preface

It is possible that Mohammed Ali Jinnah, leader of the Muslim League, simply wished to use the demand for a separate state as a bargaining chip to win greater power for Muslims within a loosely federated India. Certainly, the idea of 'Pakistan' was not thought of until the late 1930s.

One explanation for the chaotic manner in which the two independent nations came into being is the hurried nature of the British withdrawal. This was announced soon after the victory of the Labour Party in the British general election of July 1945, amid the realisation that the British state, devastated by war, could not afford to hold on to its over-extended empire.

For there were more than five hundred Princely States in existence in 1947. Each of these had its own ruler and court, and many had the trappings of fully independent states (such as railroads, CURRENCY, and stamps). All the same, they had to pay significant taxes to the British crown, and none were allowed to maintain their own armies. The Princely States were also, one might add, the most backward in India when it came to the situation of ordinary people. While British India had begun to build schools and universities, and develop the foundations of republican governance, the various Maharajahs were perfectly comfortable keeping their subjects in total, feudal subjection.

The rare piece of the drama "Partition", in 1947 warranted the scholars to rebuild the history of the cunning passages to Muslim separatism in India and the consequent blood bath of the nation.

—Editor

1

Princely States in India

PRINCELY STATES IN BRITISH INDIA

The early history of British expansion in India was characterised by the coexistence of two approaches towards the existing princely states. The first was a policy of annexation, where the British sought to forcibly absorb the Indian princely states into the provinces which constituted their Empire in India.

The second was a policy of indirect rule, where the British assumed suzerainty and paramountcy over princely states, but conceded some degree of sovereignty to them. During the early part of the nineteenth century, the policy of the British tended towards annexation, but the Indian Rebellion of 1857 forced a change in this approach, by demonstrating both the difficulty of absorbing and subduing annexed states, and the usefulness of princely states as a source of support.

In 1858, the policy of annexation was formally renounced, and British relations with the princely states thereafter were based on indirect rule, whereby the British exercised paramountcy over all princely states with the British crown as ultimate suzerain, but at the same time respected and protected them as allies.

The exact relations between the British and each princely state were regulated by individual treaties, and varied widely, with some states having significant autonomy, some being subject to significant control in internal affairs, and some being in effect the owners of a few acres of land with little autonomy.

During the 20th century, the British made several attempts to integrate the princely states more closely with British India, creating the Chamber of Princes in 1921 as a consultative and advisory body, transferring the responsibility for supervision of smaller states from the provinces to the centre in 1936, and creating direct relations between the Government of India and the larger princely states superseding political agents. The most ambitious was a scheme of federation in the Government of India Act 1935, which envisaged the princely states and British India being united under a federal government. This scheme came close to success, but was abandoned in 1939 as a result of the outbreak of the Second World War. As a result, in the 1940s, the relationship between the princely states and the crown remained regulated by the principle of paramountcy and the various treaties between the British crown and the states. Neither paramountcy nor these arrangements could continue after Indian independence. The British took the view that because they had been established directly between the British crown and the princely states, they could not be transferred to independent India. At the same time, they imposed obligations on Britain that it was not prepared to continue to carry out, such as the obligation to maintain troops in India for the defence of the princely states. The British government therefore decided that paramountcy, together with all treaties between them and the princely states, would come to an end upon the transfer of power.

Sikkim

Three princely states bordering India—Nepal, Bhutan and Sikkim—were not integrated into the Republic of India in the period between 1947 and 1950. Nepal had been recognised by the British and the Government of India as being *de jure* independent. Bhutan had in the British period been considered a protectorate outside the international frontier of India. The Government of India entered into a treaty with Bhutan in 1949 continuing this arrangement, and providing that Bhutan would abide by the advice of the Government of India in the conduct of its external affairs.

Historically, Sikkim was a British dependency, with a status similar to that of the other princely states, and was therefore considered to be within the frontiers of India in the colonial period.

On independence, however, the Chogyal of Sikkim resisted full integration into India. Given the region's strategic importance to India, the Government of India signed first a Standstill Agreement and then in 1950 a full treaty with the Chogyal of Sikkim which in effect made it a protectorate which was no longer part of India. India had responsibility for defence, external affairs and communications, and ultimate responsibility for law and order, but Sikkim was otherwise given full internal autonomy.

In the late 1960s and early 1970s, the Chogyal, supported by the minority Bhutia and Lepcha upper classes, attempted to negotiate greater powers, particularly over external affairs, in order to give Sikkim more of an international personality. These policies were opposed by Kazi Lhendup Dorji and the Sikkim State Congress, who represented the ethnic Nepali middle classes and took a more pro-Indian view. In April 1973, an anti-Chogyal agitation broke out; the agitators demanded the conduct of popular elections. The Sikkim police were unable to control the demonstrations, and Dorji asked India to exercise its responsibility for law and order and intervene. India facilitated negotiations between the Chogyal and Dorji, and produced an agreement which envisaged the reduction of the Chogyal to the role of a constitutional monarch and the holding of elections based on a new ethnic power-sharing formula. The Chogyal's opponents won an overwhelming victory, and a new Constitution was drafted providing for Sikkim to be associated with the Republic of India. On 10 April 1975, the Sikkim Assembly passed a resolution calling for the state to be fully integrated into India. This resolution was endorsed by 97% of the vote in a referendum held on 14 April 1975, following which the Indian Government amended the constitution to admit Sikkim into India as its 22nd state.

CRITICAL PERSPECTIVES ON THE PROCESS OF INTEGRATION

The integration process repeatedly brought Indian and Pakistani leaders into conflict. During negotiations, Jinnah, representing the Muslim League, strongly supported the right of the princely states to remain independent, joining neither India nor Pakistan, an attitude which was diametrically opposed to the stance taken by Nehru and the Congress and which was reflected in Pakistan's support of Hyderabad's bid to stay independent. Post-partition, the Government of Pakistan accused India of hypocrisy on the ground that there was little difference between the accession of the ruler of Junagadh to Pakistan—which India refused to recognise—and the accession of the Maharajah of Kashmir to India, and for several years refused to recognise the legality of India's incorporation of Junagadh, treating it as *de jure* Pakistani territory.

Different theories have been proposed to explain the designs of Indian and Pakistani leaders in this period. Rajmohan Gandhi postulates that an ideal deal working in the mind of Patel was that if Muhammad Ali Jinnah let India have Junagadh and Hyderabad, Patel would not object to Kashmir acceding to Pakistan. In his book *Patel: A Life*, Gandhi asserts that Jinnah sought to engage the questions of Junagadh and Hyderabad in the same battle. It is suggested that he wanted India to ask for a plebiscite in Junagadh and Hyderabad, knowing thus that the principle then would have to be applied to Kashmir, where the Muslim-majority would, he believed, vote for Pakistan. A speech by Patel at the Bahauddin College in Junagadh following the latter's take-over, where he said that "we would agree to Kashmir if they agreed to Hyderabad", suggests that he may have been amenable to this idea. Although Patel's opinions were not India's policy, nor were they shared by Nehru, both leaders were angered at Jinnah's courting the princes of Jodhpur, Bhopal and Indore, leading them to take a harder stance on a possible deal with Pakistan.

Modern historians have also re-examined the role of the States Department and Lord Mountbatten during the accession process. Ian Copland argues that the Congress leaders did not intend the settlement contained in the Instruments of Accession to be permanent even when they were signed, and at all times privately contemplated a complete integration of the sort that ensued between 1948 and 1950. He points out that the mergers and cession of powers to the Government of India between 1948 and 1950 contravened the terms of the Instruments of Accession, and were incompatible with the express assurances of internal autonomy and preservation of the princely states which Mountbatten had given the princes.

Menon in his memoirs stated that the changes to the initial terms of accession were in every instance freely consented to by the princes with no element of coercion. Copland disagrees, on the basis that foreign diplomats at the time believed that the princes had been given no choice but to sign, and that a few princes expressed their unhappiness with the arrangements. He also criticises Mountbatten's role, saying that while he stayed within the letter of the law, he was at least under a moral obligation to do something for the princes when it became apparent that the Government of India was going to alter the terms on which accession took place, and that he should never have lent his support to the bargain given that it could not be guaranteed after independence.

Both Copland and Ramusack argue that, in the ultimate analysis, one of the reasons why the princes consented to the demise of their states was that they felt abandoned by the British, and saw themselves as having little other option. Older historians such as Lumby, in contrast, take the view that the princely states could not have survived as independent entities after the transfer of power, and that their demise was inevitable. They therefore view successful integration of all princely states into India as a triumph for the Government of India and Lord Mountbatten, and as a tribute to the sagacity of the majority of princes, who jointly achieved in a few months what the Empire had attempted, unsuccessfully, to do for over a century—unite all of India under one rule.

PRINCELY STATES AND PUNJAB

The partition of Punjab in 1947 is one of the unique events as it enforced the movements of the people on the scale absolutely unparalleled in the history of world. There must be many examples in the bloody history of mankind where the extent of violence has been as great or even greater but it is probably true that there has never been such a huge exchange of population. On Direct Action day August 16, 1946 in Calcutta the violence had begun and it spread to the Bengal countryside resulting into large number of deaths. From there it moved on to Bihar, then on to the United Province and finally to the province of Punjab, where the scale of the violence and the extent of the killing exceeded even the horrors that had preceded it.

According to the fortnightly report of October 1946: Most district officers in Punjab continued to sound a grave note of warning and to say that a situation which is so essentially unstable may deteriorate quickly and dangerously without any adequate warning being given.

Yet another disturbing development during this time was the rapid growth of volunteer forces of various political parties, which were called private armies by the British, and open defiance of law by them in several provinces. There was marked increase in the activities of both the Rashtriya Swayamsevak Sangh (RSS) and the Muslim League National Guards (MLNG) in the Punjab. The strength of the latter had increased from 3,000 at the end of 1945 to 10,000 in July 1946.

The announced aim was to increase it to half a million by the end of 1946. The government of Punjab was of the view that *"both these were trouble-spreading agencies and for this reason and others which are obvious, are potentially very dangerous"*. The working committee of Provincial Muslim League also decided to launch a civil disobedience movement including the non-payment of taxes and revenue, violation of law and order, boycott of non-Muslim traders and the boycott of goods manufactured by the non-Muslims. The government of Punjab was getting increasingly worried about provocative speeches made in Muslim places of worship.

It said: Muslim are being exhorted to be prepared, not for a political campaign, constitutional or otherwise, but for a crusade. It further noted, unfortunately, the Calcutta riots do not seem to have made the communities pause and think of the grave need to avoid further bloodshed. Rather civil war is still accepted as being preferable to the abandonment of any principles and the Calcutta casualties are regarded as little or nothing compared with what is likely to happen if agreement is not reached.

In Punjab by the beginning of 1947, the RSS membership had reached the figure of 47,000 and that of MLNG 23,000. The Sikhs also decided to form *Akal Fauj* or *Sena*. In view of the increasing law and order concern on January 24, 1947, the Government of Punjab banned the Muslim League National Guard (MLNG) and the Rashtriya Swayamsevak Sangh (RSS). The Punjab government had inadvertently offered a challenge to the League without the strength to go through with it. Viceroy Wavell noted in his journal on January 27: *the action taken in the Punjab against the Muslim Guards seems to have raised a storm....* The Muslim League leaders in Punjab seised the opportunity to stir up agitation.

The ban followed routine searches of the offices of the two organisations. Though nothing really objectionable was found, workers who tried to protest and obstruct the raiding parties were arrested on January 25, when they defied a ban on processions and meetings. The League seised the opportunity and organised a massive defiance of the order. Demonstrations were held by Muslim crowds in different parts of the city. In the evening a Muslim crowd staged a demonstration in front of the Civil Lines Police Station where the League leaders were lodged.

However the demonstrators were scattered by the police, resorting to lathi charge, resulting in injuries to over a dozen persons. Khizar Hayat Khan, the Punjab Premier was really in a fix. He said in a communiqué that he had no desire to attack the Muslim League or to arrest its members, but he could not permit deliberate defiance of the ordinary law or of emergency order which had been issued solely to maintain communal peace in the province. Of course, the problems Khizar faced at that time were awful. The Premier headed a non-Muslim Government in a province where a large number of officers and employees were Muslims and had secret or even open sympathy for the League.

An overwhelming number of officers and men in the police force being Muslims, were also more loyal to the League than to the government and thus Jinnah's mass movement received indirect support from all such quarters. Keeping in mind the gravity of these problems, the Premier held a conference on the January 26, with his colleagues to discuss the situation arising out of the ban on the National Guards and also on the RSS. On that day, many Muslim League leaders were released to pacify the Muslim masses. After consultation with his ministers, he issued a statement on the January 28, withdrawing ban on the MLNG and RSS. But he made it clear that the ban on processions and meetings would continue as the government in the present state of situation considered it essential.

He further appealed to the members of all communities to support the Punjab Government in maintaining peace and communal harmony. But, the League leaders were re-arrested on the January 29, 30 and 31, when they indulged in the acts of violence. The Hindu and Sikh papers supported the action taken by the coalition ministry against the Muslim League agitation and held that agitation was unconstitutional, undemocratic and undoubtedly communal. Unfortunately, to the dismay and disappointment of the Punjab government, the British Prime Minister, Lord Attlee's declaration on the February 20, expressing his intention to transfer power to responsible Indian hands by June 1948, emboldened the Muslim League to intensify the struggle in an all out bid to get its demand of Pakistan conceded.

In view of Attlee's declaration, it became more important for the League to oust Sir Khizar Hayat Khan and take the reins of government into its own hands. On February 24, the demonstrations of the League in the Punjab were marked by clashes between the police and demonstrators at Amritsar and Jullundur. In a letter to the King dated February 24, 1947, Wavell had stated that the state of affairs in the Punjab was causing considerable anxiety.

He minded no words when he said: The situation is dangerous, since, the Hindus and Sikhs are getting restive, the rival communities are not unequally balanced, and trouble in the Punjab is likely to take violent forms.

Jenkins was also of the view that: On a long view the Punjab Muslims have already done themselves incalculable harm by their disregard of the very large non-Muslim communities.

The report also cited that Sikh leader Master Tara Singh for the first time said that Sikhs were organising their own army in response to the challenges given by MLNG. Under the influence of communal bugbear and the Muslim League politics, the Premier Khizar Hayat Khan felt so helpless that he resigned from the Premiership on the March 2, without even consulting his non-Muslim colleagues.

On the same day, he announced that he was taking this step because he felt that His Majesty's government pronouncement of the February 20, made it incumbent on him to leave the field clear for the Muslim League to come to some agreement with other parties. Meanwhile, the Nawab of Mamdot expressed his desire before the Governor to permit him for the formation of Muslim League ministry in Punjab.

Demonstrations were taken out by non-Muslims to mark their protests against the proposed League Ministry which culminated in a riot situation in the same evening.

The Governor found that he could not allow a purely Muslim League ministry, without any support whatever from Hindus and Sikhs, to be formed in the Punjab. The Muslim league having lost the confidence of Hindus and Sikhs due to its past conduct of several years and its creed of hate and violence, got no support from them. The Governor suspended the constitution and the Punjab from March 5, 1947 was to be governed directly by the Governor under Section 93 of the Government of India Act.

Just as Punjab was rapidly being overrun by violence, Jenkins (Punjab's Governor) noted the specific reasons of why a League ministry was not possible at that point: Private information suggests that Mamdot commands only three votes outside the League including, Muslim and two Scheduled Castes. Risk of installing a League Ministry of this kind with parliamentary majority is enormous... (and would) be a fraud on the constitution.

Jenkins then pointed out how the installation of a League Ministry was bound to be opposed by the Sikhs and Hindus and how police troops and myself (the British) would immediately be involved on the Muslims side in what would in fact be a civil war for possession of Punjab. In 1947, Muslims and non-Muslims in West Punjab, East Punjab and Princely States according to 1941 census were as under:

	Districts or States	Percentage in Total Population of		
	Districts of East Punjab	Muslims	Sikhs	Rest
1.	Hissar	28.2	6.0	64.8
2.	Rohtak	17.2	0.1	81.7
3.	Gurgaon	33.	5..	66.8
4.	Karnal	30.6	2.0	67.0
5.	Ambala	31.6	18.4	48.7
6.	Simla	18.2	2.7	74.3
7.	Kangra	5.1	0.6	94.3
8.	Hoshiarpur	32.5	16.9	49.8
9.	Jullundur	45.2	26.4	27.6
10.	Ludhiana	36.9	41.7	21.4
11.	Ferozepur	45.1	33.7	20.2
12.	Amritsar	46.5	36.1	15.4
13.	Gurdaspur	50.2	19.1	25.2

	East Punjab States	Muslims	Sikhs	Rest
1.	Kapurthala	56.4	25.9	16.3
2.	Faridkot	30.7	57.7	10.9
3.	Patiala	22.6	47.3	30.9
4.	Jind	14.1	11.3	74.2
5.	Nabha	20.7	36.0	42.9

	Districts of West Punjab	Muslims	Sikhs	Rest
1.	Lahore	60.7	18.3	16.8
2.	Sialkot	62.1	11.7	19.4
3.	Gujranwala	70.4	10.9	11.9
4.	Sheikhupura	63.6	18.9	10.5
5.	Gujrat	85.6	6.4	7.7
6.	Shahpur	83.7	4.8	10.2

7.	Jhelum	89.5	3.9	6.5
8.	Rawalpindi	80.0	8.2	10.5
9.	Attock	90.5	3.0	6.4
10.	Mianwali	86.2	1.4	12.4
11.	Montgomery	69.1	13.9	15.9
12.	Lyallpur	62.8	18.8	14.6
13.	Jhang	82.6	1.5	15.8
14.	Multan	78.0	4.2	16.9
15.	Muzaffargarh	86.5	0.8	12.8
16.	Dera- Ghazi Khan	88.9	0.2	11.7

Riots broke out in Lahore on March 4. The Hindu and Sikh Students of Lahore took out a big procession to demonstrate their resolve not to tolerate a Muslim league ministry. This perfectly non- violent procession was fired on by the Muslim police, which had stood hooliganism and law breaking from Muslim mobs for over a month in the province. In this firing on procession of Hindus and Sikhs, 125 were injured and 10 were killed. On March 5, under the leadership of Master Tara Singh, Sikhs, Hindus and the Congressmen got united on the same front. He appealed to every Sikh and Hindu to rise against the occasion and be ready for supreme sacrifice.

The Sikh, Hindu and the Congressmen gathered and fixed March 11, 1947 as *'Anti-Pakistan Day'* when flag will be hoisted, hartal observed and public meetings held. By the morning of March 5, the major towns across Punjab including Amritsar, Jullundur, Rawalpindi, Multan and Sialkot were up in flames. Most North and West bound trains out of Lahore were cancelled. The sale of petrol and diesel was banned in many cities of Punjab. Outgoing phone calls and telegrams from Lahore too were banned. In district Gujarat Muslim mob started murdering, burning, raping, looting and abduction. The Lyallpur which was a richest spot the Sikhs possessed in the Punjab, also affected with riots.

The March disturbances had rocked the very foundations of Punjab but it was Rawalpindi that suffered most. The story of Rawalpindi district killings was most brutal and inhuman the world has ever witnessed anywhere on the surface of the earth. Sikhs were murdered by Muslim gangs in the villages including Thamali, Doberan and Choa Khalsa. On the March 5, 1947 on hearing of the firing on the Hindu and Sikh students of Lahore, the Hindu-Sikh students of Rawalpindi took out a procession protesting against the Muslim attempt at the formation of a communal ministry in the Punjab, and the police firing the non-violent procession of Hindu and Sikh students. There were a free fight in which the Muslims got the worst of it.

Then a huge Muslim mob from the countryside, incited for attack on Hindu and Sikhs by the *Pir* of Gojra, a Muslim religious head and a leader of this area. Young women were molested and raped in open, frenzied hooligans were looting and setting fire to houses. While Punjab was burning, the Congress Working Committee ultimately decided to divide the State of Punjab on communal lines on the basis of two nation theory. On March 8, the Congress working Committee concluded its session adopting the resolution on political situation.

The draft of the Resolution to divide the Punjab prepared by Nehru. Nehru wrote two letters to Wavell on the day after the crucial CWC meeting. In one of the letters he announced the Resolution a having been passed by the CWC. He also referred to the possible division of Punjab in case the League continued to stay away from the Constituent Assembly. The resolution added that the violence had demonstrated that a way out to be found that would involve 'The least amount of compulsion'. This would necessitate a division of Punjab into two provinces, so that the predominantly Muslim part may be separated from the predominantly non-Muslim part. Upto March 11, 9000 houses were destroyed and loss of property estimated to rupees 8 crore.

On March 13, conditions in both Rawalpindi and Attock districts outside the main town were still very much unsettled. On March 14, reports were received of riots, arson and murder from village in Chakwal tehsil in Jhelum district. Dhudial was attacked by a mob of 2500 men, a grim exchange of fire took place between the looters and army stationed there. In the end the army was able to evacuate most of the people of Dhudial to safer places. The narration of atrocities by district officers to Nehru and Liaquat Ali on the joint tour of several districts of East and West Punjab were unnerving.

Nehru after going through their stories of violence remarked: I think the disturbances will end completely within a few days.... A man who is panickly is a useless citisen and a danger to others... all that has happened is intimately connected with political affairs.... The Punjab has had a lesson, let it learn from it."

But the Governor Jenkins was not happy with his tour. He wrote to the viceroy and said that political leaders particularly members of the Interim Government were putting a great strain on the administration by their travels in Punjab. The complaint did not mention Nehru by name, but the fact that the letter to Wavell followed almost immediately after Nehru had visited Punjab and that some journalists too had been touring Punjab at the time possibly indicated that the Government was not too keen to see Nehru in this part of country. In fact, Nehru had met Jenkins in Lahore on March 14, and even as the meeting was on, a message was received at Government house, Lahore from the Viceroy for Nehru requesting, him not to visit Peshawar.

Nehru agreed not to go, but only grudgingly. There had been numerous complaints across Punjab against officials of the Punjab police who were said to be under the Muslim League's influence. One police official in Multan even brought along camels to take away looted goods. Not a single temple remained in the vicinity of Rawalpindi and Multan. Punjab had become the 'Ulster of India'. In March 1947, over 18,000 troops, in addition to two squadrons of Air Force and Parachute, were in action to suppress communal violence in Punjab. Penderal Moon observed, "*What had been seen in Punjab in March 1947 was only a curtain raiser. The main tragedy was still to come.*" By April 13, over 8,000 arrests had been made in Multan alone.

The government initiate many measures, one was its old and tried method of collective fines. A fine of ₹ 10 lakh was imposed within the Municipal limits of Multan. Those families who had lost members as killed or suffered serious damage of property were exempted. On May 14, in Lahore, 9 persons were killed and

20 injured. On May 19, 1947, the early hours of Sunday, saw most serious incidents which had taken place in Lahore since, disturbance took place on May 14. The entire province of Punjab had declared a disturbed area on May 31, 1947.

The tension in the Punjab at the end of May and in the beginning of June was so acute that most people kept a night vigil on housetops, or slept with their hands on the trigger of the pistol under the pillow. Lord Mountbatten sensed this tension, not only did he increase military precautions in the tense districts, but he arranged broadcasts from Nehru, Jinnah and Baldev Singh appealing of peace and communal harmony. On June 23, the communal situation in Lahore was worst with widespread arson, bomb explosions, life in the city being completely paralysed, firing by troops and mobs running amuck to kill people of different religion. The NWFP too was declared a 'disturbed area' with the Governor and the leaders of political parties making an appeal for peace. On June 23, the Punjab Legislative Assembly adopted a resolution in favour of the partition.

The partition committee gave way to a more powerful Partition Council and latter agreed to invite Sir Cyril Radcliffe to become Chairman of the Boundary Commission. In the beginning of July 1947, Sir Cyril Radcliffe arrived in Delhi to demarcate boundaries. His only qualification was that he did not know anything of Indian reality. In July attacks on the life and property of Hindus and Sikhs were going on as usual. Gujranwala, Sargodha and Sialkot too had started in right earnest the process of the elimination of minorities. In his visit to Lahore on July 20, Mountbatten was told that 50 per cent of the Hindu population were believed to have left the city. By the beginning of August there were 80,000 refugees in Delhi itself.

It has been estimated that nearly 21 lakhs of Muslim refugees had move into West Punjab since, August 1, 1947, and during the same period 20 lakhs of non-Muslims had left for East Punjab. In the beginning of August 1947 rioting broke out all over the Punjab and situation worsened as the date of transfer of power drew nearer. The Pakistan Government subsequently brought a number of brochures to prove that mainly the Sikhs were responsible for these riots. It was argued that in order to carve out their state, the Sikhs had plans to kill Muslims in an organised manners.

It has been estimated that nearly 21 lakhs of Muslim refugees had moved into West Punjab since, August 1, 1947, and during the same period 20 lakhs of non-Muslims had left for East Punjab. Nehru sent a telegram to Liaquat Ali Khan on August 9, 1947, expressing his anxiety at the rapidly deteriorating situation in West Punjab. He referred to the happenings in the previous week in Gujaranwala, Wazirabad and Lahore. As the date on which Pakistan was to be established that was August 15, was drawing nearer Muslims everywhere in the Muslim majority districts and in some places even in the East were growing aggressive.

With the line of demarcation between Eastern and Western Punjab still unknown and uncertain Muslims of districts like Amritsar, Jullundur and Ferozepur held strong hopes of these districts or anyway some portions of them, being awarded to Pakistan. The attitude with which the Muslims looked upon non-Muslims was that the latter were to be held by them as a subservient people from whom a less than human treatment would just be good enough.

Shri Kiron Shankar Roy, the well known leader of Bengal, in a statement to the press on July 22 said about the temper of East Bengal Muslims: There is a notion among ordinary Muslims in the Eastern Pakistan region that after August 15 houses and land of the Hindus will automatically pass into the possession of Muslims, and that the Hindus will be a sort subject race under the Muslims of that area.

What Mr. Roy said about the Muslims of Bengal, applied with still greater force to the Muslims of the Punjab, about whom the *Civil and Military Gazette* of Lahore said in its issue of the December 30, 1947 that each one of them thought that he had become a *Nawab*. After August 12-15, people started migrating from West towards East Punjab and the Muslims towards the West Punjab. Causes of mass migration were many; some writers are of the view that Sikhs and Hindus left Pakistan in order to cripple it economically as they held important positions in the west Punjab.... L.F. Rushbrook William writes that in Lahore and Lyallpur exodus not only concentrated of men of substance but also clerks and minor officials.

Even prosperous Sikh farmers said to have left their land on assurance that they would be able to return within six weeks. But the west Punjab government was determined to drive them out. Giani Kartar Singh stated that Jinnah had instructed the Governor of west Punjab to expel all the Sikhs from Pakistan. This was confirmed by the letter Sir Francis Mudie (Governor, West Punjab) addressed to Jinnah and interpreted by the East Punjab police. Sir Mudie frankly declared that he was telling everyone not to care how the Sikhs get across the border, the great thing was to get rid of them as soon as possible. The Muslim refugees in order to avail themselves of houses and business of the non-Muslims created panic and disorder to turn out Hindus and Sikhs. On August 14, Pakistan was officially born.

The advent of Pakistan was signalled by hundreds of fires raging in various parts of the city. The Punjab situation was getting worse. There were deserted tracts and town in West Punjab for miles and miles and town after town, the entire countryside from Lahore to Gujranwala lying along the G.T. Road presented a picture of desolation, smouldering ruins, empty houses and closed shops. In the last days of August, Nehru and Liaquat Ali Khan decided to fly to Lyallpur and Lahore to study the refugee problem. When the first wave of blind violence had passed in the West Punjab, the lure of loot was the chief motive for violence; calculated homicide succeeded indiscriminate violence, it was no longer a fanatic's leap in the dask but an adventurer's firm foothold on a house, a shop, or a factory.

In his book An Australian in India, Mr. Casey, the ex-Governor of Bengal, writes: In other words I believe that the principal present day motive behind Pakistan is the economic urge on the part of the Muslims (particularly in the cities) to advance themselves economically.... I believe that when the Muslims in a village or a small town think of Pakistan, they think in terms of the little village or town store being owned by a Muslim and not by a Hindu. When the city Muslims think of Pakistan, I believe he thinks largely in terms of the mills and shops and business houses being owned by Muslims instead of by Hindus.... But the fact remains that Pakistan or no Pakistan, Hindus and Muslims have got to continue to live together.... Pakistan would not result in the village store being owned by a Muslim. It would not put the mills and the business houses into Muslim hands. The only way Muslims can advance themselves economically is to achieve education, and to learn how to complete successfully with the Hindus, which means a vast amount of hard work and the passage of time. It can not be achieved by political means."

It must be admitted that the milk of human kindness did not dry up all at once. *There were extraordinary instances where neighbourly attachment was not shaken by popular passion or even the fear of the mob. J. Nanda wrote*: I have feared of men and women who were hidden under haystacks or cold ovens by kind neighbours. I can picture the scene when the hooligans arrived to check-up; the beating hearts in the oven and the hay stack must have stilled as the assassins suspiciously scored the place for the 'condemned' men; the protectors, perhaps a little pale, are likely to have put on a considerable amount of bravado and righteous indignation at not being taken at their word. Such steadfastness was, however, the exception because the hooligans were better organised and better armed than the majority of peaceful citisens in villages and towns; neighbours are generally kind folks but not of the stud from which martyrs are made."

Some raiding parties brought camels, donkeys and carts to carry off the booty Inevitably, old personal scores were paid off in a few cases, but as a rule the raid on the minority of a village was not made by the majority community of the same village, but of a different village. In the district of Western Punjab it was not uncommon for a false alarm to be raised in the villages that a Sikh band (*Jatha*) was around the corner; and this alarm signal was doubly useful in collecting women and children in one place and in forming the male adults into a party for raiding villages in the vicinity. At Lahore on September 25, a Muslim mob of several thousand strong, attacked a Sikh-Hindu refugees train at Kamoke, about 25 miles west of Lahore killing 340 Sikhs and Hindus and wounding 250. About 1000 abducted women were recovered from

Sheikhupura district by military evacuation. On October 1, a convoy of lorries from Lakki to Bannu were attacked. Attack on Muslim columns, 9 miles west of Amritsar and a Hindu and Sikh refugee camp at Tandianwala (Lyallpur) were the main incidents reported by the military spokesman.

Nearly 115 refugees had been killed, 45 wounded in the attack at Tandianwala. Penedral Moon had pointed, on the whole, a somewhat rosy picture of situation in Bahawalpur state, adjoining Punjab because, *"we escaped the worst scenes of misery."* But this assessment was not shared by the Hindus and Sikhs. Neogy, Minister for rehabilitation, told to Constituent Assembly of India (CAIL) on November 18, 1947 that, "a rough estimate of migration from Bahawalpur is 80,000". During the debate on refugee matters repeated pleas were made by the members to the government to take speedy measures to ensure early evacuation of refugees from that state.

In October 1947, the refugee population from West Punjab in Indian camps was well over 7,20,000. On October 3, 1947, according to the government's report following number of refugees were awaiting for evacuation. Hindus and Sikhs:

Rawalpindi	3,66,500	Muzaffargarh	1,05,000
Sargodha	32,500	Dera Ghazi Khan	50,000
Sialkot	90,000	Multan	1,48,000
Gujranwala	32,000	Montgomery	8,500
Sheikhupura	2,59,600	Lyallpur	1,67,500
Jhang	59,000	Lahore	8,000

After the resignation of Khizar Hyat Khan, riots broke up in United Punjab's two main cities – Lahore and Amritsar. Amritsar was the main affected city from March onwards. It faced huge communal massacres in its inner area. This was the second most populous and commercially developed city after Lahore of the colonial Punjab. From March to August 1947, it experienced endemic communal conflict. The Muslim League's six week agitation from January 24, 1947 ostensibly in the name of civil liberties, but in reality designed to unseat the Unionist coalition government heightened communal tension in Amritsar. This had already been raised by the election campaign which the Muslim League had presented as a referendum on Pakistan. The death of a Sikh constable in the city on February 24, led the Akali leader Master Tara Singh to claim that the Muslim League was fighting a communal, rather than a political campaign. Rioting begun in Amritsar on March 5, and rapidly became more serious than Lahore. By the evening of March 6, the city was completely out of control. The SGPC report blames the Muslims.

It was in Chowk Moni in Hall Bazaar that the first Sikh, Bhai Mangal Singh got killed. The report maintains that Muslims from the neighbouring areas congregated at the Khair-ud-Din Mosque and at the nearby MAO College before setting fire to Hindus and Sikh shops in the Hall Bazaar and the adjoining Katra Jaimal Singh. Students and the Muslim National Guards organisation which boosted some 8,000 numbers played a leading role in orchestrating the violence. Weapons were stockpiled in Muslim schools and colleges, notably at MAO College and at the textile mills of such notables as Shiekh Sadiq Hasan, the President of the Amritsar District Muslim League.

In his report dated March 7, to Wavell, Jenkins (Governor) gave horrendous accounts of communal conflagration in Amritsar: By the evening of March 6, the city was completely out of control. There was some difficulty in securing reinforcements. We also so tied up now that neither the area commander nor I wish to commit reserves until we are quite sure about the need for committing them. The death toll does not seem to be very high. Most of the population seem to have produced arms, including fire-arms, and many buildings are burning. Masses of people, including many women and children, running away from the city added to the confusion with the looting.

Peace was restored only after British, Gurkha and Indian troops were deployed in the region. On April 11, reported a clash between Muslims and Sikhs outside the ruins of the Chowk Pragdas mosque in Amritsar in which nineteen persons were killed and more than sixty injured. The aim of the communal war of succession in both Lahore and Amritsar was to make it impossible for a rival community to continue living in a territory claimed for the majority. On March 6, nine cases of stabbing were also reported from Ludhiana. After this extensive police patrolling took place during the night with a curfew from 6 p.m. to 7 a.m. Companies of troops were sent to Ludhiana, to control the situation. The curfew extended for one week.

The superintendent of police visited a number of villages to re-assure the population. Jullundur was also highly affected by communal riots. On March 6, a large Muslim mob gathered, shouting slogans and molesting individual Hindus and Sikhs, though as yet no widespread attacks had begun. Babu Labh Singh (former President of Akali Dal) appeared among Muslims requesting them with folded hands to keep away from fighting and try to save Punjab from destruction. This appeal fell flat on Muslims, who continued their shouting and attacks, and stabbed Babu Labh Singh to death. His murder sent a wave of horror among the Hindus and Sikhs of Jullundur and the situation became tense. Incidents of loot and murder took place.

The Governor of Punjab accompanied with Inspector General, visited the Northern areas of Jullundur, withstand by order to military to meet any emergency. He underlined that in the past, communal trouble had seldom occurred in two important places at the same time Lahore and Amritsar. He also brought out two special factors in these riots. The first was that the Sikhs were likely to retaliate for the losses they had suffered when they were taken unaware. The second was the Congress Working Committee's resolution demanding the partition of the Punjab which was likely to be treated as an affront by the Muslims. In the northern Mewat, the trouble started about March 26, when some Meos stole a buffalo from Nurpur, a Hindu Ahir Village. When they recovered buffalo, they were attacked by the Meos, on their way back. On March 29, Hindus assembled in large number near Hasanpur.

An attempt to hold a *Panchayat* on March 30, failed and burnt the Gujar village of Koha Khandelwala. Next day the Hindus retaliated by burning four Meo villages – Sakatpur, Ghairatpur, Dehri and Gangani. On the April 1, the Meos responded by burning Badgujar, Bisal, Akabarpur, Kharki and Baghanki. Up to the point all villagers had been evacuated before being burnt. By the end of April, over 50,000 refugees had reached Haridwar and every major railway station in East Punjab bore the look of a refugee township. Shortage of food and clothing and lack of sanitation were acute. Before the national boundaries were drawn, Hindus and Sikhs had starting leaving the areas that had witnessed the worst violence.

It was about this time (May, 1947), that the Hindus and Sikhs in Amritsar and Lahore began to hit back. Sikhs made no attempt to conceal their warlike preparations. Master Tara Singh was exhorting his followers to go out Smite the Amalekites. In one of the speeches in the Golden Temple at Amritsar, he declared, *'remember Rawalpindi: revenge our people: spare no one who stands in the way of Sikh rights in our land'*. Inflammatory leaflets were being distributed and instructions sent to various Sikh communities to prepare themselves for action. Trains were to be attacked, the headworks of the canals dynamited, refugees ambushed and Muslims were to be driven from their homes.

Michael Edwards was in the Punjab at that time and when he was passing through a village a few miles from Amritsar, he was actually invited to watch assemblage of about three hundred Sikhs drilling with rifles and tommy guns. In April and May, 1947, Michael Edwards, saw the actual spots of trouble of Northern India but also some of these places which were as yet untouched by the spectre of communal violence. He saw armouries of weapon some stolen, some bought, some manufactured in secret workshops. In one place, he even saw light artillery, mortars and a small tank. Some of the Princes were engaged in increasing the strength of the state forces and not only for the purpose of defending themselves. The Commissioner, Ambala Division, reported on June 10, that, strength of the troops... (was) inadequate to deal with armed bands roaming about the district. On July 10, armed gang attacked villagers in Ferozpure. Seven persons were killed and 4 seriously injured in village of Tarewala as a result of attack of 19 persons armed with guns, pistol and spears.

Garhshankar in Hoshiarpur saw a major communal clash on July 19, leading to 20 deaths. It started when a women of one community was abducted, leading to retailiation from the other side. By the beginning of August, there were 80,000 refugees in Delhi itself. In the UP, no less than thirty three out of the forty-nine districts had reported influx of refugees numbering over 100,000. Thousands of others had found temporary homes in the towns and villages in East Punjab.

In his letter dated August 15, 1947 to Jinnah, Mudie (Governor of West Punjab) wrote: "A serious incident is reported from the Gurdaspur-Sialkot border, where Muslims attacked a train and are said to have killed 100 Hindus and Sikhs..."

At the joint defence council meeting Nehru raised his concern as to why the trains were being attacked despite being provided with a military escort. Auchinleck (Commander-in-Chief Field Martial) described the *modus operandi* of the gangs as either entering the train on a station and then attacking suddenly, *"or put one man on the train to pull the chain at the spot where the rest of the gang was ready."* Auchinleck said that protection of railways was imposing a heavy strain on the troops. In the Jullundur, Hoshairpur and Gurdaspur rural areas the situation had deteriorated.

August 15 was strongly celebrated in the Punjab, during the afternoon a Sikh mob paraded a number of Muslim women naked through streets of Amritsar, raped them and then hacked some of them to pieces with Kirpans and burnt the other alive..." Wolpert had stated: In and around Amritsar, bands of armed Sikhs killed every Muslim they could find, while in and around Lahore, Muslim gangs sharpened their knives and emptied their guns at Hindus and Sikhs. Entire trainloads of refugees were gutted and turned into rolling coffins, funeral pyres on wheel, food for bloated vultures who darkened the skies over the Punjab and were sated with more flesh and blood in those final weeks of August than their ancestors had enjoyed in a century.

According to Penderal Moon casualties in the East Punjab were heavier than the West Punjab. Though the Radcliffe Award was ready on August 9, 1947, the government withhold it to avoid repercussions and responsibility. Sir Cyril Radcliffe left India on August 15, and the Award was published on August 17, 1947. This also enhanced violence. On August 17, the Prime Ministers of

India and Pakistan met at Ambala to bring peace, order and security to the Punjab and made joint appeal for peace.

Ian Morrison, who had previously been its war correspondent in North America, Burma and elsewhere, after his tour of about three weeks in riot affected areas in the Punjab, sent the following cable to his newspaper on August 24, 1947: More horrible than anything we saw during the war is the universal comment of experienced officers, British and Indian on the present slaughter in East Punjab. The Sikhs are clearing East Punjab of Muslims, butchering hundreds daily, forcing thousands to flee westwards burning Muslim villages and homesteads, even in their frenzy levels of Sikh leadership, and it is being done systematically, sector by sector. Some large towns like Amritsar are quarter, because there are no Muslim left. In a two hours air reconnaissance of the Jullundur district at the week-end I must have seen 50 villages aflame.... The Sikh Jathas, armed mobs from 50 to 100 strong, assemble usually in the Gurdwaras, their place of worship, before making a series of raids.

Towards the end of August, a camp for about six thousand Muslims was set up in Hansi, district Hissar which was attacked by *Jats, Rajputs* and *Banias*. It resulted in heavy loss of Muslim life. There were several attacks on trains between Jullundur, Ludhiana and Rajpura. It will be remembered that by this time Sikhs had become the special targets of Muslims attacks in the West Punjab. A Sikh was not safe anywhere and was killed at sight. On August 31, Patel went to Jullundur in a bid to protect and evacuate East Punjab Muslims. In his letter to Nehru the next day, he wrote, *Both on my onward and return journeys, I saw several villages on this side of the Sutlej in flames*. In the beginning of September, the ethnic cleansing had reached gigantic proportions. The number of refugees crossing the border daily was between 100,000 and 150,000. He blamed the Sikhs particularly for this mass migration. On September 25, situation in the East Punjab again worsened. From Alwar state, 45,000 Muslims started their journey to Lahore by train. In the way, 3000 Muslims were mercilessly killed. In Gurdaspur district a village was attacked by a Muslim mob, including men in police uniform. Several looters were arrested in Hoshiarpur.

A refugee camp was attacked between Doraha and Sahnewal. The escort shot dead about 150 attackers, two subinspectors were suspended for failing to protect Muslim refugees in Ferozepur district. A large number of illicit weapons were recovered at Karnal district. After the communal broke up of the provincial services the police force in East Punjab had divided from 17000 to 3000. It could not protect refugee camps like the one at Kurukshetra with 2,70,000 refugees from Pakistan. The movement of Hindu and Sikh refugees coming on foot from Pakistan to India had been seriously affected by the floods that had breached roads and damaged bridges.

Nearly 2100 Hindus and Sikhs were brought to Amritsar from Khanewal and 100 Muslim refugees left Beas on October 3. On October 12, 1947 Lady Mountbatten concluded her two days tour in the East Punjab. She saw herself the pitiable state of sufferers coming from Pakistan.

At the indo-Pakistan borders, she complained to the Pakistan authorities of searches carried on and properly snatched by them. She learnt that Muslims from across Pakistan side made 27 raids and 16 minor attacks on Indian villages with the help of Pakistan police, army and national guards. On October 13, about 500 Sikh and Hindu refugee were killed out of the convoy of 2400 refugees bound for the East Punjab. On 1 week of October, an attack was made on a Muslim foot convoy in Ferozepur. Casualties were 500 and 1000.

The Government of Punjab by its telegram dated October 23, 1947, conveyed their anxiety to Government of India at the increasing number of reports of Muslim passengers being thrown out of trains on Bina-Katni and Jhansi-Itarsi railway lines. In four days (22-23 September), 2700 Muslims and 600 non-Muslims were killed or injured in railway trains alone. In his reply to the debate in CAIL, N. Gopalaswamy Ayyangar, minister without Portfolio, said that on the October 20, 1947, about 28 lakh Muslims were in India awaiting evacuation and about 11 lakh non-Mulsims had to be brought over to India from West Punjab and the NWFP. In the first ten days period from October 21-31, 6 lakh Muslims entered India.

From November 1-10, 6.5 lakh Muslims entered Pakistan and 1.3 lakh non-Muslims entered India. Such massive movement continued and by about November 25, the balance that remained to be moved was about 4 lakh Muslims from India and about three lakh non-Muslims from Pakistan. This insubordination was greatly fuelled by a complete breakdown in the communications network. So bad was it that in many cases orders from state headquarters could not be conveyed even by Deputy Commissioners. Ch. Lehri Singh, Food Minister of East Punjab said that, "*Smooth working was impossible because of the practical non-existence of communications, particularly the telephone network*".

It was only around the first week of November that telephone calls from Simla could be put through to Amritsar. A transmitter of the All India radio became operational in Jullundur from November 1. Interestingly on many occasions the government of East Punjab began conveying orders to its field officers through the radio, with officers being instructed to keep their sets tuned for messages between regular radio programmes. Governor Trivedi even believed that one fallout of the poor communications was that peace appeals made by senior leaders did not reach the grass-roots workers in time. Reports of looting by the police and other officers were routine. Jogendar Singh, sub-inspector of police, Beas Police Station was arrested by SP, Amritsar, Ch. Ram Singh, for possessing vast amounts of looted goods. While participating in a debate in the East Punjab Legislative Assembly, Sardar Sajjan Singh remarked that, *there was hardly a policeman in entire Amritsar district, except one head constable who had not been a party to loot.*

It was only after the present SP Ch. Ram Singh (came) that things had changed. Among the Amritsar police, there was another problem which, in fact led Governor Trivedi to initiate a special drive to overhaul it. The problem was that over 70 per cent of the Amritsar force had been Muslim, who to the last man had left East Punjab. These vacancies were filled by people who came from the Western Punjab districts, many of whom as chance would have it had suffered personal tragedies. As a result they were filled with hatred and a desire for revenge and therefore rarely lost an opportunity to loot Muslim property or even facilitate attacks on

Muslims. It was only towards the end of November 1947 that Swaran Singh, Home Minister of East Punjab, could declare in a press conference that there was complete peace in East Punjab. *Any man can go about anywhere in East Punjab without any escort or fear.*

We have fully recovered from the shock of partition and our administration is now well tuned. He said (of the thirty-two lakh non-Muslims in West Punjab and NWFP) only 2,58,000 Hindus and Sikh evacuees were left in West Punjab. Some of them desired evacuation and some did not. He emphasised that no one will be forced to evacuate in spite of the formal decision for total exchange of population between the two Punjab.

The Governor of East Punjab assured that evacuation would be over by the end of November 1947. A broadcasting station started functioning in Jullundur on November 1, 1947, followed by a relay station in Amritsar thereafter. All schools and colleges in East Punjab reopened on November 17, 1947. Princely states also faced the disaster of partition violence. *The Dawn* in an article addressed to the Viceroy, reported that the state of Faridkot had distributed over 1,000 firearms to the Sikhs in the state and that every Sikh household had been adequately fortified.

The report said that the ruler had done this in the belief that the exist of the British would be followed by chaos in the region, during the course of which the lands of weaker neighbours could be grabbed as had happened in the 19 century. In Patiala state, Muslim population of the state was 1/3, which had been virtually rather wiped out or had been expelled out. In the city, on August 15, 500 rioters including police and troops in uniform attacked Mohalla Kucha Rangrazan and killed 1000 Muslims. Muslims took refuge in Bahadurgarh Fort numbering 23,000. Nearly 14,000 Muslims had been butchered in Patiala state. The number of refugees in other was as such: Dera Bassi camp - 15,000, Sirhind – 60,000, Samana – 10,000, Talwandi – 10,000 and Nauli – 40,000. Out of total Muslim population of 4,36,539 nearly 1,88,000 Muslims shifted to the refugee camps.

A large number of Muslim girls were forcibly married. On August 22, City Muslim League President of Ludhiana reported that at Doraha Railway Station, UP-Bombay Express had detained on August 21, by Sikhs. About one thousand Muslims were attacked and butchered with swords and Bhalas. But when enquires were made by the state these allegations proved false and baseless, and made to calculate to execute communal bitterness. Again City Muslim League President of Bhatinda reported that in Tappa Mandi, a general massacre of Muslims had taken place and in Patiala five Muslims had murdered at Railway Station on 25 August. In reaction the State Government imposed a 24-hour curfew. Yadwinder Singh was worried about these incidents.

He wrote to Patel: "As regards minorities I have assured them many times that their interests will be safeguarded and they shall be protected but what are we to do with certain people or groups who always want to create mischief and want nothing settled".

On August 29, Ghazanfar Ali expressed anxiety to Patel: "Over the reported murder of Muslims and loot and arson in Patiala between Rajpura and Ludhiana and Rajpura and Bhatinda requested Maharaja to take necessary steps to end the upheaval".

But in response Maharaja Patiala stated that allegations of extensive loot, arson and murder in Patiala state territory grossly exaggerated. Maharaja added that every effort being made to protect life and property of Muslims but our endeavours greatly handicapped by gruesome stories of Muslim atrocities on minorities in West Punjab brought by refugees and coming otherwise. To protect the Muslims, State deployed army to travel with the trains running between Ambala and Bhatinda. In September, the Patiala State Government issued a press communiqué It said that communal disturbances broke out in certain parts of Patiala state and city proper, where the situation took a turn for the worse. On September 3, Sikhs decorated a special train with Pakistan flags and picked up thousands of Muslims under pretension for the Pakistan.

Armed military Sikhs attacked train at Fatehgarh station and killed many. A few survivors escaped through the dead bodies, and reached Karachi. Though the authorities took all precautions and imposed curfew and military patrolling to prevent communal clashes yet certain elements got out of control. The military had to open fire on several armed groups. As a result of widespread rioting and military action several hundred persons were killed and wounded. Patiala state forces also sustained casualties.

It was decided that small pockets of one community should be segregated to places predominantly inhabited by their own community.

This was execute by the military authorities, with the result that no further loss of life and property was reported. In the 2 week of September, Maharaja Patiala issued ordinance in Punjab States Banning Assembly of more than five armed persons and giving authority to escorts both army and police whether of Indian or East Punjab States to shoot those who contravene this regulation. Of the total of 24,000 Muslims, nearly 18,000 were evacuated to Bahadurgarph fort, where a refugee camp was opened under military guard. Arrangements for free board and lodging were provided by the state. More than 2000 persons left Patiala on their own.

A few reported missing. A Pakistan special was attacked by a Sikh armed band near Sirhind on September 21. On October 10, a refugee train carrying mostly Muslim Kashmiri collies was attacked near Koti Railway Station, 5 miles from Kalka, 5 Muslim men were killed and 25 were missing. In retaliation Muslim from Malerkotla attacked village Darogwala, near Dhuri on the night of October 5, murdered 3 persons and injured one with fire arms. Near about 15,000 Muslims collected in villages Shergarh, Galauli, and Thana Arno. 50 armed Muslims attacked Bareta village. Muslims of Daska attacked villages in small parties resulting looting murder. Mohammedans also burnt and ruined the village Lehra Mohabbat.

By his letter dated September 23, 1947 to Maharaja of Patiala, Secretary to Governor East Punjab, urged: It is obviously most essential in the interests of Sikhs and Hindus awaiting evacuation from West Punjab, if on no other ground, the attacks like these must not only cease forthwith but that any other unlawful activities of armed bands operating in and from Patiala state should be swiftly suppressed.... Situation is serious and unlawful incidents this side only lead to reprisals in West Punjab.

An observer who watched the progress of column of Muslim refugees from Kapurthala state, said: I saw a long column of Muslim men, women and children proceeding from Kapurthala to Jullundur. The column was guarded by a few military sepoys. The women and children walking in the centre, flanked on either side of the road. Every now and again one of the these groups would make sudden sally at the column of Muslims, drag out two or three Muslim women and run away with them. In this process, they would kill or injure the person who tried to resist them. The military sepoy did not make serious attempt to resists. By the time column arrived at Jullundur almost all the women and young girls had been kidnapped in this manner.

A Madras based weekly observed that: A five mile caravan of Muslim refugee crawling at a snail's pace into Pakistan over the Sutlej bridge. Bullock carts piled high with pitiful chattels, cattle being driven alongside. Women with babies in their arms and wretched little tin trunks into the promised land not because it is the promised land, but because bands of Hindus and Sikhs in state in Ferozepur district had hacked hundreds of Muslims to death and made life impossible for the rest.

The worst sufferers of partition were women. The attacks on the women were made on two levels: firstly, women as an embodiment of the community honour and secondly, their bodies as the site of community reproduction. The modus operandi included gang rapes, stripping, parading naked women through the town, branding the breasts and genitalia with slogans like *Pakistan Zindabad* or *Hindustan Zindabad*, amputating the breasts, knifing open the womb and killing the foetuses. The rape especially was used as a weapon not just to humiliate the 'other', but also to sow one's own seed in the enemy womb.

Thus each community acknowledged the role of women as the bearers of future generation. Those women who were impregnated with the 'bad seed' were at timed forced to undergo abortion to maintain the purity of the community. It has, however, been pointed out that women were not only victims but also sometimes provided "moral support or backing for at least a proportion of the violence that occurred." This was not limited only to women alone but also brought men in its orbit. The men were either castrated or forcibly circumcised in many cases. Likewise the attack on children was based on a similar premise and the perpetrators showed no mercy to a generation which could become belligerent in future. Many women were abducted, they were mercilessly treated with inhuman activities, *i.e.*, either raped or forcibly married.

On the night of August 25, 1947, a scene so dreadful, which illuminated the outskirt of Gurgaon itself, and consuming their inmates men, women and children. Two dainty teenaged girls, daughter of a well known Muslim lawyer of Hissar were on their way to Delhi by train, expected to be included in refugee convoy going to Pakistan. The lustful gang attacked the train and dragged the girls out. The two were then taken to P.W.D. rest house where they were repeatedly raped by Magistrate and his accomplice. On September 10, 1947, Muslims carried out mass conversion of Hindus and Sikhs, forcible marriages and organised loot in Jhelum district and in the surrounding villages of Pind Dadan Khan tehsil. The Muslim *Pir* called 'Shahzada' was responsible for the marriages of a number of Brahmin girls to Muslims.

The converted Hindus and Sikhs were made to eat one meal at his house. On October 3, Muslim soldiers accompanying Muslim convoy at Amritsar kidnapped five Hindu women. On October 1, 1947, a refugee convoy that started from Risalpur in military trucks was suddenly attacked near Khairabad, 240 women were said to have abducted. In one village of Rawalpindi, some ninety women committed suicide by throwing themselves into a well, while at another place thirty-two women were put to the sword by their own men when their capture by Muslim attackers was seen to be imminent. In East Punjab 'large scale' abduction of Muslim women was blamed on the Sikh *Jathas* and on refugees from the West. But here, too, the local police and military frequently participated in the abduction and distribution of women

Anis Kidwai, later recalled what generally became of these women: The 'better stuff' would be distributed among the police and army while the 'small coin' would be given to the rest (of the attackers). After this the girls would go from one hand to another, and after being sold four or five times would become showpieces in hotels, or they would be kept in safe-custody in the house for the enjoyment of police officials.

A mob of 10,000 to 12,000 persons armed with deadly weapons attacked the train at Kamoke on October 1. About 400 girls were abducted from the train. Another Muslim mob appeared at Harppur and abducted 60 girls, mob consisted of Khewara labourers. A non-Muslim convoy from Bahawalpur heading towards Jodhpur on October 4, was attacked near Rahimyar Khan, 700 women and girls were abducted. Zia-ul-Islam states that in the Eastern Punjab nearly 55,000 Muslim women were abducted. K.L. Gauba has given the approximate figures of women abducted and raped and also of the children.

Abducted	West Punjab	–	100,000 (approximately)
	East Punjab	–	50,000 (approximately)
Raped	West Punjab	–	50,000 (approximately)
	East Punjab	–	
Children	Murdered or maimed for life	–	1,00,000 approximately

Murders, abductions and conversions became common scene. No community lagged behind. Ethics and morals took the back seat and criminalisation of human instinct assumed prominence. Figures can only give flash but these figures represented living human beings. According to Mosley, in the nine months between August 1947 and the spring of the following year, over 600,000 Hindus, Sikhs and Muslims were killed. Ian Stephens believes that 500,000 persons died in the 1947 holocaust.

This death toll is comparable with the official tally of commonwealth deaths (in World War II), civilian as well as military, between September 1939 and August 1945 of about 5,40,000. According to Penderal Moon, the total casualties from August onwards in the West Punjab and Bahawalpur was 60,000, the total casualties in the East Punjab had been heavier than the West Punjab. Sumit Sarkar quoting Penderal Moon gives the approximate figures 1,80,000 of which 60,000 in the West and 1,20,000 in the East. By March 1948, 60,00,000 Muslims and 45,00,000 Hindus became refugees. On the whole Muslim suffered most lives, Hindus and Sikhs lost most property. So the partition created complex problems for the people. The people were butchered mercilessly on a massive scale. The women were soft targets physically and psychologically. Sexually assaulted women were acceptable to none.

The displacement of over twelve million people at the time of partition remains the largest migration in contemporary history. There are countries where a mass of humanity has been deported for forced labour or even exterminated. At times war has been resulted in exchange of population as a repatriation movement. Invariably a forced migration of population results in loss of citisenship to the refugees. But when men and women from Pakistan sought refuge, they met neither with hostility nor coolness or reserve. They were hailed as co-religionists, "*Compatriots re-entering the fold.*" They were integrated at once in the country of their refuge. Their integration was almost instantaneous and complete. Hence, to call such persons, "*refugees*" is inaccurate to a certain extent. There is no single definition of "refugee" that is suitable for all purposes.

The refugee is an involuntary migrant, a victim of politics, war or natural catastrophe. Every refugee is naturally a migrant, but not every migrant is a refugee. A migrant is one leaves his residence (usually for economic reason) in order to settle elsewhere, either in his own or in another country. A refugee movement results when the tensions leading to migration all so acute that what at first seemed do be a voluntary movement becomes virtually compulsory. The up rooted become either internal refugees that is "*national refugees*" (persons who have been displaced in their own country) or "*International refugees*" (persons outside their country of origin). "*Refugees*" or "*displaced persons*" are individuals who have involuntarily left their homes or communities and have been compelled by forces over which they have little or no control-war, invasion, persecution or natural disaster to change their place of residence, often from country to country. The strain of prolonged displacement from their homes and communities, often combined with prolonged residence in temporary camps, serves to intensely the adjustment problems of refugees.

The detachment and "*normlessness*" as well as the physical deprivation which accompanies this status, often result in what has been called "*DP Apathy*", namely an initial attitude of passivity and lack of initiative. This is also the result of dependency patterns that tend to develop in situations, such as in refugee camps, where all basic needs are met by the authorities. A refugee therefore, may be defined as a person who would not like to migrate from his homeland but for reason beyond his control, political, religious or economic that might have rendered his life unbearable and unlivable. Thus, for all intents and purposes, the migrants from the West Punjab are refugees. Under the U.P. Refugee Registration and movement act, 1947, a refugee is defined as a person who has migrated into the state in consequence of communal disturbance from the area which now constitutes Pakistan.

The legal documents used terms like "*displaced persons*" or "*evacuees*", while the official writings used the term "*refugees*" to describe the plight of migrants. The term 'refugee' technically pertains to those who seek shelter outside their own national borders, which in the case of partition migrants did not happen till August 15, 1947. The large scale migration after this date was, however, across the international borders between India and Pakistan, which in the process created refugees in international legal terminology. Thus, it will be safe to deduce that a category of refugees existed within the overall category of partition migrants of whom not all can be classified as refugees for the reasons.

While mass migration was largely induced under threat and coercion, individuals and families used different strategies of exit, of which not all were undertaken in chaotic circumstances. Many people had begun migrating long before partition took place, while others had evacuated and secured their belongings without state sponsorship. The important difference lies in the relationship the migrants had with the state, since, statelessness is a prime factor in the legal and conceptual understanding of refugees. Word "*Muhajir*" is used in Urdu for refugee.

The Muslim migrants from India with their labels as *Muhajir* come to Pakistan feeling that they had sacrificed their homes and livelihood to facilitate the making of a Muslim state. Their migratory status later become the rallying point for creating a separate *Muhajir* political identity and demands for provincial autonomy. M.A. Ispahani lamented that, *"There appears a trend to treat Mohajirs as something like second class citisens"*.

The word refugee, hurt the self-respect of those who were the worst sufferers of partition and many of them objected to this nomenclature. B. Pattabhi Sitaramayya made this point forcefully both as the President of AICC and also as a member of the Constituent Assembly of India (CAIL).

Speaking in the CAIL on 29 November 1947, he urged: "I take objection to the word 'refugee'. It is an abominable word. The people that come to us in India in a helpless state from West Punjab are not refugees. They are natives of this country, born of the soil, brought up in the midst of surroundings in which we grew. They have title and a light to live in these portions of the country. It is not as if they are strangers, coming to seek refuge and shelter at your hands.... I would call them Pravasis or evacuees. A pravasi is one who had been exiled, they had been either voluntarily or unvoluntarily exiled."

Sitaramayya made the same plea in his presidential address at the session of Indian National Congress at Jaipur on 18 December 1948, when he said: "May we not preferably call them evacuees, and in our own national language Pravasis or better Nirvasis rather than Saranarthis.... They have not come here to seek shelter or to beg protection. It is the nation's approval of partition that has compelled this mass migration."

Khurshed Lal, member of CAIL, too emphasised this point during the debate and stated: "The word 'refugee' implies as if they were some foreigners, some aliens who have come to our land to take shelter, and they resent this word.... They belonged to a part of the country which had to be torn asunder so that India may be free. They have paid the real price for freedom and they have suffered for it, and it is time that we tried to share this burden with them."

Renuka Ray, another member (CAIL), said that the word, 'refugee' symbolises an "attitude of mind" and should be substituted by the word 'evacuees'. The first wave of evacuees consisted of the upper middle class migration occurred quite early as a precursor to the impending mass migration in the months after March. These were mainly from NWFP and the Rawalpindi Division and able to take with them a part of their moveable property. As a precautionary measure, many people with substantial properties and businesses left the trouble prone areas long before the partition took place. They would either take up temporary residence in Hindu-dominated cities or proceed to the hill stations of Simla or Mussorie for early summer vacation, while waiting to see if the situation would normalise.

The second wave of evacuees started after the June 2, 1947 announcement from the Rawalpindi Division. These consisted of Hindus and Sikhs from the Lahore and Rawalpindi Divisions. The third wave after July 21, became a panic flight. Wholesale shooting and murder of minorities with the active help or connivance of the Muslim Police and Balochi troops became the chief task of the Muslim League in all the Districts of Lahore division.

The fourth wave of evacuees consisted of the rural Hindu and Sikh population, mainly the owners and tillers of the soil in the rich canal colonies of Montgomery, Sheikhupura and Lyallpur. They had stayed behind to the last moment firmly resolved to remain in Pakistan if they could be assured of an honorable living. But the Pakistan Government had by that time decided to get rid of them.. The Muslim Mob organised by the police and the Baloch Military actually hunted them out from every nook and corner of these colonies and forced them to move to relief camps set up for evacuation. The fifth wave of evacuees consisted of the people stranded here and there in small towns and villages and in other small pockets who could not move to a bigger town or a railway station without danger to their lives. They were brought out by Motor Transport by Military Evacuation Organisation.

These consist mostly of the *Meghs*, the *Choohras*, the odes and other menial classes whom the Pakistan Government not allow to migrate to Hindustan or those who have since, then been forcibly converted to Islam. The class difference between Hindu, Sikh and Muslims was the possible ground for conflict, fearing which the Hindu and Sikh landlords made arrangements to flee long before.

The class conflict inherent in the partition violence needs to be unmasked of its religious veil. Evidently, it was only the class difference between Hindus and Sikhs and the Muslims that defined the Partition exodus, but the internal class hierarchy among Hindus and Sikhs that also shaped how migration took place. Migration also provides an opportunity to unscrupulous people, which made their fortunes.

Of the drivers of cars, the police, and the military detained to protect the convoys, the Liaison agency, the organisers of the camp and the custodians with whom the people left their trunks and luggage a few were in the racket. Later on when the luggage left behind was retrieved, the owners found that gold, silver and other ornaments had mysteriously been filched away though the locks were still there. The Muslim Military and police detained on convoy duty was more 'straight forward' in robbing Hindus and Sikhs. After taking way and pooling together for distribution among themselves later on the booty so obtained they would start searching the rest of the luggage.

The heavy trunks and beddings would be thrown on the road side and every article scattered. The only alternative was to strike a bargain and handover anything to which the soldiers took a fancy or to give cash concealed by the evacuees on their persons or in the luggage. Pakistan military was so bold and reasonable as to agree to accept the payment, if necessary, on arrival at Amritsar. It was open loot in those days and as stark ruin faced the West Pakistan minorities in the face. It was clear that organised violence had left their home to take shelter in camps for their strength lay in numbers and safety in togetherness.

The reconstruction of the journey shows a class divided process which could not be abridged by as momentous an event as partition migration. The duration of journey, and the means of transport used to undertake the journey, were crucial indicators of the class differences that significantly after the experience of displacement.

The clusters of differing migration experiences can be:

- *Built around the*: Foot Columns: Those who walked hundred of miles over several days or weeks.

- *Railway Journey*: A shorter journey but under taken in highly cramped and difficult conditions.
- *Military Trucks*: Used for short distance travel but not available easily and finally.
- *The Air Travel*: That was swift, safe but available only to those who could pay the exorbitant price. The level of danger also increased dramatically as the mode and duration of the journey become shorter.

The Earliest means as also the most popular with rural people was the foot convoy. These convoys enabled them to bring with them their bullock carts and cattle and were to be moved from remote villages where transport facilities were not available. The route for these convoys was the Lyallpur-Balloki-Chunian-Ferozpur road. The major portion of the population of districts of Lyallpur, Montgomery, Sheikhupura and Sialkot was evacuated by means of organised convoys. At the head were the bullock carts, each carrying a whole family together with its few remaining possessions. There were innumerable cows, bulls and buffaloes and occasionally a stray dog could be seen following its master. The caravan was moving at snail's pace because both men and beasts were too tired and hungry to walk any faster and they take requires a special effort on their part. The Caravans were vulnerable to attacks while passing hostile towns and villages. So a degree of organisation was necessary for survival. They were organised with young women and children in middle, Older men and women around them with the last protective ring thrown around them by young men with crude weapons like *lathis* or some times rifles.

The urge among the columns was to escape from Pakistan and to cover the journey in the quickest possible time. Safety was only in movement, as gangs of looters and armed mauraders were hovering like vultures, and made short work of stragglers. Some of these caravans were fairly well-armed with weapons legal as well as illegal. During the day time the arms were concealed under the bundles of their belongings in bullock-carts and at night these were taken out for the sake of protection. The caravans of bullock carts, as well as foot columns travelled by day and bivouacked along the roadside at night time. On the average, they covered 15 to 20 miles a day. To feed the cattle, they cut fodder from the fields along the roadside, mostly belonging to Hindus and Sikhs who were on the move.

Although these convoys were protected by mobile units of army, they were attacked a number of times because it was not possible for these units to be present everywhere on the scores of miles long route. The Lyallpur-Balloki-Chunian-Ferozepur road was the funnel through which approximately 50 to 60 thousand evacuees poured in to Ferozepur every day. The biggest evacuee caravan consisting of three lakhs of people came into India from the districts of Lyallpur and Montgomery in first week of October. Small shopkeepers, landlords, artisans, doctors, labourers, even dogs, starved cattle, so vast was the size that it took eight days for it to cross a given point.

The convoy had left Layallpur on September 11, to slowly trudge the 150 kilometre route into India. It seemed as if nature too had decided to teach the people a lesson. Many of the central districts as the catchments areas of the rivers *Sutlej* and *Beas* received heaviest rainfall in the year 1947. *Hindustan Times* report said, *"Today the attacks and the attacked are alike in flight from the waters of the Beas, Sutlej and Ravi."* The report said over 1,00,00 evacuees were seen waiting in miserable conditions on the eastern mudbanks of the *Beas,* with another about 300,000 standard on the bank of the *Ravi. The Dawn* Wrote: *"to the sorrows of Punjab have been added the disaster of the floods."*

In the last week of September more than half of all structures in Ferozepur collapsed. Around Lahore about 120 villages were completely washed away. Because of the flood damage, in the Punjab the net value of rice was expected to fall from ₹ 20 crore to less than ₹ 10 crore in 1947. The outbreak of cholera epidemic was therefore only a nature sequel. Even troops were affected the Dogra Regiment lost four soldier to Cholera. In the Western districts cholera was widespread in towns like Kasur, Jhang and Okara. While foot columns were the preferred means of evacuation for the rural masses, railways were deployed to ferry the urban populace. Over a million non- Muslims were estimated to have been evaluated by rail during the peak period from August 27 to the end of November, 1947 over 1.3 million Muslims in the opposite direction. In this situation the Government of India and Pakistan decided to prepare a joint Evacuation Movement Plan (JEM) on October 20. According to the 1941 census there were 5.3 millions Muslims in Eastern Punjab and 3.8 million non-Muslims in West Punjab. It was estimated that since, August 1, 1947, 2.1 millions Muslims had left Eastern Punjab and 2 million non-Muslims Western Punjab. The JEM Plan arranged for rail evacuation with contributions from India and Pakistan of 20 and 30 railway trains respectively or a pool of stocks for evacuees movement.

These refugee trains were known as "*India Special*" or "*Pakistan Special*". Though the evacuees trains was started to evacuate the people, it served an altogether different purpose for attackers. Instead of launching random attacks, now one could indulge in "wholesale slaughter" because these trains carried members of a single community. The incidents of retaliation were especially in cases of train attacks. Whenever a *ghost* train laden with dead bodies arrived on one side another would immediately be sent in the opposite direction. Several trains were attacked. Even though train journey was fraught with danger, it was much in demand as a quick mean to get away from risk zones.

The special trains were free for the evacuees who could travel to any destination with in the country of their choice. But to get a place on the train was not that simple. A simple reason was that often the train timetables and their platform would not be revealed until about half an hour before the departure as a safety precaution. Through their networks, the railway employees could address information more easily than anybody else. They could place themselves at the right time and place to board the train before the rush started. Many refugees tried to get names scaled up in priority through their personal connections or by bribing the officer in charge even an acquaintance in the railway department could prove to be valuable in such circumstances as some refugees experienced. By the first week of September, the evacuation of displaced persons from West Punjab was taken over by a new command of the Army- the Military Evacuation Organisation with its head quarter at Amritsar under Brigadier Chimni.

By the end of October, the MEO were using nearly, 1200 military and civilian vehicles for the movement of refugees. Of the ten Motor Transport Companies each consisting of 150 vehicles, which were raised for the MEO. There were four main routes form Pakistan Punjab to India Punjab: Narowal-Dera Baba Nanak, Lahore-Amritsar, Kasur-Ferozepur and Montgomery-Fazilka. Military trucks were used for short distance. In order to facilitate the speedy clearance of refugees on both sides, the East Punjab Government and the West Punjab Government entered into an agreement by which no train or motor vehicle was to cross the border without evacuees.

It implied that no Indian Motor Vehicle or train could enter Pakistan without Muslim refugees, nor could any Pakistan motor vehicle or train enter Indian territory without Hindu and Sikh refugees. This naturally implied the control and checking of such vehicle. The Indian motor convoy commandant complained that, "the convoys from the East Punjab with Muslim evacuees first go to the Walton Training School. There they were made to wait for a considerable time and were asked to carry other Muslim evacuees to the districts where they might be going.

In this way, about six hours were spent at the Walton Training School. Again at the bridge of River *Ravi*, they were not allowed to cross unless every truck was full to the maximum capacity and if any vehicle was found to carry a smaller number of evacuees than the expected number, the passengers of those vehicles are transhipped to other vehicles and empty vehicles sent back. This procedure was repeated at many places on the way. But trucks were important source for short Journey. Around 1, 200 military and civilian trucks were deployed by the MEO (India) with an additional pool of 1,000 trucks at the peak period.

By the middle of November, around 3,13,400 non- Muslims and 2,09,440 Muslims had been transported in this way. Military trucks also became victims of violence in several places. While all the means of surface transport were prone to risks of one kind or another, air transport was free from all such dangers to life and property. The Rehabilitation Ministry set up a transfer Bureau, an agency specially created to cater to the state employees, who were affected by the violence and population movement. The migration course followed by the Government employees was different from ordinary people since, their travel, stay and continued employment was arranged by the state.

"The staff that come to Delhi were of three categories; those who were posted permanently to Delhi, those who were to posted elsewhere in India: and those who had left Pakistan on account of disturbances. Each category was being dealt within an appropriate to receive all those who arrived by air and to look after them and sent them to allotted residences. Evidently, the Government as an efficient guardian of its employees was able to transfer them out safely. For this purpose as early as the end of August 1947, 10 air craft were mobilised from various transport companies for six to seven daily trips between India and Pakistan. The scheduled flights between Delhi, Karachi, Quetta, Lahore, Rawalpindi and Peshawar were intensified.

Facilities were provided for private individuals to charter planes to evacuate refugees from Sialkot, Sargodha, Lyallpur and Dera Ismail Khan. For the organisation and coordination of the air services the Government appointed a special officer called the controlling authority, '*Air Transport for Refugees*'. In October 1947, maximum aircrafts were used for the evacuation of refugees R.I.A.F. squadrons, retained in the country at the request of both the disturbed areas in the East and West. About 1200 Royal Pakistan Air Force Personnel were flown out of the NWFP.

In addition, many special flights were undertaken to fly important government official on their various missions. Also senior Commanders of the Armed Forces of the two dominions were provided with aircrafts to meet their requirements. A total of 12,769 passengers were carried. The aircrafts of these squadrons had flown a total of 6,43,000 miles. In addition, a fleet of British Overseas Airways Corporation (BOAC) was added to the available air resources. The BOAC fleet consisted of 18 Dakota and two York Aircrafts and could carry out 962 flights at the height of evacuation between September 15 and December 7.

During this period it transported 28,000 people from Pakistan and 18,000 in the reverse direction. In one day alone these aeroplanes flew 13,000 miles between the two dominions with full loads in each direction. However these official figures exclude larger unaccounted estimates of passengers carried by companies such as Indian National Airways. From August 31 onwards, the company promised that one of its Delhi-Lahore flights, could call daily at Amritsar in both directions. The passengers could obtain information from Faletti's Hotel at Lahore, an elite spot for the rich. Thus the displaced persons moved their new created dominion with different means of transportation. Kirpal Singh gives the table to show their evacuation with different means.

Modes of Transportation	Numbers
Foot Columns	1, 036, 000
Special Trains	10, 00, 000
Motor Transport	31, 34, 000
Air Transport	28, 000

The evacuation of non-Muslims from Sindh has been proceeding by sea and rail. In addition to the regular Persian Gulf Line steamers of the British Indian Steam Navigation company, pick up evacuees from Karachi on their way to Bombay, nine steamers had chartered by the Government of India, but clearance from Karachi was restricted to only 2,000 a day, as the port authorities had pleaded inability to handle more. By November 21, nearly 133,000 non-Muslim evacuees had been cleared from Sindh by Steamers and country craft. On September 3, 1947, a conference in Lahore met to work out camps. This was attended by Sardar Patel Ghazanfar Ali, the commander in chief of the Indian Army, General Rob Chart, General Kiani of Pakistan, the Governor and all the Provincial ministers of the East and West Punjab. It was decided that the entire responsibility of the Evacuees Camps would be of the Government in whose territory they were situated. The main concentration of evacuees was in East Punjab, Delhi, U.P., Bombay, the East Punjab States, Bikaner, Jodhpur and other Rajputana states. It was estimated towards the end of November that the total number of evacuees in camps all over India was about 1,250,000 including 5,00,000 in East Punjab, 2,50,000 in Kurukshetra, 1,50,000 at Delhi, and the rest in camps of other parts of the country. The daily expenditure on camps runs into several hundred thousands of rupees. During 1947-48 a budget of ten crores of rupees had been sanctioned for relief.

There were several non-Muslim evacuees camps functioning in East Punjab accounted for 721,000 evacuees towards the end of December 1947. The displaced persons in East Punjab were to first report at the transit camps opened at the entry points like Fazilka, Ferozepur, Khemkaran, Attari, Amritsar and Dera Baba Nanak, from where they were to proceed to the areas allocated to them under the central plan.

They could stay in the relief camp of the area till alternative arrangements for their settlements were made for them either by the state or by their friends or relations. A separate rescue home for women was also set up at Jullundur, with accommodation for 800 to 900 women.

Displaced persons were also lodged in localities evacuated by Muslims, in Charitable and religious institutions and in schools and colleges, some of the localities having been declared as "relief camps". Some camps were larger than even some of cities. As per the 1951 population census in India and Pakistan, the total number of displaced persons in the two countries was found to be 15.63 million. The evacuees population in India was estimated as 7.48 million against 7.15 million in Pakistan. The responsibility of resettlement of the million of uprooted people, both urban and rural and unattached women and children, presented a colossal problem of providing immediate relief finding housing accommodation lands, shops, business concerns, factories and in large number of cases new vocations.

Accordingly, the plan for rehabilitation was divided into three stages. Immediately after evacuation the evacuees were put up in relief camps. Afterwards, there was a gradual dispersal of the camp residents to the rural or urban areas as the case might be. A large number were still left in the camps for whom no source of income could be found. They constituted the third group. Apart from this general programme of relief to the incoming evacuees, there was a group of unattached and recovered women and children which offered a formidable problem.

2

The Indian States

India is a land of diversities linguistic, ethnic, cultural, and religious as well as many others. This has led to the formation of a large number of small states. As observed by Gurmukh Nihal Singh: "Nature has made India a more or less self-sufficient unit, but historical accidents have divided her into a large number of separate political entities". Even in the earlier stages of civilization there had never been an occasion when the whole country had completely been under a single government. The political integration of the country was never possible.

Moreover, the concept of a nation also did not exist. India, instead of being a nation, was divided into a number of small states. These were having a separate entity of their fighting among themselves all the time. Political unity among these states was thus non- existent. However, they were able to defend themselves against external aggressions either singularly or collectively. The rulers of these states used to look after the welfare of their subjects; they had managed to establish a kind of brotherhood among the people. There was no party system and the states were governed by the kind who supposedly gained legitimacy through heredity as an accepted head. Democratic institutions were non- existent in these small states.

Attempts were, however, made by some rulers to consolidate the country into one unit. Rulers like Ashoka of the Mayura dynasty, Chandra Gupta of the Gupta dynasty, Harshavardhan of the northern India had made attempts in this direction but their success was not remarkable. The problem of the Indian states assumed a more serious dimension particularly during the British rule. The states which existed during the earlier period, assumed a different status under the colonial government. The beginning of the British domination in India was, basically, through a series of treaties with the various rulers of the country from time to time.

Even after deploying the armed forces, the British Government was not fully successful in extending its control to the entire country; it had to enter into treaties with powerful native kings. At the beginning of the British rule, the various native states could not come together for the purpose of political freedom. To start with, the East India Company, which was a trading company, entered into treaties with the native rulers from 1757 upto Lord Minto's Governor-Generalship in 1813. The company wanted a footing in India. At the time of Wellesley, it was decided that the British should take up permanently political power in India; also the princes should be allowed to retain their personal insignia of sovereignty by surrendering their political independence.

This was maintained by the British rulers in subsequent period. The new policy was formulated by Metcalfe who, in a letter written in 1816 stated: "They said that some power in India had always existed, to which the peaceable states submitted and in return obtained protection against the invasion of upstart chiefs and armies of lawless banditti; that the British Government now occupied the place of that protecting power and was the natural guardian of weak states..." Till the breaking out of the First World War, nationalism in India did not grow to such an extent as to pose a threat to the British rule. There was no upsurge of mass consciousness for the establishment of a responsible Government in the country. The great war of 1914-1919 acted as a catalyst towards accelerating the temper of the Indian nationalism. The doctrine of paramountcy was a peculiar strategy evolved by the British for governing the relations with the states.

As observed by Shankar: "Paramountcy meant that the States accepted Suzerainty of the British government and the government of India, to carry out directions given to them by the Government of India. It was convenient to the British government to refuse to define paramountcy".

Paramountcy was a special system concerning the relationship of the states with the British government. The states had to cooperate with the government on matters of all-India policies in respect of railways, post and telegraphs, and defence. The crown representatives sometimes used to station an army, construct railways on a part of the states, and used to take the administrative control of the area. States had a series of agreements with the British government. In addition to that, the crown representative could seek military assistance from the government of India in case he found it necessary for the protection of the ruler from an external aggression an internal revolt. The relation of the states with the paramount power was based on latter's military strength and the states were the subordinate allies. The relationship between the states and the British crown thus remained as long as the British power existed in India. The position of the Indian states and their relation with the British Government were well-defined through various treaties and declarations by the British Government from time to time.

As early as 1858, the proclamation of Queen Victoria stated: "We hereby announce to the native princes of India that all treaties and engagements made with them by or under the authority of the Honourable East India Company are by us accepted and will be scrupulously maintained. We shall respect the Rights, Dignity and Honour of Native Princes as Our Own".

The same assurance was further confirmed by Lord Morley, then secretary of state for India on February 23, 1909. At a later date, during World War-I in 1914, King George V observed: "Paramount regard for treaties, faith and pledged word of ruler, and peoples is the common heritage of England and India". The position of the states became very much critical at the time of the transfer of power in 1947. It was a question whether with the lapse of paramoutcy, the states would attain complete freedom or not.

There were two possibilities with regard to the position of the states after the lapse of paramountcy. At the time of the withdrawal of the British power in India, one possibility was that the states might become completely free and independent sovereign states without having any control exerted over them by the two newly formed states of India and Pakistan. Such a possibility was very much dangerous since, the result would have been that the country would be divided into a number of states which would not have sufficient resources of their own for their liabilities.

Such a proposition would have led to the complete Balkanisation of the country. The second and the most practical possibility was that with the withdrawal of the British power, the states would develop new relationship with either of the states-India or Pakistan, depending upon the geographical continuity and political situation prevalent. In order to maintain the unity of the country, such a solution was a must, but it was difficult to ascertain whether the Princes of the states, liked to surrender their power and join the newly formed states as federating units. If considered from the point of view of the individual gain, it was obvious that the second possibility might not be welcomed, but taking into consideration the overall interest of the country, the rulers might agree to sacrifice their personal interest and merge their states with the Indian union. The steps towards more autonomy for India, after the Government of India Act, 1935, were the proposals made by Sir Stafford Cripps in 1942 when the Second World War was in full swing. The British Government assured independence to India after the end of world war provided India participated in the war in their favour.

At the time of independence, the position of the native states was also defined in Cripps Mission. The British Government desired that power should be handed over to the Indian leaders after framing a constitution and if the states desired so, they should also be allowed to take part in the constitution making. In case the states did not agree to accept the new constitution and wanted to retain their independent status, they could accede to the new Dominion at a later date. The treaty with the British Government for the Indian states would be revised to meet the changed circumstances, irrespective of whether the states would adhere to the constitution or not.

In case the states decided to join the constitution-making body, they could send representatives proportionate to their population. As regards the position of the states after the transfer of Power, Cripps observed, that would, however, be open to an adhering state to negotiate and make suitable arrangements on these matters in the new Union. Though the states expressed their desire to cooperate with the new union in framing a constitution, they however appealed that they should be permitted to form a Union with all non-acceding states. The Cabinet Mission Plan of 16 May, 1946 gave a clear picture of the transfer of power and the position of the native states in the new set up of free India. The future of the country depended much on the decision of the Princes regarding their participation in the new constitution and the merging of their princely states with the Indian Union.

Thus the native states' role in free India was very much important and unless those princes were properly guided towards integrity of the country, the very idea of building a united Indian nation would have been at stake.

CONGRESS ATTITUDE TOWARDS THE STATES

The Congress, in late nineteenth century, was just like a voluntary organisation and the functions were three-fold:

1. It acted as a social reformer and the same was preached by leaders like Raja Ram Mohan Roy, Iswar Chandra;
2. It tried to maintain the traditional values of the Indian society as enunciated by Dayanand Saraswati; and
3. It acted as a political organisation.

On political ground, its movement was confined to the British India only. In 1893, Dadabhai Naoroji, the President of the 9th session of the Indian National Congress, which was held in Lahore spoke about paramount power and the princes. He stated: "Another subject of our future work to which I need only touch now is the relations of the government with the native states". The idea about the states developed in the 31st session of the Congress at Lucknow in 1916, when the then President A.C. Mazumdar referred to the native states with regard to intellectuals as he remarked that many brilliant persons had shown their excellence in the princely states. The congress did not want to interfere with the internal affairs of the princes though it had full sympathy for the princes with regard to their rights and privileges.

APPEAL TO THE PRINCES

Sardar had close contacts with the princes. He explained that by acceding to the Indian Union the future of the country, and simultaneously the future of the princely states, would be brighter; even peace would return to the country. Sardar appealed to the princes for their good-will and for peaceful accession of their States to India. He tried to impress upon the princes that for the integrity of the country, the princes should co-operate with the Congress to form a United India.

He said: "...I have a few words to say to the Rulers of Indian states among whom I am happy to count many as my personal friends...Let not the future generation curse us for having had the opportunity but having failed to turn it to our mutual advantage..."

He thus gave a personal touch to the problem of the princely states by considering the princes as his friends and was sure that his appeal would rouse patriotism in the minds of native rulers. His appeal had an electrifying effect on the princes as can be seen from the various encouraging letters he received from the rulers of the several states. Sardar, could, thus, inspire them by restoring confidence in them with a message that it would be good for them to join the Dominion of India. They realised that for their own security and prosperity as well as in the interest of the country, they should accede to the Indian union. This act of Sardar substantiated his contribution in the formation of a strong Indian nation with the support of a majority of the princely states. He could realise that that was the most opportune moment for the States to be brought into the Indian Union, in order to avoid the creation of a third force which would be disastrous for the country's unity.

PROCESS OF THE INTEGRATION OF STATES

When we study the process of the integration of the various states and the part played by Sardar in it, we realise the important role that Sardar had in the integration of the country. The states included Saurastra (including Junagadh) Hyderabad, Travancore, Cochin, Kashmir and other small states. Sardar's role in each of these states was vital.

Saurastra (including Junagadh)

Since, the smaller states of West Gujarat, which were virtually ebbing out, but had a good organisation for rousing the political consciousness of the people in so far as the Congress was concerned they attracted the attention of Sardar Patel in his very first attempt towards their integration. The West Gujarat known as Saurastra constituted a number of small states which did not have much potential from the point of view of economic and political independence. In all, 327 such States existed in Gujarat. These States were attached to some of the adjoining bigger States in April, 1943, as per the attachment scheme. But the attachment scheme terminated with the lapse of paramountcy on August 14th, 1947. The Home Department prepared a revised Instrument of Accession for these states.

In the new Instrument of Accession, the States were to be freed from the attaching states and to be administered by the Government as in the pre-attachment period. The states would vest all residuary powers and jurisdiction in the Central Government. The modus operandi was very simple, as those states did not have any capability of declaring independence with the lapse of paramountcy. There was also no possibility for those states to accede to Pakistan due to political and geographical conditions. Sardar succeeded in bringing the small states together and it was a very important step towards national solidarity. It was reported that the Jam Saheb of Nawanagar was strengthening his armed forces with a desire to be the overlord of Kathiawad.

Sardar had a very good contact with the people of Kathiawad states as he was associated with some of State's Peoples' Union. Sri U.N., Dhebar was Sardar's disciple and was the leader of the people of the Kathiawad States. It was reported that the rulers of Kathiawad, on the advice of the political agent, met under the leadership of the Jamsaheb to form a union of Kathiawad, covering the whole of the peninsula and decided to declare sovereign independence subject to the right of Junagadh to declare separate independence or to join Pakistan. The Jamsaheb would be the president of the Union comprising seven states, *viz.* Jamnagar, Bhavnagar, Gondal, Probandar, Morvi, Dhrangadhra and Junagadh.

They were helped by the political agent with the intention of Balkanising the country. Sardar, on receipt of such information and with the help of his comrades like Dhebar and other leaders of the people's conference of the states, tactfully dealt with the situation and ultimately persuaded the princes to join the Indian Union.

Sardar wrote to B.L. Mitter on 28th June, 1947: "The question of smaller states will now engage my attention as a Member in charge of the new states' department. Along with these will come the question of ports? I have no doubt, I shall find your note of assistance in this respect"....

Sardar, then fully concentrated on the states of Kathiawad and with his efforts and support from the people of the states, he could bring the rulers to agree to the accession. Junagadh created a big problem for the solidarity of the country. It was one of the strongest States in Saurastra at that time and was ruled by a Muslim ruler but the inhabitants were mostly Hindus. Geographically, it was close to India, though it had direct access to the sea through its port of Veraval. In the beginning, Junagadh assured that it would accede to India. Such impression was created by the *Dewan,* A.K.M. Husen and his brother Nabi Baksh, the Constitutional Adviser. But Husen had to go abroad for treatment and in his absence his place was taken over by Shah Nawaz Bhutto.

The *Nawab* was not at all serious about the administration and welfare of the people. The change of *Dewan* occurred on 10th August, 1947 and the *Nawab* was virtually a prisoner in the hands of his new Dewan. Junagadh was so much connected with other States that a part of its territory fell into the area of the States which had acceded to India. There were two other small States called Babariwad and Mangrol headed by Muslim rulers under the control of the Junagadh State, that had acceded to India, but the *Nawab* argued that Mangrol had no authority to negotiate any instrument of accession without the permission of Junagadh. Till 14th August, 1947, Junagadh did not accede either to India or to Pakistan.

However, on 15th August, 1947, the people of the state were shocked on hearing that the state had acceded to Pakistan and that the accession had been accepted by the other party. The people resented such an undemocratic action Sardar agreed that the armed forces on surrounding Junagadh would be kept in readiness so that they could be deployed in no time. V.P. Menon was sent to meet *Nawab* and explain about his wrong decision. The Government of India press Communiqué dated 25th September, 1947, strongly denounced such action of *Nawab* and asserted firmness in dealing with the situation. Under the leadership of Shamaldas Gandhi, who had taken consent of Sardar Patel, Kathiawad People's Front was formed and supplies to Junagadh were stopped. Bhutto appealed to Pakistan for help but in vain. Violence started in the State and encouraged by the Kathiawad people's Front, the subjects of the State started a demonstration against the *Nawab*, who fled to Karachi with his family.

On October 27th, Bhutto admitted that the people did not accept the *Nawab*'s accession to Pakistan. Bhutto fled to Pakistan after requesting the Union Government to take over the administration. The people's verdict and ultimately found support and Junagadh came under India, due to the tactful handling by the States' Department headed by Sardar Patel. Sardar, in his speech on November 13, 1947 at Junagadh, explained at length the strategy adopted by the Government of India. He explained that the Government had tried its best through negotiations to come to a peaceful settlement in the interest of the country.

Though the things were moving in the proper direction, the Government of India had to take drastic steps due to a sudden change in the *Nawab*'s policy, to bring the state under its control, which he thought as the correct step. Finally Junagadh merged was merged in Kathiawad States, which became a part of the Gujarat state. U.N., Dhebar, a dedicated Congressman and Sardar's follower, became the first Chief Minister of Kathiawad states.

The way Junagadh was made to accede to India was very clear from legal and democratic point of view. Junagadh's accession to Pakistan raised lot of Public controversy; but from the point of the guideline of the British Government's partition programme, Junagadh had to accede t India on geographical and economical grounds, though the state was ruled by a Muslim ruler. Taking the population into consideration the state having a majority of Hindus should be a part of India. On similar consideration, Bahawalpur, a state adjacent to India and Pakistan was allowed to accede to Pakistan. Sardar, thus acted in a finest way in his handling of the Junagadh situation without keeping any loopholes open for any controversy in future.

ACCESSION OF THE STATES

From June to August 15, 1947, 562 of the 565 India-linked states signed the instrument of accession. Despite dramatic political exchanges, Travancore, Jodhpur and Indore signed on time. Patel was also willing to take on other Indian leaders for the sake of accomplishing the job. The *privy purse* pledge was offensive to many socialists, and Prime Minister Nehru had complained of Patel by-passing the Cabinet to make the pledge to the Princes. Patel described the pledge as an essential guarantee of the Government's intentions, and it was duly incorporated into the Constitution. (In 1971, Prime Minister Indira Gandhi's Congress Party would repeal the clause through a constitutional amendment.) Patel defended their right to retain property and contest elections for public office, and today, especially in states like Rajasthan and Madhya Pradesh, descendants of the formerly royal families play an important role in politics. However, in the strenuous process of integration three major conflicts arose that posed a major threat to the Union:

Junagadh

Junagadh was a state on the southwestern end of Gujarat, with the principalities of Manavadar, Mangrol and Babriawad. The Arabian Sea stood between it and Pakistan, and over 80% of its population was Hindu. Possibly on the advice of his *Dewan*, Sir Shah Nawaz Bhutto, who was prominent in the Muslim League, the Nawab of Junagadh Mahabhat Khan acceded to Pakistan. The accession was announced on August 15, 1947, when Pakistan had come into being. When Pakistan confirmed the acceptance of the accession in September, the Government of India was outraged that Muhammad Ali Jinnah would accept the accession of Junagadh despite his argument that Hindus and Muslims could not live as one nation. Patel believed that if Junagadh was permitted to go to Pakistan, it would exacerbate the communal tension already simmering in Gujarat.

Patel gave Pakistan time to void the accession and hold a plebiscite in Junagadh. Samaldas Gandhi formed a democratic government-in-exile, the *Arzi Hukumat* (in Urdu: *Arzi*: People's Request, *Hukumat*: Government) of the people of Junagadh. Eventually, Patel ordered the forcible annexation of Junagadh's three principalities. Junagadh's court, facing financial collapse and no possibility of resisting Indian forces, first invited the *Arzi Hukumat*, and later the Government of India to accept the reins. A plebiscite was conducted in December, in which approximately 99% of the people chose India over Pakistan.

Kashmir

Maharaja Hari Singh, a Hindu, was equally hesitant about acceding to either India — he felt his mostly Muslim subjects would not like joining a Hindu-majority nation — or Pakistan — an eventuality which he would personally prefer to avoid. He personally believed that Kashmir could exercise its right to stay independent; a belief in which he was backed by Sheikh Abdullah, the leader of Kashmir's largest political party, the National Conference. However, Pakistan coveted the Himalayan kingdom, while Indian leaders including Gandhi and Nehru hoped that the kingdom would join India. Hari Singh signed a *Standstill Agreement* (preserving status quo) with Pakistan, but did not make his decision by August 15.

Pakistan, concerned about the lack of movement on the front, attempted to force the issue by permitting the incursions of tribals from the North-West Frontier, followed in September 1947 by regular forces. India offered military assistance to the Kashmiri Government, which was totally without an organised military; such assistance, however, was conditional on the Maharaja signing the Instrument of Accession, which he then did. By this time the raiders were close to the capital of Srinagar. Indian troops secured Jammu, Srinagar and the valley itself during the First Kashmir War, but the intense fighting flagged with the onset of winter, which made much of the state impassable.

Prime Minister Nehru, recognising the degree of international attention brought to bear on the dispute, declared a ceasefire and sought U.N. arbitration with the promise of a plebiscite. Patel had argued against both, describing Kashmir as a bilateral dispute and its accession as justified by international law. Patel had feared that the U.N.'s involvement would stall the process and allow Pakistan to reinforce its presence in Kashmir; in addition, it was far from clear, which way a plebiscite would go. In 1957, Kashmir was officially integrated into the Union, but with special provisions made for it in the Constitution's Article 370. The northwestern portion that remained under control of the Pakistan army is today Pakistan-administered Kashmir. In 1962, China occupied Aksai Chin, the northeastern region bordering Laddakh.

Hyderabad

Hyderabad was a state that stretched over 82,000 square miles (over 212,000 square kilometres) in the centre of India and with a population of 16 million, 85% of whom were Hindus. Its ruler was Nizam Osman Ali Khan, and had always enjoyed a special relationship with the British Raj. When the British ruled out dominion status, the Nizam set his mind upon independence, under the influence of Muslim radical Qasim Razvi. Without Hyderabad, a large gap would exist in the centre of the united nation envisioned by Indian nationalists and the Indian public. Patel believed that Hyderabad was looking to Pakistan for support, and could pose a constant threat to India's security in the future.

Patel argued that Hyderabad was essential for India's unity, but he agreed with Lord Mountbatten that force should not be used immediately. A *Standstill Agreement* was signed — an agreement made with no other princely state without an explicit assurance of eventual accession. However, Patel required Hyderabad promise it would not join Pakistan. Mountbatten and India's agent K.M. Munshi engaged the Nizam's envoys into negotiations. However, no deal was reached that both sides found acceptable, and the Nizam alleged that India had created a blockade. India, on the other hand, charged that Hyderabad was receiving arms from Pakistan, and that the Nizam was allowing Razvi's Razakar militants to intimidate Hindus and attack villages in

India. Lord Mountbatten crafted a proposal called the *Heads of Agreement*, which called for the disbandment of the Razakars and restriction of the Hyderabad army, for the Nizam to hold a plebiscite and elections for a constituent assembly, and for eventual accession. While India would control Hyderabad's foreign affairs, the deal allowed Hyderabad to set up a parallel government and delay accession. Hyderabad's envoys assured Mountbatten that the Nizam would sign the agreement, and he lobbied Patel hard to sign for India. Patel signed the deal but retained his belief that the Nizam would not accept it. The Nizam, taking Razvi's advice dismissed the plan.

In September 1948, Patel made it clear in Cabinet meetings that he intended to use force against the Nizam. He obtained the agreement of the new Governor-General Chakravarthi Rajagopalachari and Prime Minister Nehru after some contentious debate, and under Operation Polo, sent the Army to invade Hyderabad.

Between September 13 and 18th, Indian troops fought Hyderabadi troops and Razakars and defeated them. Patel retained the Nizam as the head of state as a conciliatory gesture. The main aim of Mountbatten and Nehru in attempting to achieve integration through diplomacy had been to avoid an outbreak of Hindu-Muslim violence. Patel insisted that if Hyderabad was allowed to continue its independence, the prestige of the Government would be tarnished and then neither Hindus nor Muslims would feel secure in its realm. The successful annexation of Hyderabad was praised by many Indian Muslim leaders, and there were no episodes of civil violence.

Conflicting Agendas

Different theories have been proposed to explain the designs of Indian and Pakistani leaders in this period. Rajmohan Gandhi postulates that an ideal deal working in the mind of Patel was that if Muhammad Ali Jinnah let India have Junagadh and Hyderabad, Patel would not object to Kashmir acceding to Pakistan. In his book *Patel: A Life*, Gandhi asserts that Jinnah sought to engage the questions of Junagadh and Hyderabad in the same battle. It is suggested that he wanted India to ask for a plebiscite in Junagadh and Hyderabad, knowing thus that the principle then would have to be applied to Kashmir, where the Muslim-majority would, he believed, vote for Pakistan. In a speech at the Bahauddin College in Junagadh following the latter's take-over, Patel said:

"If Hyderabad does not see the writing on the wall, it goes the way Junagadh has gone. Pakistan attempted to set off Kashmir against Junagadh. When we raised the question of settlement in a democratic way, they (Pakistan) at once told us that they would consider it if we applied that policy to Kashmir. Our reply was that we would agree to Kashmir if they agreed to Hyderabad."

Patel's opinions were not India's policy, nor were they shared by Nehru, but both leaders were angered at Jinnah's courting the princes of Jodhpur, Bhopal and Indore. In her book *The Sole Spokesman*, Ayesha Jalal argues that Jinnah had never actually wanted partition, but once created, he wanted Pakistan to become a secular state that was inclusive to its Hindu minority and strategically secure from a geographically-larger India, thus encouraging Hindu states to join.

When Jinnah remained adamant about Junagadh, and when the invasion of Kashmir began in September 1947, Patel exerted himself over the defence and integration of Kashmir into India. India and Pakistan clashed over Kashmir in 1965 and 1971, as well as over the sovereignty of the Rann of Kutch in August, 1965.

INDIAN INTEGRATION OF JUNAGADH

Junagadh was a former princely state of India, located in what is now Gujarat, outside but under the suzerainty of British India. In the independence and partition of India and Pakistan of 1947, the 565 princely states were given a choice of whether to join India or Pakistan or to remain independent.

The Muslim Nawab of Junagadh, Muhammad Mahabat Khanji III, whose ancestors had ruled Junagadh and small principalities for some two hundred years, decided that Junagadh should become part of Pakistan, much to the displeasure of the people of the state, an overwhelming majority of whom were Hindus. The Nawab acceded to the Dominion of Pakistan on 15 August 1947. Pakistan accepted this on 13 September. When Pakistan confirmed the acceptance of the accession in September, the Government of India was outraged that Muhammad Ali Jinnah could accept the accession of Junagadh despite his argument that Hindus and Muslims could not live as one nation. Sardar Vallabhbhai Patel believed that if Junagadh was permitted to go to Pakistan, it would exacerbate the communal tension already simmering in Gujarat.

The princely state was surrounded on all three sides by India, with an outlet to the Arabian Sea. The unsettled conditions in Junagadh had led to a cessation of all trade with India and the food position became precarious. The region was in crisis and the Nawab was forced to flee to Karachi with his family fearing for his life and established a provisional government with his followers.

Patel offered Pakistan time to void the accession and to hold a plebiscite in Junagadh. Samaldas Gandhi formed a government-in-exile, the *Aarzi Hukumat* (in Urdu:*Aarzi*: Temporary, *Hukumat*: Government) of the people of Junagadh. Eventually, Patel ordered the forcible annexation of Junagadh's three principalities. Junagadh's state government, facing financial collapse and lacking forces with which to resist Indian force, invited the Government of India to take control. A plebiscite was conducted in December, in which approximately 99% of the people chose India over Pakistan.

Background

After the announcement by the last Viceroy of India, Lord Mountbatten, on 3 June 1947, of the intention to partition British India, the British parliament passed the Indian Independence Act 1947 on 11 July 1947, as a result, the native states were left with these choices: to remain independent or to accede to either of the two new dominions, the Union of India or the Dominion of Pakistan.

The Indian Government made efforts to persuade Nawab Sahab of Junagadh to accede to India, but he remained firm. The Indian minister V. P. Menon came to request an accession to India, threatening consequences in case of denial. The Nawab however decided to accede to Pakistan, and an announcement to this effect was made in the gazette of Junagadh (*Dastrural Amal Sarkar Junagadh*) on 15 August 1947 as follows:

Published by Authority

Friday 15th August, 1997

Extra Ordinary

The following communique has been published by Junagadh State.

The Government of Junagadh has during the last few weeks been faced with the problem of making its choice between accession to the Dominion of India and accession to the Dominion of Pakistan. It has had to take into very careful consideration every aspect of this problem.

Its main preoccupation has been to adopt a course that would in the long run make the largest contribution towards the permanent welfare and prosperity of the people of Junagadh and help to preserve the integrity of the State and to safeguard its independence and autonomy over the largest possible field. After anxious consideration and careful balancing of all factors the Government of the State has decided to accede to Pakistan and hereby announces its decision to that effect. The State is confident that its decision will be welcomed by all loyal subjects of the State who have its real welfare and prosperity at heart.

Now that the Dominions of India and Pakistan have been admitted to the fellowship of independence sovereign State on an equal footing, it is to be hoped that vast avenue of the progress will be thrown open to the people, of the both Dominions in every walk of life and that the peoples of both Dominions will combine to derive the fullest benefit from the opportunities which will now be made available to them in peace and cooperation with each other. The Government of Junagadh will continue to make every endeavour to secure for all classes of the people of Junagadh without distinction in fullest measure the blessing of security, peace and prosperity and is confident that in the furtherance of this object, it will receive the fullest cooperation from all classes and sections of the subjects of His Highness the Nawab Saheb Bahadur.

Instrument of Accession

Immediately after making the announcement in *Dastrural Amal Sarkar Junagadh,* the Jungadh government communicated to Pakistan its wish to accede, and a delegation headed by Ismail was sent to Karachi with the Instrument of Accession signed by the Nawab. The Constitutional Assembly of Pakistan considered the proposal in detail and approved it. The Quaid-e-Azam, Muhammad Ali Jinnah, as Governor General of Pakistan, counter-signed the Instrument of Accession on 15 September 1947.

The Instrument of Accession dated 15 September 1947 reads as follows:

HYDERABAD

Sardar's greatest role in the integration of states was his able handling of the Hyderabad crisis. Most of the states acceded to India, Hyderabad, the largest of the native states with a Muslim ruler and 86 per cent Hindu population created a threat to the solidarity of the country. Hyderabad was surrounded by the Indian Territory on all sides and did not have nay access to the sea; but the ruler, the Nizam, had high aspirations and wanted to proclaim sovereignty after the paramountcy was withdrawn. In order to negotiate with the Nizam, Lord Mountbatten was chosen and Sardar agreed to this, knowing fully well its pros and cons.

Sardar knew that, if the problem was handled by Mountbatten, it would be good for India since, international and communal repercussions could be avoided. Moreover, as Walter Monckton, the adviser of the Nizam, was a friend of Mountbatten, negotiations would be easier. However, the decision on any point of controversy beyond the agreed formula was vested in the Congress High command only. Thus, Sardar was sure that, it would not be dangerous for India even if the negotiations were carried on by Lord Mountbatten. On the contrary, Sardar would formulate the policy without coming into direct confrontation with the Nizam. The negotiations with the representatives of the Nizam started in July, 1947 but an accord could not be reached.

Sardar, in his letter dated 24th August, 1947 to Lord Mountbatten, clearly indicated that Nizam should accede to the

Dominion of India in line with the instrument of Accession prepared for the other states. Sardar stated that the Nizam should follow the same path as the other states and in case he did not agree to the same, he should agree to allow the people of the state to decide the issue of accession. But, in spite of the best efforts of Mountbatten, the negotiations failed. Ultimately with great reluctance an extension of two months was granted to Hyderabad to decide about the accession.

Sir Walter Monckton, in his note dated 15th September, 1947, stated: "I know that Mr. Patel was and is against any extension of time to Hyderabad and that the Viceroy prevailed over the cabinet of the Dominion to allow him personally two months time to see whether I, could find a compromise satisfactory to both sides"....

Sardar could foresee the difficult situation which the country was facing and in his letter dated 19th September, 1947 to Mountbatten, Sardar explained the situation in Hyderabad and stated about the steps that would be necessary in future due to the wrong policy of the Nizam as he had created his own *Frnakentstein-Ittehadul-Mussalmeen*. After some more discussions with a number of delegates from Hyderabad, some concessions were granted by Sardar to the Nizam and the Standstill Agreement for one year and the collateral letters were signed on 29th November, 1947.

The same day Sardar made a statement in the Constituent Assembly and explained that the period of one year granted to the Nizam would be helpful for final accession. Thus, he agreed with the settlement reached by the government on the ground that accession of Hyderabad would be peaceful. It is said that Razvi, a member of the Ittehad-ul-Mussalmeen, and controlling the policy of the Nizam, met Sardar Patel in Delhi to try for additional concessions from him; but Sardar quickly disposed him and firmly indicated that there was no possibility of accepting Hyderabd as being independent.

When Razvi indicated that Sardar should realise their difficulties, and that in case Sardar did not concede his request, Hyderabad would fight tooth and nail, Sardar remained unmoved and replied: "How Can I stop you from committing suicide if you want to"?

This proves that Sardar was confident that in the course of time he would be able to merge Hyderabad with India. As per the new agreement, K.M. Munshi a trusted man of Sardar was sent to Hyderabad as Agent General of India and detailed reports about the political conditions were received through him. Sardar also kept in touch with the members of the Hyderabad Congress and formulated his policy on the basis of the information he received from time to time. Sardar was not at all hopeful about the settlement in Hyderabad in line with the Stand still Agreement for one year... Inspite of Standstill Agreement for one year, the Nizam did not give up his hope of attaining complete independence with the help of foreign powers.

His doubtful actions, were reported to Sardar by K.M. Munshi, other trusted people and the reports of the news-papers regarding the reign of terror and the oppression of the Hindu Community. The Razakars started arson and looting in the neighbouring States. The Nizam wanted to represent his case to the Security Council to internationalise the issue. People, in India became impatient but Sardar was preparing for the final assault and counting the days.

In his letter to Nehru, Sardar stated: "I have already decided to issue instructions to Hyderabad and Bhopal States regarding the composition of their armed forces. We are telling them that we are bound to take it into account in making allotments of arms and equipments and that the composition of these forces should be readjusted in order to create more confidence among the non-Muslim majority"...

When the situation was becoming alarming, Sardar intimated Nehru that the time came to tell Hyderabad that the Nizam should accede unconditionally. Sardar wanted that the situation should be tackled firmly so that it did not go out of hands. In his letter dated 21 June, 1948 to N.V. Gadgil, Sardar cautioned that the decision about Hyderabad's accession should be similar to that of the other States and the situation could be brought under control. He advised the Indian Military to be alert as he apprehended that the trouble, any time, might demand immediate military action. Sardar sought information from defence ministry and was informed that in case of nay military action, it would not take more than three weeks.

In spite of his illness, Sardar kept in close touch with the day to day events on Hyderabad. Though Nehru was hesitant due to the international reaction, Sardar was firm in his stand. It was decided that military would march into Hyderabad, on 13th September, 1948 and Sardar did not agree to postpone the operation. At the instance of Sardar, C. Rajagopalachari, the then Governor-general called a meeting of the cabinet to regularise the action. Sardar's assessment was correct and Hyderabad was captured practically without any bloodshed within a week's time. It was a great achievement. Sardar's conviction regarding the action taken against Hyderabad was very clear. He was very confident that actions taken by him were without flaw and would sand against any criticism.

On October 30th, 1948 he boldly said: "We shall do what the interests of the people of Hyderabad demand and what they themselves desire. It would be for them to take a decision and no outside interference can succeed in keeping the Nizam on the throne if people wish otherwise"....

There were suggestions regarding the dividing Hyderabad into three linguistic parts but Sardar indicated that this would be done at an appropriate time, if necessary. With the merger of the State with India, the next step for financial and social integration started automatically and ultimately it gave birth to a new linguistic state called Andhra Pradesh which contributed to a greater consolidation in removing all doubts of any disintegration at a later date. A bold step taken at, an appropriate time has strengthened the process of Nation-building in India.

KASHMIR

Kashmir was also a problem. The state was ruled by a Hindu ruler, whereas the population was Muslim. It occupied a strategic position. Till August 15th, 1947 Kashmir did not accede to India. Sardar knew the importance of Kashmir from its geographical position and wanted to tackle the problem himself as the Minister of the States, but, Nehru was willing to deal with Kashmir, and Sardar did not object to it. But Sardar too did not fail to give his best advice in this regard.

As observed by Allen Campbell Johnson in his book 'Mission with Mountbatten': "Indeed the states Ministry under Patel's direction, went out of its way to take no action which could be interpreted as forcing Kashmir's hand and to give assurances that accession to Pakistan would not be taken amiss by India"....

When the Maharaja of Kashmir agreed to accede to India, in similar lines as the other states, the question of sending the army to Kashmir to help the Maharaja rebuff an armed attack by the intruders was discussed at a meeting. Everybody including army generals, Nehru and Mountbatten could not find a solution but Sardar got up and said that Kashmir should be defended at all costs. The committee decided to send an agent to Kashmir and Kunwar Sir Daleep Singh was posted as Agent in Jammu.

At the instance of Mountbatten, the Kashmir dispute was referred to the United Nations on 1st January, 1948, but Sardar was not present in Delhi at that time. Sardar, however was skeptical about the reference to the United Nations. Had Sardar's advice on Kashmir been heeded by Nehru, the problem we are facing now would not have risen at all.

At K.M. Munshi said: "But for Jawaharlal Nehru, who, under the influence of Sheikh Abdullah, took away the portfolio of Kashmir from Sardar's States Ministry, Kashmir would never have become the problem that it has been"...

Kashmir still poses a problem for the country; but the steps taken by the Indian leaders in sending the army to Kashmir at the request of the Maharaja was in the Cabinet Mission Plan.

The action regarding Kashmir was defended by the Prime Minister when he informed the Prime Minister of the U.K., that: "Helping Kashmir is an obligation of national interest to India...I should like to make it clear that the question of aiding Kashmir in this emergency is not designed in any way to influence the States to accede to India"...

Sardar also played his role by holding a secret meeting with Ramchandra Kak, the Prime Minister of Kashmir. The position of Kashmir, as it stands today, is much better for India from the strategic point of view, and such a political situation created in

Kashmir is a kind of an interim solution and has helped the country to stand against any onslaught from the external powers. The solidarity of the country has been strengthened with the accession of Kashmir to India.

INSTRUMENT OF ACCESSION (JAMMU AND KASHMIR)

The Instrument of Accession is a legal document executed by Maharajah Hari Singh, ruler of the princely state of Jammu and Kashmir, on October 26, 1947. With the formal acceptance of the Governor General of India, it settled the question of the accession of the Jammu and Kashmir princely state (including Jammu, Kashmir, Northern Areas, Laddakh, Trans-Karakoram Tract and Aksai Chin) to the Dominion of India. "Whereas the Indian Independence Act, 1947, provides that as from the fifteenth day of August, 1947, there shall be set up an Independent Dominion known as India, and that the Government of India Act 1935 shall, with such omission, additions, adaptations and modifications as the governor-general may by order specify, be applicable to the Dominion of India.

And whereas the Government of India Act 1935, as so adapted by the governor-general, provides that an Indian State may accede to the Dominion of India by an Instrument of Accession executed by the Ruler thereof. Now, therefore, I Shriman Inder Mahander Rajrajeswar Maharajadhiraj Shri Hari Singhji, Jammu and Kashmir Naresh Tatha Tibbetadi Deshadhipathi, Ruler of Jammu and Kashmir (princely state), in the exercise of my sovereignty in and over my said State do hereby execute this my Instrument of Accession and I hereby declare that I accede to the Dominion of India with the intent that the governor-general of India, the Dominion Legislature, the Federal Court and any other Dominion authority established for the purposes of the Dominion shall, by virtue of this my Instrument of Accession but subject always to the terms thereof, and for the purposes only of the Dominion, exercise in relation to the State of Jammu and Kashmir (hereinafter referred to as "this State") such functions as may be vested in them by or under the Government of India Act, 1935, as in force in the Dominion of India, on the 15th day of August, 1947, (which Act as so in force is hereafter referred to as "the Act")." It is further specified that. "I accept the matters specified in the schedule hereto as the matters with respect to which the Dominion Legislature may make law for this State." Thus the power of the Dominion to make laws was restricted to the matters mentioned in the Schedule namely Defence, Foreign Affairs and Communications and a few ancillary subjects specified in the schedule. For all other matters concurrence of the State Government was essential. The accession was accepted by Lord Mountbatten of Burma, Governor General of India, the following day (October 27, 1947). Mountbatten in his letter of acceptance wrote that "I do hereby accept this Instrument of Accession

COMPLETING INTEGRATION

The Instruments of Accession were limited, transferring control of only three matters to India, and would by themselves have produced a rather loose federation, with significant differences in administration and governance across the various states. Full political integration, in contrast, would require a process whereby the political actors in the various states were "persuaded to shift their loyalties, expectations, and political activities towards a new centre", namely, the Republic of India.

This was not an easy task. While some princely states such as Mysore had legislative systems of governance that were based on a broad franchise and not significantly different from those of British India, in others, political decision-making took place in small, limited aristocratic circles and governance was, as a result, at best paternalistic and at worst the result of courtly intrigue. Having secured the accession of the princely states, the Government of India between 1948 and 1950 turned to the task of welding the states and the former British provinces into one polity under a single republican constitution.

Fast-Track Integration

The first step in this process, carried out between 1947 and 1949, was to merge the smaller states that were not seen by the Government of India to be viable administrative units either into neighbouring provinces, or with other princely states to create a "princely union". This policy was contentious, since it involved the dissolution of the very states whose existence India had only recently guaranteed in the Instruments of Accession. Patel and Menon emphasised that without integration, the economies of states would collapse, and anarchy would arise if the princes were unable to provide democracy and govern properly.

They pointed out that many of the smaller states were very small and lacked resources to sustain their economies and support their growing populations. Many also imposed tax rules and other restrictions that impeded free trade, and which had to be dismantled in a united India. Given that merger involved the breach of guarantees personally given by Mountbatten, Patel and Nehru initially intended to wait until after his term as Governor-General. An Adivasi uprising in Orissa in late 1947, however, forced their hand. In December 1947, princes from the Eastern India Agency and Chhattisgarh Agency were summoned to an all-night meeting with Menon, in the course of which they were persuaded to sign Merger Agreements integrating their states into Orissa, the Central Provinces and Bihar with effect from 1 January 1948. Later that year, 66 states in Gujarat and the Deccan were merged into Bombay, including the large states of Kolhapur and Baroda. Other small states were merged into Madras, East Punjab, West Bengal, the United Provinces and Assam. Not all states that signed Merger Agreements were integrated into provinces, however. Thirty states of the former Punjab Hill States Agency which lay near the international border and had signed Merger Agreements were integrated into Himachal Pradesh, a distinct entity which was administered directly by the centre as a Chief Commissioner's Province, for reasons of security.

The Merger Agreements required rulers to cede "full and exclusive jurisdiction and powers for and in relation to governance" of their state to the Dominion of India. In return for their agreement to entirely cede their states, it gave princes a large number of guarantees. Princes would receive an annual payment from the Indian government in the form of a privy purse as compensation for the surrender of their powers and the dissolution of their states. While state property would be taken over, their private property would be protected, as would all personal privileges, dignities and titles. Succession was also guaranteed according to custom. In addition, the provincial administration was obliged to take on the staff of the princely states with guarantees of equal pay and treatment.

Although the Merger Agreements were principally intended for smaller, nonviable states, they were also applied to a few larger states. Kutch in western India, and Tripura and Manipur in North-East India, all of which lay along international borders, were also asked to sign Merger Agreements, despite being larger states, following which they became Chief Commissioners' Provinces.

Bhopal, whose ruler was proud of the efficiency of his administration and feared that it would lose its identity if merged with the Maratha states that were its neighbours, also became a directly administered Chief Commissioner's Province, as did Bilaspur, much of which was likely to be flooded on completion of the Bhakra dam.

FOUR-STEP INTEGRATION

Merger

The bulk of the larger states, and some groups of small states, were integrated through a different, four-step process. The first step in this process was to convince groups of large states to combine to form a "princely union" through the execution by their rulers of Covenants of Merger. Under the Covenants of Merger, all rulers lost their ruling powers, save one who became the Rajpramukh of the new union.

The other rulers were associated with two bodies—the council of rulers, whose members were the rulers of salute states, and a presidium, one or more of whose members were elected by the rulers of non-salute states, with the rest elected by the council. The Rajpramukh and a deputy Rajpramukh, or *Uprajpramukh*, were chosen by the council from among the members of the presidium. The Covenants made provision for the creation of a constituent assembly for the new union which would be charged with framing its constitution. In return for agreeing to the extinction of their states as discrete entities, the rulers were given a privy purse and guarantees similar to those provided under the Merger Agreements.

Through this process, Patel obtained the unification of 222 states in the Kathiawar peninsula of his native Gujarat into the princely union of Saurashtra in January 1948, with six more states joining the union the following year. Madhya Bharat emerged on 28 May 1948 from a union of Gwalior, Indore and eighteen smaller states. In Punjab, the Patiala and East Punjab States Union was formed on 15 July 1948 from Patiala, Kapurthala, Jind, Nabha, Faridkot, Malerkotla, Nalargarh, and Kalsia. The United State of Rajasthan was formed as the result of a series of mergers, the last of which was completed on 15 May 1949. Travancore and Cochin were merged in the middle of 1949 to form the princely union of Travancore-Cochin. The only princely states which signed neither Covenants of Merger nor Merger Agreements were Kashmir, Mysore and Hyderabad.

Democratisation

Merging the administrative machineries of each state and integrating them into one political and administrative entity was not easy, particularly as many of the merged states had a history of rivalry. In the former Central India Agency, whose princely states had initially been merged into a princely union called Vindhya Pradesh, the rivalry between two groups of states became so bad that the Government of India persuaded the rulers to sign a Merger Agreement abrogating the old Covenants of Merger, and took direct control of the state as a Chief Commissioner's State.

As such, the mergers did not meet the expectations of the Government of India or the States Department. In December 1947, Menon suggested requiring the rulers of states to take "practical steps towards the establishment of popular government". The States Department accepted his suggestion, and implemented it through a special covenant signed by the rajpramukhs of the merged princely unions, binding them to act as constitutional monarchs. This meant that their powers were *de facto* no different from those of the Governors of the former British provinces, thus giving the people of their territories the same measure of responsible government as the people of the rest of India.

The result of this process has been described as being, in effect, an assertion of paramountcy by the Government of India over the states in a more pervasive form. While this contradicted the British statement that paramountcy would lapse on the transfer of power, the Congress position had always been that independent India would inherit the position of being the paramount power.

Centralisation and Constitutionalisation

Democratisation still left open one important distinction between the former princely states and the former British provinces, namely, that since the princely states had signed limited Instruments of Accession covering only three subjects, they were insulated from government policies in other areas. The Congress viewed this as hampering its ability to frame policies that brought about social justice and national development. Consequently, they sought to secure to the central government the same degree of powers over the former princely states as it had over the former British provinces.

In May 1948, at the initiative of V. P. Menon, a meeting was held in Delhi between the Rajpramukhs of the princely unions and the States Department, at the end of which the Rajpramukhs signed new Instruments of Accession which gave the Government of India the power to pass laws in respect of all matters that fell within the seventh schedule of the Government of India Act 1935.

Subsequently, each of the princely unions, as well as Mysore and Hyderabad, agreed to adopt the Constitution of India drafted by the constituent assembly as the constitution of that state, thus ensuring that they were placed in exactly the same legal position vis-à-vis the central government as the former British provinces. The only exception was Kashmir, whose relationship with India continued to be governed by the original Instrument of Accession, and the constitution produced by the state's Constituent Assembly.

The Constitution of India classified the constituent units of India into three classes, which it termed Part A, B, and C states. The former British provinces, together with the princely states that had been merged into them, were the Part A states. The princely unions, plus Mysore and Hyderabad, were the Part B states. The former Chief Commissioners' Provinces and other centrally administered areas, except the Andaman and Nicobar Islands, were the Part C states. The only practical difference between the Part A states and the Part B states was that the constitutional heads of the Part B states were the Rajpramukhs appointed under the terms of the Covenants of Merger, rather than Governors appointed by the central government. In addition, Constitution gave the central government a significant range of powers over the former princely states, providing amongst other things that "their governance shall be under the general control of, and comply with such particular directions, if any, as may from time to time be given by, the President". Apart from that, the form of government in both was identical.

Reorganisation

The distinction between Part A and Part B states was only intended to last for a brief, transitional period. In 1956, the States Reorganisation Act reorganised the former British provinces and princely states on the basis of language. Simultaneously, the Seventh Amendment to the Constitution removed the distinction between Part A and Part B states, both of which were now treated only as "states", with Part C states being renamed "union territories". The Rajpramukhs lost their authority, and were replaced as the constitutional heads of state by Governors, who were appointed by the central government. These changes finally brought the princely order to an end. In both legal and practical terms, the territories that formerly were part of the princely states were now fully integrated into India and did not differ in any way from those that were formerly part of British India. The personal privileges of the princes—the privy purse, the exemption from customs duty, and customary dignities—survived slightly longer, but were abolished in 1971.

POST-INTEGRATION ISSUES

The Princes

Although the progressive integration of the princely states into India was largely peaceful, not all princes were happy with the outcome. Many had expected the Instruments of Accession to be permanent, and were unhappy about losing the autonomy and the guaranteed continued existence of their states they had expected to gain.

Some felt uneasy about the disappearance of states that generations of their family had controlled, while others were unhappy about the disappearance of administrative structures they had worked hard to build up and which they believed to be efficient. The majority, however, despite the "strain and tension" of adapting to life as private citizens, were content to retire on the generous pension provided by the privy purse. Several took advantage of their eligibility to hold public offices under the central government. The Maharaja of Bhavnagar, Col. Krishna Kumarasingh Bhavasingh Gohil, for example, became the Governor of Madras State, and several others were appointed to diplomatic posts overseas.

Colonial Enclaves

The integration of the princely states raised the question of the future of the remaining colonial enclaves in India. At independence, the regions of Pondicherry, Karikal, Yanam, Mahe and Chandernagore were still colonies of France, and Daman and Diu, Dadra and Nagar Haveli and Goa remained colonies of Portugal. An agreement between France and India in 1948 provided for an election in France's remaining Indian possessions to choose their political future. A plebiscite held in Chandernagore on 19 June 1949 resulted in a vote of 7,463 to 114 in favour of being integrated with India. It was ceded to India on a *de facto* basis on 14 August 1949 and *de jure* on 2 May 1950.

In the other enclaves, however, the pro-French camp, led by Edouard Goubert, used the administrative machinery to suppress the pro-merger groups. Popular discontent rose, and in 1954 demonstrations in Yanam and Mahe resulted in pro-merger groups assuming power. A referendum in Pondicherry and Karaikal in October 1954 resulted in a vote in favour of merger, and on 1 November 1954, de facto control over all four enclaves was transferred to the Republic of India. A treaty of cession was signed in May 1956, and following ratification by the French National Assembly in May 1962, *de jure* control of the enclaves was also transferred.

Portugal, in contrast, resisted diplomatic solutions. It viewed its continued possession of its Indian enclaves as a matter of national pride and, in 1951, it amended its constitution to convert its possessions in India into Portuguese provinces. In July 1954, an uprising in Dadra and Nagar Haveli threw off Portuguese rule.

The Portuguese attempted to send forces from Daman to reoccupy the enclaves, but were prevented from doing so by Indian troops. Portugal initiated proceedings before the International Court of Justice to compel India to allow its troops access to the enclave, but the Court rejected its complaint in 1960, holding that India was within its rights in denying Portugal military access. In 1961, the Constitution of India was amended to incorporate Dadra and Nagar Haveli into India as a Union Territory.

Goa, Daman and Diu remained an outstanding issue. On 15 August 1955, five thousand nonviolent demonstrators marched against the Portuguese at the border, and were met with gunfire, killing 22. In December 1960, the United Nations General Assembly rejected Portugal's contention that its overseas possessions were provinces, and formally listed them as "non-self-governing territories". Although Nehru continued to favour a negotiated solution, the Portuguese suppression of a revolt in Angola in 1961 radicalised Indian public opinion, and increased the pressure on the Government of India to take military action.

African leaders, too, put pressure on Nehru to take action in Goa, which they argued would save Africa from further horrors. On 18 December 1961, following the collapse of an American attempt to find a negotiated solution, the Indian Army entered Goa, Daman and Diu. The Portuguese took the matter to the Security Council but a resolution calling on India to withdraw its troops immediately was defeated by the USSR's veto. Portugal surrendered on 19 December. This take-over ended the last of the European colonies in India. Goa was incorporated into India as a centrally administered union territory and, in 1987, became a state.

Sikkim

The former princely state of Sikkim, located at a strategically important point on the border between India and China, was integrated into India in 1975 as its 22nd state.

Three princely states bordering India—Nepal, Bhutan and Sikkim—were not integrated into the Republic of India in the period between 1947 and 1950. Nepal had been recognised by the British and the Government of India as being *de jure* independent. Bhutan had in the British period been considered a protectorate outside the international frontier of India. The Government of India entered into a treaty with Bhutan in 1949 continuing this arrangement, and providing that Bhutan would abide by the advice of the Government of India in the conduct of its external affairs.

Historically, Sikkim was a British dependency, with a status similar to that of the other princely states, and was therefore considered to be within the frontiers of India in the colonial period. On independence, however, the Chogyal of Sikkim resisted full integration into India.

Given the region's strategic importance to India, the Government of India signed first a Standstill Agreement and then in 1950 a full treaty with the Chogyal of Sikkim which in effect made it a protectorate which was no longer part of India. India had responsibility for defence, external affairs and communications, and ultimate responsibility for law and order, but Sikkim was otherwise given full internal autonomy.

In the late 1960s and early 1970s, the Chogyal, supported by the minority Bhutia and Lepcha upper classes, attempted to negotiate greater powers, particularly over external affairs, in order to give Sikkim more of an international personality. These policies were opposed by Kazi Lhendup Dorji and the Sikkim State Congress, who represented the ethnic Nepali middle classes and took a more pro-Indian view. In April 1973, an anti-Chogyal agitation broke out; the agitators demanded the conduct of popular elections. The Sikkim police were unable to control the demonstrations, and Dorji asked India to exercise its responsibility for law and order and intervene.

India facilitated negotiations between the Chogyal and Dorji, and produced an agreement which envisaged the reduction of the Chogyal to the role of a constitutional monarch and the holding of elections based on a new ethnic power-sharing formula. The Chogyal's opponents won an overwhelming victory, and a new Constitution was drafted providing for Sikkim to be associated with the Republic of India. On 10 April 1975, the Sikkim Assembly passed a resolution calling for the state to be fully integrated into India. This resolution was endorsed by 97% of the vote in a referendum held on 14 April 1975, following which the Indian Government amended the constitution to admit Sikkim into India as its 22nd state.

Secessionism and Sub-nationalism

While the majority of princely states absorbed into India have been fully integrated, a few outstanding issues remain. The most prominent of these is in relation to Kashmir, where a violent secessionist insurgency has been raging since the late 1980s.

Some academics suggest that the insurgency in Kashmir is at least partly a result of the manner in which it was integrated into India. Kashmir, uniquely amongst princely states, was not required to sign either a Merger Agreement or a revised Instrument of Accession giving India control over a larger number of issues than the three originally provided for. Instead, the power to make laws relating to Kashmir was granted to the Government of India by Article 5 of the Constitution of Jammu and Kashmir and was, under Article 370 of the Constitution of India, somewhat more restricted than in relation to other states.

Widmalm argues that during the 1980s, a number of Kashmiri youth began to feel that the Indian government was increasingly interfering in the politics of Jammu and Kashmir. The elections of 1987 caused them to lose faith in the political process and begin the violent insurgency which is still ongoing. Similarly, Ganguly suggests that the policies of the Indian government towards Kashmir meant that the state, unlike other parts of India, never developed the solid political institutions associated with a modern multi-ethnic democracy. As a result, the growing dissatisfaction with the *status quo* felt by an increasingly politically aware youth was expressed through non-political channels which Pakistan, seeking to weaken India's hold over Kashmir, transformed into an active insurgency.

Separatist movements also exist in two other former princely states located in North-East India, Tripura and Manipur. These separatist movements are generally treated by scholars as being part of the broader problem of insurgencies in Northeast India, rather being a result of specific problems in integrating the princely states into India, as the Kashmir problem is and, in particular, to reflect the failure of the Government of India to adequately address the aspirations of tribal groups in the Northeast, or to tackle the tensions arising from the immigration of people from other parts of India to the northeastern areas.

The integration of former princely states with other provinces to form new states has also given rise to some issues. The Telengana region, comprising the Telugu-speaking districts of the former Hyderabad State, were in many ways different from the Telugu-speaking areas of British India with which they were merged. In recognition of these differences, the States Reorganisation Commission originally recommended that Telengana be created as a separate state, rather than as part of a broader Telugu-speaking entity.

This recommendation was rejected by the Government of India, and Telengana was merged into Andhra Pradesh. The result was the emergence in the 1960s of a movement demanding a separate Telengana state. The demand has been accepted by the Union Government in December 2009. A similar movement, although less strong, exists in the Vidarbha region of Maharashtra, which consists of the former Nagpur state and the Berar region of the former Hyderabad state.

OTHER STATES

Regarding the accession of the other states, Sardar acted like a magic-stick. In no time, he could merge the States of Orissa,

Chhatishgarh, Rajasthan, Punjab and so on. He realised that the people of states were supreme and by organising the States', people for establishment of popular government, he could achieve success. He had, with him, able workers and supporters who had worked untiringly to bring such a merger in record time.

The *Maharaja* of Mysore was not inclined to join the Union of India after withdrawal of British power. His Dewan M. Sankar Lingegowda had a series of correspondence with Sardar through which he expressed that after the lapse of paramountcy, the Maharaja of Mysore should get back the territory ceded in 1799 and sovereignty should return to the King, Sardar, clearly explained to him, in his reply, that even in England the sovereignty rested with the people with the King as the head of the State. Similarly, in a democratic country, the authority of the people is supreme.

He also warned that Maharaja should carefully note that after June, 1948, paramountcy would evaporate in air and he would have a hard time; hence, to maintain his honourable position even after the lapse of paramountcy, the Maharaja should take the Mysore Congress into confidence. Sardar's advice had sobering effect on the King and ultimately he joined the Constituent Assembly and sent seven representatives there out of which few were elected representatives of the people of the state. Sardar's handing of the situation was not in the normal way but he gave a human touch while he pointed out the future of the King after departure of the British power. He acted on the basis of information he used to get from various sources through reliable party cadres. Indore was also a trouble spot.

At the beginning Maharaja Holkar of Indore in collaboration with *Nawab* of Bhopal wanted to attract some more states like Jodhpur to form a group against accession to Indian Union. But in Indore the State's People Conference was very active. Maharaja was given an ultimatum that by May 25, 1947 popular government had to be established, which was not acceded by the King. On the other hand without the consent of Praja Mandal, the King appointed one Mr. Horton, a Britisher as his Prime Minister. Praja Mandal launched a statewide agitation and invited Sardar Patel to intervene. Maharaja did not succeeded in his negotiations for remaining independent but his accepted Instrument of Accession was not received by the States' Department before 15th August, 1947.

To create pressure on the King, it was indicated to him that since, the Instrument of Accession was not received in time the terms and conditions would be revised. Sardar met Maharaja of Indore on 19th August, 1947 and the King signed the revised Instrument of Accession and acceded to India, Sardar's careful handling of the Indore affairs and timely action could pave the way for integration of Indore. It is interesting that afterwards the King became friendly with Sardar.

Bhopal was a State ruled by a Muslim ruler; but geographically it had no connection with Pakistan. The *Nawab* of Bhopal was very powerful and he was the chairman of the negotiating committee of the Chamber of Princes.

The *Nawab* had no intention to accede to Indian Union, rather he was keen in maintaining his sovereignty or joining hands with Pakistan. The *Nawab* and King of Indore had a joint interview with Mountbatten, the viceroy on 4 August, 1947 when Viceroy intimated that he did not have any authority to alter the terms and conditions of accession and final decision rested with Sardar Patel.

He, however, assured that Sardar Patel would not be unkind to them. After a considerable time *Nawab* did not find any alternative, so he acceded to India. In spite of his earlier anti-Indian attitude, Sardar realised that the *Nawab* was a changed man when he admitted his fault and apologised to him.

Sardar took him as his friend and exchanged his cordial relation in the coming years. *Nawab* in later years was very helpful in tackling the refugee problem. Sardar thus gave a humanitarian touch to politics of integration of States. There are innumerable instances where Sardar could bring down the rulers of the States to terms and agree them to accession to India as per the terms and conditions stipulated by the Government of India. Sardar had to deal with diversified Kings having different attitude with caution and applying varied, human, social, political and psychological approach. Sardar will always be remembered as the man who laid the foundation stone for a United India.

The complex process of integration of the Princely State, which ended with success, has paved the way for the stability and prosperity of the country.

In the face of partition, it was not sure whether the departure of the British power from India would create a vacuum and leave behind the possibility of creating a third force contributing towards the balkanisation of the country. Even the initiators of partition were not fully convinced regarding the establishment of peace and harmony in the post-partition period. The Congress leaders, baffled by the thrust created through disturbance and communal riots by the Muslim League. Had to look for a solution to such a calamity and had to reconcile to the idea of partition, without looking deeply into the problems that might come ahead, while Sardar was prepared to face the consequences.

His conviction was crystal clear, when he brought an analogy between a riot-stricken country and a mutilated leg of a person which needed amputation to save the rest of the body. Even on the eve of partition Sardar was fully aware that the post-partition period would be full of immense problems and the first and foremost task would be to integrate all the Princely States into the Union of India a positive step directed towards the unity of the country as the prerequisite for nationbuilding.

His actions, aimed at establishing a sovereign democratic country in divided India, were too commensurate with the need of the time. The immediate requirement after partition was the unification of the country by merging the princely states in the Indian Union and Sardar could decide upon the speed with which the action was to be undertaken. The integration of the princely states in India was handled in a well-organised manner by Sardar.

The pattern of integration was also not identical in case of all the states. Sardar could visualise the socio-political environment in the various states based on which, his action-plan was formulated to suit the requirement. It is interesting to find that his approach to the problem had a broad base and diversified modalities wee adopted. It is unimaginable what a spade work he did to obtain the political information of the various states to formulate his action plan. His association with the State's people was very close.

By virtue of his ingenuity, he followed the path of persuasion with friendly states, threats with smaller states and even confrontation with the states which were found to be unmanageable through normal channels of action programme.

In all such cases, Sardar followed a well-organised path of action, keeping in view peace and harmony and preparing the country for a better future and promising its citisens overall prosperity as a nation of the world. The after effect of the integration process is also interesting from the point of the contribution it had made in the nation-building activity.

Though at the time of merging the states into the dominion of India, certain complexities like misunderstanding and enmity developed between the ruling Congress party and the rulers of the States, the same did not persist for a long time but ended in a happy note of mutual adjustment. As Sardar could generate confidence in the minds of the people of the various states, his task in bringing back normalcy and healthy administrative set up in the integrated states became easier.

The mechanics of integration of the states turned out to be so simple that the total number of five hundred and odd states could be integrated in a short span of time without even a single drop of blood being shed.

Sardar's overall management of the integration system has proved to be far superior to any other integration process in the world surpassing the ingenuity of Bismark, the great unifier of Germany.

His multipronged attack with definite objective of homogenisation of the country, his stage play in the integration drama with the help of his Lieutenant like V.P. Menon, U.N., Dhebar, K.M. Munshi, J.N. Chaudhari, V. Shankar and others has proved to be a great success as we can see from the results which have followed in the successive years.

The efforts of Sardar have led the country towards democratisation and prosperity through the economic steps which were taken in the post-integration period. The absence of a third force has resulted in the solidarity of the country and we are now poised for great promises in the coming years as one of the recognised nations of the world. Sardar's role in the dynamics of nationbuilding through the process of integration has paved the way for a glittering future of the country. "If this integration of princely states" writers Geoffrey Tyson in 'Nehru' "had not been carried out with a skilled and sure had by the late Sardar Patel the sub continent might easily have suffered division into a third major segment in which the smaller princely states would have grouped themselves round the more powerful rulers in independent blocks, with resultant balkanisation of a large part of the land". The integration of the princely states thus acted as a synchronising phenomenon and established a State of balance between chaos and segmentation and solidarity of the newly born Indian Union.

3

Jinnah, Partition and Leaders

QUAID-I-AZAM MUHAMMAD ALI JINNAH

Quaid's message to the people of Pakistan was "search your hearts and see whether you have done your part in the construction of the new and mighty state. It is now upto you to work and work: and we are bound to succeed. And never forget our motto: Faith, Unity and Discipline." Syed Sharifuddin Pirzada, renowned legal luminary and Advisor to the Chief Executive on Foreign Affairs, Law, Justice and Human Rights declared while addressing at the seminar held at the Quaid-e-Azam's Mazar on 25th December, 2001 commemorating the concluding day of the Quaid's 125th year of birth.

In his very informative speech, Syed Shariffudin further said: "It is indeed my great pleasure and proud privilege to speak on this special occasion when we are holding a colloquium on Quaid-e-Azam Mohammed Ali Jinnah to cap the observance of the Quaid-e-Azam year.

I warmly welcome General Pervez Musharraf, President of Pakistan, who took initiative in this behalf. The deep devotion of General Pervez for the founding father is reflected in the picturesque park surrounding Quaid's Mazar which, under his orders, was completed speedily and for renaming the Convention Centre at Islamabad as Jinnah Hall. I am also grateful to Mr. Tressler and the Ministry of Culture Dr. Z.H. Zaidi and the members of the National Committee of the Quaid-e-Azam Year for the cooperation extended to me as its Chairman.

Mr. Jinnah was an outstanding jurist, a polished parliamentarian and indeed a statesman of all seasons. Dadabhai Nooroji had full confidence in him. Tilak trusted him and was a party to the famous Lucknow Pact. Gokhle described Jinnah as the Ambassador of Hindu-Muslim unity. At the session of the Congress at Nagpur (1920) Mr. Jinnah opposed Mr. Gandhi's resolution on noncooperation and said that it would lead to mob hysteria and violence and urged that the constitutional way should be followed.

From Curzan to Cripps, fro Minto to Mountbatten, from Nagpur Congress to the Nehru Report, from Lucknow Pact to Lahore Resolution, from 14 points to 14th August are the landmarks on the pathway to Pakistan. M.H. Hodson writes: "Jinnah was the man who framed and accomplished the colossal ambition of destroying India's unity by carving from her body a new Islamic Nation." "Jinnah's objective was long-term and perpetual-to seize from the moment of history what might be a millennium of national identity for ninety million Indian Muslims." Not even his political enemies ever accused Jinnah of corruption or self-seeking. He could be bought by no-one, and for no price. Nor was he in the least degree a weathercock, swinging in the wind of popularity or changing his politics to suit the chances of the times. He was a steadfast idealist as well as man of scrupulous honour."

Dr. Ambedkar and Mahatma Gandhi had publicly acknowledged that Mr. Jinnah was incorruptible. In fact, among the third world leaders, Mr. Jinnah was accepted by all as Mr. Clean. I wish the politicians of Pakistan had followed the path paved by the Quaid. The emergence of Pakistan stands out as a landmark in modern history as well as a personal triumph for Quaid-e-Azam. Unlike most other leaders of the colonial era, he was neither a rebel nor an agitator, but a constitutionalist to the core. While he shunned agitational politics, he struggled with success to wrest from the unwilling hands of the British and the Indian National Congress an independent Muslim state in South Asia through debate, discourse logic and negotiations.

There are probably two occasions when Mr. Jinnah had to make exceptions. At the farewell reception of Lord Willingdon, the Governor of Bombay, Mr. Jinnah's protests prevented presentation of address to him. Jinnah and his wife Ruttie, and their supporters were forcibly hustled by the Commissioner of Police out of the Hall. Citizens of Bombay hailed him as a great hero and erected People's Jinnah Hall to commemorate the historic incident. The second occasion was when Pandit Nehru and the Congress tried to wriggle out of the grouping provisions of the Cabinet Mission Plan. Quaid addressing the council of the Muslim League declared: "Today we have said goodbye to constitutions and constitutional methods." 16 August 1946 was declared as a day of Direct Action. The riots in Calcutta and other places led the British to announce Transfer of Power to India and Pakistan.

Quaid-e-Azam's speeches of 11 and 14 August, 1947 in the Constituent Assembly articulate his faith in the fundamental human rights, underpinned by the equality of all citizens, irrespective of religion, caste or creed. Quaid-e-Azam firmly believed in Tolerance, Transparency, Rules of Law, and Independence of Judiciary. Jinnah had identified "Peace within and peace without" as the goal of Pakistan's foreign policy. He declared that Pakistan wished to live in peace and to maintain cordial and friendly relations with the world at large, and that it had no aggressive designs against anyone. He reiterated Pakistan's desire to abide by the Charter of the United Nations and to make its full contribution to the peace and prosperity of the world. His message to the Muslim states was one of friendship and goodwill.

Quaid-e-Azam strongly supported the just struggle for self-determination of the people of Palestine and Kashmir. To our great misfortune, Jinnah was not destined to live long enough to see a constitution framed by the Pakistan Constituent Assembly. He did, however, specify certain broad parameters for the future constitution. In a broadcast to the people of the United States in February 1948, he said that while the constitution had yet to be framed, he did not know "what the ultimate shape of his constitution is going to be, but I am sure that it will be of a democratic type, embodying the essential principles of Islam... Islam and its idealism have taught us democracy. It has taught equality of men, justice and fair play.... We are the inheritors of these glorious traditions and are fully alive to our responsibilities and obligations as framers of the future constitution of Pakistan. In any case, Pakistan is not going to be a theocratic State-to be ruled by priests with a divine mission."

Quaid-e-Azam was conscious of Nuclear deterrence and gave clear indication as to the course to be adopted by Pakistan. On January 2, 1948 he said: "The destruction caused by the First World War pales into insignificance as compared to the devastation and havoc resulting from the last World War and now with the discovery of the Atom Bomb, one shudders to think of the pattern of future wars.

The war-weary humanity is watching with fear and hope the evolution of the United Nations Organisation for its ability to successfully deal with the causes of war and threats to world peace will depend on the salvation of mankind and the future of civilization. Pakistan, which has recently been admitted to the United Nations Organisation will do everything in its power to strengthen the Organisation and help in the achievement of the ideal which have been set up as its goal. While giving the fullest support to the principles of the United Nations Charter we cannot afford to neglect our defence.

However strongly the United Nations Organisation might be, the primary responsibility for the defence of our country will rest with us and Pakistan must be prepared for all eventualities and dangers. The weak and the defenceless in this imperfect world invite aggression from others. The best way in which we can serve the cause of peace is by removing the temptation from the path of those who think that we are weak, and therefore, they can bully or attack us.

That temptation can only be removed if we make ourselves so strong that nobody dare entertain any aggressive designs against us." The compelling circumstances in which Pakistan had to conduct nuclear tests on May 28, 1998 are well known. We must salute our scientist, specially Dr. Qadeer Khan, the valiant armed forces and the Presidents and the Prime Ministers who, notwithstanding the pressures persisted in proceeding with the nuclear programme. The people of Pakistan are proud that Pakistan is now the 7th nuclear State in the world.

Quaid-e-Azam was one of the great leaders of the 20th century. Mr. Jinnah had the charisma of Churchill, dignity of De Gaulle, magnetism of Mandela, and the rationality of Roosevelt. 11 September 2001 may be an international tragedy when terrorists attacked the two towers in New York and the Pentagon in Washington. But 11 September 1948 is a real national tragedy when the Father of the Nation died. Quaid gave his life so that Pakistan should live as a stable, progressive and prosperous State. To conclude, Quaid's message to the people of Pakistan was: "Search your hearts and see whether you have done your part in the construction of the new and mighty state. It is now upto you to work and work: and we are bound to succeed. And never forget our motto: Faith, Unity and Discipline."

JINNAH A PORTRAIT

An anglicized barrister who ended up founding a separate Muslim majority state is an apparent paradox but not really so, because had this urbane lawyer been any more religious he would have been unable to maintain unity amongst the ranks of his constituents, the deeply fractured and disjointed millions in the Muslim community. He would either be denounced as a Sunni or Shia or Barelvi or a Deobandi or something else.

Throughout his struggle for the Muslims, he maintained a very deliberate distance from them, for had he fraternized with one section, the other section would be alienated. Jinnah had to be quintessentially aloof and isolated, in an unapproachable ivory tower of impartiality. This, which was his greatest strength, is often presented as a paradox *i.e.* the paradox of a Bond street gentleman with no apparent hint of religiosity leading the unwashed and deeply religious masses of the subcontinent.

Indeed this was his solution to the deep divisions between Indians and India that had been his first and most important love. The young Lincoln's Inn returned Barrister, perhaps the youngest to be called to bar, could not find any reason why a United India could not work. He had opposed his co-religionists on the issue of separate electorates. Walking in the footsteps of Dadabhai Naoroji and Gokhale, he saw himself as an Indian first, second and last.

Such was his unwavering faith in this national goal that he made it a precondition to his joining the Muslim League in 1913 while remaining simultaneously a Congressman.

His advocacy of Hindu Muslim Unity won him the accolades of his countrymen and he was widely hailed as the Best Ambassador of "Hindu Muslim Unity." At the height of his legal career he represented Tilak against the sedition charges levelled by the British government. It was around this time that he led a successful protest against Lord Wellingdon, which the British broke up by sending the police. In his honour there stands the Jinnah Memorial hall and education trust even today, serving each and every community equally and fairly, in the city that he loved the most- Bombay.

What was the nature of his relationship with the British rulers? He was their harshest critic but never a rebel. While the Indian nationalist movement increasingly cried out "Free India or sink to our level", Jinnah said "Free India or raise us to your level". His vigorous campaigning got Indians the right to serve in army as officers and equals of the British.

Muhammad Ali Jinnah was by nature and role a lawyer and a legislator. He was instrumental in passing of such monumental bills as the restraint of child marriages, which he did so against the will of the obscurantist elements within the Muslim community, declaring forcefully as he had always done that legislation had nothing to do with religion and this certainly wasn't a religious matter. On several occasions he rose to defend some Indian dissident or the other, none more famous than Bhagat Singh, the young Sikh revolutionary who had been left high and dry by the so called national leadership.

In what was in my estimate his finest speech, he castigated the British for ignoring the long held standards of British justice and what he considered tyranny of the worst kind. And what of his most famous rival, the one the world considers one of the greatest ever? Jinnah respected Gandhi as a man of conviction but was uncomfortable with his style of mass politics. Gandhi had the finger on India's pulse. He gave up his western dress and law practice to become the "Mahatma" of the masses. He became one with them and in doing so he released, perhaps inadvertently, those dark forces that Jinnah had always feared.

Not only did Gandhi appeal to religious superstitions of the Hindu masses who were ready to worship him like a God, but he also encouraged Muslim divines to topple secular leadership like Jinnah and take matters into their own hands. Perhaps the approach would have worked, but the benefits were short lived as soon the dark forces turned on each other.

It was not out of some temporary irritation or annoyance that Jinnah, this secular and nationalist Congressman, turned to separatism, as some would have us believe. Nor was it some opportunism. H V Hodson ruled it out by saying that even his doughtiest opponents acknowledged his incorruptibility and steadfast idealism. He was supremely a man of honour and integrity, prompting Dr. Ambedkar to say that there was no other politician in the whole of South Asia to whom the word "incorruptible" more fittingly applied. In the mid 1930s when a group of Muslim students visited Jinnah in London with their "Pakistan scheme", he is supposed to have told them to "stay away, before I think of you as stooges of British imperialism". Then what changed? Why did Jinnah become the separatist mass politician that he himself had once despised? This question awaits its historian, but Woodrow Wyatt offers a simpler explanation. In an interview with Christopher Mitchell, the producer of a documentary on the life of Mr. Jinnah, Wyatt said that Jinnah was a lawyer brought up in England and lawyers brought up in England have a funny habit of fighting for justice.

Having taken up the case of the Muslim shariat and nobility in 1937, Jinnah slowly broadened the base of his litigants to include the entire Muslim community. This he was forced to do after the Congress party had refused to share power with the Muslim League in places where it had won all Muslim constituencies. In what was to seal the fate of a United India, Jawaharlal Nehru had taunted the Muslim League and its leader challenging them to find their own inherent strength.

It was then, that for the first time Jinnah had concluded that the Muslim minority of South Asia could no longer depend on small mercies by the majority. Like any good lawyer, and he considered him exactly that, he thus set out to win the case but what was the brief? The nuanced idea of a secular state with a Muslim majority is not always easy to relate to. Even harder is the idea of such a demand being a bargaining counter for ironclad safeguards within the union. It is here that Jinnah is cut down to size by occam's razor into a Darth Vader like figure, which he never was. "My father never wanted separation," declared Dina Wadia famously. Recent discoveries seem to favour her assertion. Jinnah's idea was of a loose federal union of India constituting Hindu majority and Muslim majority areas, which was to many a logical solution to a communal problem that had existed for centuries and a problem that Jinnah certainly did not invent or ascribe to at any point in his life.

But one thing is clear. Throughout his agonizing last few years, dying of Cancer and Tuberculosis, he was forced to take on not just the Congress Party or the British but also the Mullahs, who in large numbers opposed the Pakistan demand using the most humiliating and disgraceful language against him. There was pressure from within to declare an Islamic state based on Quran and Sunnah which he resisted tooth and nail, even expelling from the party his close friend the Raja of Mahmudabad. The impetuous Raja later repented and was allowed back in.

As Pakistan became certain, he showed his hand. His vision of Pakistan, which he repeated on numerous occasions, was one where sovereignty rested unconditionally with the people regardless of religion, caste or creed. On 11th August 1947, speaking to the constituent assembly he made plain that a person's religion was a personal matter and would have nothing to do with the business of the state. Citing the example of Catholic and Protestant conflict in England, Jinnah spoke of a modern nation state which would rise up above these differences and work towards the betterment of the people of Pakistan without distinction.

As if to cement his words, he appointed a Hindu Law minister to undertake the task of lawmaking in the new state. Sadly today every dictum laid down by him has been ignored as Pakistan is an avowed Islamic Republic. What did he imagine Pakistan's relations to be with India? He certainly did not foresee a nuclear arms race. He once told a young lady, who happens to be author Tariq Ali's mother, that he wanted open borders between Pakistan and India. Kuldip Nayyar, the Indian writer and parliamentarian, recalls often how Jinnah had told him that Pakistan would stand side by side India in the common defense of the subcontinent against all foreign invasions. On the eve of his departure from India he had appealed to let bygones be bygones and start afresh, an appeal no one has paid any heed to.

Many tributes have been paid to the life and times of Mr. Jinnah in the past. None greater than Saadat Hassan Manto's famous "Mera Sahab" or M N Roy's obituary for him, which are two of a kind because Manto was not the kind of person who wore his political opinion on his sleeves and M N Roy was a secular humanist of international stature. He has been described as Pakistan's George Washington, its King Emperor, its arch bishop of Canterbury, its Prime Minister all rolled in one, but I have a feeling he would have settled for much less. Nay he would have preferred to be called South Asia's Clarence Darrow, for like Darrow, Jinnah too had been a champion of unpopular causes, like the Suffrage movement with which he was deeply associated in England in the 1890s.

Jinnah too had championed reason and logic over superstition and he too had taken on a figure like William Bryan Jennings, said to be the greatest figure in American history since Thomas Jefferson. In the end Jinnah wanted to be acknowledged as a lawyer above all and he was, for his portrait today graces the most hallowed hall of British legal tradition *i.e.* the Great Hall of Lincoln's Inn, where he stands with some of the finest legal minds produced in 500 years

HISTORY OF JAMMU & KASHMIR

Jammu and Kashmir came into being as a single political and geographical entity following the Treaty of Amristar between the British Government and Gulab Singh signed on March 16, 1846. The Treaty handed over the control of the Kashmir State to the Dogra ruler of Jammu who had earlier annexed Ladakh. Thus a new State comprising three distinct religions of Jammu, Kashmir and Ladakh was formed with Maharaja Gulab Singh as its founder ruler. The feudal dispensation in the State, however, was too harsh for the people to live under and towards the end of a hundred years of this rule when their Indian brethren were fighting for independence from the British under the inspiring leadership of Mahatma Gandhi and Pandit Jawahar Lal Nehru, the Kashmiris led by a towering personality, the Sher-I-Kashmir Sheikh Muhammad Abdullah, rose against the autocracy. The autocratic rule came down heavily on the people's freedom movement. However, the people laid their lives in the cause of freedom and to uphold the ideals of secularism, equality, democracy and brotherhood.

The high point of the movement was July 13, 1931 when 22 protesters were martyred. The event strengthened the movement and contrary to the expectations of the then rulers, the peopled emerged more determined in their resolution to seek an end to autocratic rule. By the time the rulers could realise the futility of breaking the will of the people with the might of the State, the National Conference, headed by Sheikh Muhammad Abdullah, had become a mass movement and a force to reckon with. It broke the barriers of region and religion and became a popular and secular voice of the people of the State whose collective yearning was freedom from autocracy and the establishment of a popular rule. The people's movement spearheaded by the National Conference saw several ups and downs with its leaders particularly the Sher-I-Kashmir suffering vissitudes and long internment.

Accession

Jammu and Kashmir was one of about 565 princely States of India on which the British paramountcy lapsed at the stroke of midnight on August 15, 1947. While the power was transferred to the people in British India, the rulers of the princely States were given an option to join either of the two Dominions – India or Pakistan.

The Government of India Act 1935, as adopted in the Indian Independence Act, 1947, provided, "An Indian State shall be deemed to have acceded to the Dominion if the Governor General has signified the acceptance of an Instrument of Accession executed by the rule thereof." India, Pakistan and even Britain were party to these provisions. So the choice of joining either of the Dominions was left to the Rulers of the States concerned. Moreover, in the Indian Independence Act, 1947, there was no provision for any conditional accession.

The Ruler of Jammu and Kashmir, Maharaja Hari Singh did not exercise the option immediately and instead offered a proposal of Standstill Agreement to both the Dominion, pending final decision on State's accession. On August 12, 1947, the Prime Minister of Jammu and Kashmir sent identical communications to the Government of India and Pakistan which read, "Jammu and Kashmir Government would welcome Standstill Agreement with Union of India/Pakistan on all matters on which there exists arrangements with the outgoing British India Government." Pakistan accepted the offer and sent a communication to J&K Prime Minster on August 15, 1947. It read, "The Government of Pakistan agrees to have Standstill Agreement with Jammu and Kashmir for the continuation of existing arrangements ...". India did not agree to the offer and advised the Maharaja to send his authorized representative to Delhi for discussion on the offer.

The Story Behind

Pakistan, though entered into Standstill Agreement, had an eye on Jammu and Kashmir. Even before the lapse of the British paramountcy on J&K, Mr. Muhammad Ali Jinnah, author of two-nation theory, had plans to grab the Paradise on Earth. He had once boastfully declared that "Kashmir is blank cheque in my pocket." The Pakistan's designs on Kashmir could be well judged from the comments appearing on August 24, 1947 issue of its semi-official daily Dawn, "... the time has come to tell the Maharaja of Kashmir that he must make his choice and choose Pakistan.... Should Kashmir fail to join Pakistan the gravest possible trouble will inevitably ensue." In his bid to woo Sher-I-Kashmir Sheikh Mohammed Abdullah, the undisputed leader of Kashmir, Mr. Jinnah visited Srinagar a couple of times, but failed to achieve his objective. Even his arrogance and browbeating tactic did not pay him.

The Maharaja was already facing a formidable challenge from the people who had launched the Quit Kashmir movement under the leadership of Sher-I-Kashmir Sheikh Muhammad Abdullah against the autocratic rule. Quit Kashmir movement ran parallel to the national movement with Sheikh Muhammad Abdullah having close association with the leaders of the national movement against British rule.

The national leaders like Mahatma Gandhi and Pandit Nehru too espoused the cause of the people of Kashmir seeking political freedom from autocratic rule. To deal with the people's upsurge, Maharaja had even detained Sheikh Abdullah on May 20, 1946 for spearheading 'Quit-Kashmir' movement. Faced with new alarming situation arising out of repeated violations of the Standstill Agreement by Pakistan and blocking of Pindi-Srinagar road, the Maharaja set him free on September 29, 1947. Sher-I-Kashmir, as he was fondly called by the people for his unmatched courage, deputed his close aide Kh.G.M.Sadiq to Pakistan to tell Pak leaders about the sentiments of the people who can not be taken for granted and coerced to join them. This plain speaking did not desist Pak for her designs.

While addressing a mammoth public meeting at Hazuri Bagh, Srinagar on October 1, 1947, Sher-I-Kashmir had made things about the future of the state obvious when he said, "Till the last drop of my blood, I will not believe in two-nation theory." It was yet another rebuff to Mr. Jinnah. Finding their designs on Kashmir not fructifying, Pakistan rulers launched an armed attack on Jammu and Kashmir to annex it. Tribals in thousands alongwith Pak regular troops entered the State on October 22, 1947 from several points and indulged in bloodshed and mayhem. The bewildered people of the estate were not expecting an attack from Pakistan especially in view of the Standstill Agreement.

Bowing before the wishes of the people as reflected by Muslim dominated National Conference and to push back the invaders, the Maharaja signed the Instrument of Accession in favour of India on October 26, 1947 on the prescribed terms and conditions.

This was accepted by the Governor General of India, Lord Mountbatten next day. The Instrument of Accession executed by Maharaja Hari Singh was the same which was signed by other rulers of the princely States. Similarly, the acceptance of the Instrument of Accession by the Governor General was also identical in respect of all such instruments. He was to write, "I do hereby accept the Instrument of Accession." It could not be conditional as mere acceptance by the Governor General was complete and final.

With J&K becoming legal and constitutional part of Union of India, the troops were rushed to the state to push back the invaders and vacate aggression from the territory of the state. The first batch of Indian Army troops arrived at Srinagar airport immediately after the Accession was signed. On October 30, 1947 an Emergency Government was formed in the State with Sheikh Muhammad Abdullah as its head. The Army fought sustained battle with the tribals and after several sacrifices pushed them out of the Valley and other areas in the Jammu region.

Meanwhile, the people of Kashmir under the towering leadership of Sher-I-Kashmir were mobilised and they resisted the marching columns of the enemy. Till the arrival of the troops, it were mainly the Muslim volunteers under the command of Sheikh Muhammad Abdullah who braved death to push back invaders. Lt.General P.C.Sen who as Brigadier functioned as Commander of 161 Infantry Brigade in Srinagar during 1947-48, wrote in his book, 'Slander was the Thread', "These volunteers moved across the mountains and forests with speed and gave accurate information the army about enemy's strength, location and movements". While the army pushed back the invaders, there are several instances where people put up a gallant resistance and stopped the advance of the invaders. The most glaring examples of people's resistance was the martyrdom of Muhammad Maqbool Sherwani and Master Abdul Aziz.

Shaheed Sherwani, a staunch follower of Sher-I-Kashmir, did not oblige the invaders when they enquired from him the route to Srinagar. Instead, he put them on a wrong track gaining time for troops to come. Somehow the tribesmen came to know about his tactics and nailed him at a Baramulla crossing and asked him to raise pro-Pakistan slogans. He did raise slogans but these were different. These were pro-Hindu Muslim amity and in favour of Sher-I-Kashmir. Engaged by this, the ruthless tribesmen emptied their guns on him.

The sacrifice of Master Abdul Aziz too was exemplary. The invaders who raped the nuns and wanted other non-Muslim women to handed over to them, Master Abdul Aziz, a tailor by profession, held the holy Quran in his hand and said that they can touch the women only over his dead body and the holy Quran. The brutal killers did not spare him.

On January 1, 1948 India took up the issue of Pak aggression in Jammu and Kashmir in UNO under Article 35 of its charter. The Government of India in its letter to the Security Council said, "...Such a situation now exists between India and Pakistan owing to the aid which invaders, consisting of nationals of Pakistan and tribesmen... are drawing from Pakistan for operations against Jammu and Kashmir, a State which has acceded to the Dominion of India and is part of India.

The Government of India requests the Security Council to call upon Pakistan to put an end immediately to the giving of such assistance which is an act of aggression against India. If Pakistan does not do so, the Government of India may be compelled, in self defence, to enter into Pakistan territory to take military action against the invaders." After long debates, cease-fire came into operation on the midnight of January 1, 1949. Presence of Pak regular troops in the Valley was attested even by UNCIP documents (UNCIP first report).

At the time of cease-fire, Pakistan was holding 78114 sq.Kms illegally and this aggression on that territory continues even today. On March 5, 1948, the Maharaja announced the formation of an interim popular Government with Sheikh Muhammad Abdullah as the Prime Minister. Subsequently, the Maharaja signed a proclamation making Yuvraj Karan Singh as the Regent.

During one of the debates in UN Security Council on February 5, 1948, Sher-I-Kashmir, said "aggression and not the accession is the issue." The Security council, however, passed a resolution on plebiscite in Jammu and Kashmir subject to certain conditions. The resolution had three parts, one relating to cease-fire while the second, the most important and relevant, was a truce agreement which provided the mechanism for plebiscite. As per the agreement, Pakistan Government agreed to withdraw its troops from the State and undertake to secure the withdrawal of its tribesmen and nationals who had invaded the State. The territory thus evacuated by the Pakistani troops would be administered by local authorities under the surveillance of UN Commission for India and Pakistan.

The second part of this agreement related to the obligation of Government of India which would have come into force after Pakistan had fulfilled its obligation in part A of the agreement and thereby terminated the situation which occasioned the presence of Indian troops. On being notified that Pakistan had withdrawn its forces, the Government of India would begin withdrawal of bulk of its forces in stages but she will maintain the minimum strength of its forces necessary for law and order with the Commission stationing its observers.

The third part related to reaffirmation of both the countries to determine the wish of the people. Pakistan, knowing well the fate of such plebiscite at that time did not take any step to fulfil its obligations under the agreement and continued to hold the territory of the State illegally and forcefully even today. The issue plebiscite was linked with the condition of withdrawal of Pakistani forces and tribesmen from the occupied territory of the state which it never fulfilled, making the resolution absolutely irrelevant. On the other hand, J&K after attaining political freedom, marched ahead to strengthen democratic structure. Moreover, the truce agreement on plebiscite was superseded by the Simla Agreement between India and Pakistan signed on July 3, 1972 itself, the two countries undertook to resolve all differences bilaterally and peacefully. Pakistan, through its commitments enshrined in this Agreement, accepted the need to once and for all shift the Kashmir question from the UN to the bilateral plane.

In 1951, the State Constituent Assembly was elected by the people. The Assembly met for the first time in Srinagar on October 31, 1951. Close on the heels of this, the Delhi Agreement was signed between the two Prime Ministers of India and Jammu and Kashmir giving special position to the State under the Indian Constitutional framework. The Constituent Assembly elected the Yuvraj as the Sadar-I-Riyasat on November 15, 1952, thus bringing to end the 106 year old hereditary rule in Jammu and Kashmir. The State Constituent Assembly ratified the accession of the State to the Union of India on February 6, 1954 and the President of India subsequently issued the Constitution (Application to J&K) Order under Article 370 of the Indian Constitution extending the Union Constitution to the State with some exceptions and modifications.

The State's own Constitution came into force on January 26, 1957 under which the elections to the State Legislative Assembly were held for the first time on the basis of adult franchise the same year. This Constitution ratified the State's accession to Union of India. Section 3 of the Constitution makes this historic fact a reality. This section 3 of the Constitution says, "The Sate of Jammu and Kashmir is and shall be an integral part of the Union of India." The Section 4 of the Constitution defined the territories which on the fifteenth day of August, 1947, were under the sovereignty of suzerainty of the Ruler of the State." Since then eight assembly elections have been held in the state besides Lok Sabha elections where the people exercised their franchise freely.

While the people of the state continue to march ahead for socioeconomic emancipation as per the Naya Kashmir charter for better quality of life, Pakistan continued with her plans to grab Kashmir through force. Pakistan waged two wars in 1965 and 1971 to annex Kashmir but the people gave her befitting reply and repulsed her attacks with the help of army like they did in 1947-48. Failing to match India's military power, it launched a low intensity war through militancy in 1990 which took a toll of 20,000 human lives besides destroying private and public property.

THE WAY OF JINNAH

Muhammad Ali Jinnah, at Lahore, October 24, 1947: "I would like to impress upon every Musalman who has at heart the welfare and the prosperity of Pakistan, to avoid retaliation and to exercise restraint, because retaliation and violation of law and order will ultimately result in weakening the very foundations of the edifice you have cherished all these years to erect. Do your duty and have faith in God. There is no power on earth that can undo Pakistan." Wise words of warning, that went unheeded or unheard. Jinnah's Pakistan died with him, with the death knell of September 11, 1948, and it took his talented countrymen a mere 23 years to undo what remained. By December 1971 the nation lay sundered in half.

Now, after the passage of over half a century, we have a leadership that is attempting to rebuild the country and the nation in the mould as visualized by its maker, Jinnah. Speaking to the people from Jinnah's Mazar on December 25, commemorating the 125th anniversary of his birth, President General Pervez Musharraf told them that the way forward, the way he was attempting to take them, was Jinnah's way, as defined by him. But to move forward "we will have to step very cautiously." Whatever decisions he takes, said Musharraf, are taken with Jinnah's vision of Pakistan in mind. Jinnah's vision encompassed a welfare state drawing inspiration from the tenets of true Islam, built on the foundations of democracy, with respect and protection for the individual, with equal rights for men, women and children irrespective of their religious faith or political views.

He quoted from the speech made long ago, in 1941 by the country's maker to the Punjab Muslim Students Federation : "There are at least three main pillars which go to make a nation worthy of possessing a territory and running a government. One is education. Next, no nation and no people can ever do anything very much without making themselves economically powerful in commerce, trade and industry. And lastly, you must prepare yourselves for your defence, defence against external aggression and to maintain internal security."

In tune with Jinnah's enunciation of his creed in his never to be forgotten and always to be repeated time and time again speech of August 11 1947, Musharraf asked his countrymen to "sink all religious and sectarian differences and show tolerance of each other's beliefs, views and thoughts, to shun religious differences," as had the nation's father when addressing the members of the

Constituent Assembly. Religious intolerance, said Musharraf, has utterly blurred Jinnah's vision. The nation has deviated from that vision to the extent that aside from being unable to tolerate other religions, "we refuse to accommodate the views of the various sects of our own religion. We are killing each other for differences in fiqhs and maslaks. We have undermined Islam to a level that people of the world associate it with illiteracy, backwardness, intolerance, obscurantism and militancy."

And what was it that Jinnah told his assembly members? "You are free, free to go to your temples, you are free to go to your mosques or to any other places of worship in this state of Pakistan. You may belong to any religion or caste or creed that has nothing to do with the business of state. As you know, history shows that in England conditions some time ago were much worse than those prevailing in India today.

"The Roman Catholics and the Protestants persecuted each other. Even now there are some states in existence where there are discriminations made and bars imposed against a particular class. Thank God, we are not starting in those days. We are starting in the days when there is no discrimination, no distinction between one caste or creed and another. We are starting with this fundamental principle that we are all citizens and equal citizens of one state.

The people of England in course of time had to face the realities of the situation and had to discharge the responsibilities and burdens placed upon them by the government of their country and they went through that fire step by step, today, you might say with justice that Roman Catholics and Protestants do not exist, what exists now is that every man is a citizen, an equal citizen of Great Britain and they are all members of the nation. Now I think we should keep that in front of us as our ideal".

Now, from the very beginning, from the outset, the leaders of Pakistan who have followed Jinnah have distorted his words to suit their immediate expedient self-serving purposes. This particular passage from his most important address has been subject to deliberate distortion and misinterpretation, having inspired the dishonest dogmatists who misappropriated the country after his death. In the official biography of Jinnah commissioned by the Government of Pakistan, written by Hector Bolitho and published in 1954, it was brutally bowdlerized to falsely read: " You may belong to any religion or caste or creed-that has nothing to do with the fundamental principle that we are all citizens and equal citizens of one state. Now, I think we should keep that in front of us as our ideal...".

We had to wait for an American, Professor Stanley Wolpert, to write what is the definitive biography of the man Jinnah as he really was-and he was commissioned by no one but himself. Yet, when the book was published in 1984 its distribution in Pakistan was proscribed because of one passage he had quoted from M C Chagla's book, 'Roses in December' which referred to Jinnah's eating and drinking preferences.

Wolpert was put under much pressure (as he reminded us when he spoke at the Aga Khan University auditorium this December 26) when the government of General Zia-ul-Haq offered to buy thousands of copies of his book were he to excise that particular passage. Of course, he refused. The amount of research Wolpert has put into his book can be gauged from the 40-odd pages of Notes and Bibliography. Back to MAJ and February 19, 1948, when he again stressed : "But make no mistake, Pakistan is not a theocracy or anything like it. Islam demands from us the tolerance of other creeds and we welcome in closest association with us all those who of whatever creed are themselves willing and ready to play their part as true and loyal citizens of Pakistan."

As he was to say a few days later: "In any case, Pakistan is not going to be a theocratic state to be ruled by priests with a divine mission. We have many non-Muslims-Hindus, Christians and Parsis. They are all Pakistanis. They will enjoy the same rights and privileges as any other citizens and will play their rightful part in the affairs of Pakistan.

What he tried to make clear on August 11, 1947 to the future legislators and administrators of his country is that "the first duty of a government is to maintain law and order, so that the life, property and religious beliefs of its subjects are fully protected by the state." He told them he would not tolerate the evils of bribery, corruption, blackmarketeering and "this great evil, the evil of nepotism and jobbery," the daily bread of powermongers. Little did he know that day that these prime evils were to become prerequisites for the survival of the politicians in and out of uniform and of the administrators of all ranks and grades for the maintenance of their power.

Musharraf admitted this on December 25 that "corruption and nepotism have eaten the nation like termites from within". He made an appeal to the so-called 'elite', the rich elite (most of them undeserving of the appellation) : "Let society treat the corrupt with contempt so that the fear of God is put into them and they at least hide and feel ashamed instead of showing off their ill-gotten riches." Yes, general, you are right. But then would Muhammad Ali Jinnah approve of your National Accountability Bureau when it makes 'deals' with the corrupt, with the robbers, and rather than extracting what it can from their ill-gotten gains, and then letting them stand trial and be sentenced and hopefully be sent to jail, it frees them, as reportedly is happening with the former chief of our Navy?

However, and whatever may happen, Jinnah's enunciated vision for his country cannot be changed, no matter how invasive the censorship and bowdlerizing of his words. If we do now have a man intent upon focusing upon that vision, and with the strength and support to see that the vision becomes reality, we should be a grateful nation.

At Last, A Fair and Accurate Book on the Life and Politics of Jinnah

Whenever India's independence from Britain is mentioned, two names connected with the event dominate: 'Mahatma' Karamchand Gandhi and Jawaharlal Nehru. Meanwhile, Muhammad Ali Jinnah, the founder of Pakistan, is either mentioned only in passing, usually as villain of the piece, or totally ignored.

Such is the prejudice Jinnah experienced from both British and Hindu politicians in his life. This prejudice existed before, during and after the independence of India. Jinnah was undermined by Hindu politicians to their own loss because the pretence not to understand him led to the partition of the subcontinent. The ultimate result was that the country was carved out in such a haphazard manner that its consequences still linger on. This new book, part of the Oxford University Press's Jubilee Series, analyses how the State of Pakistan was created and reappraises the personality and politics of the State's founder, 'Quaid-i-Azam' (the great leader) Muhammad Ali Jinnah.

Perhaps the first point to make is that, for a change, both authors are sympathetic and knowledgeable on Pakistani affairs. Professor S M Burke is a former professor and consultant in South Asian Studies at the University of Minnesota. His co-author in this venture is another scholar, Mr Salim Al-Din Quraishi, Head of the Modern South Asian Section of the British library.

Among the history makers of this century Muhammad Ali Jinnah is perhaps the most misunderstood. The reasons for this are twofold. First, the history of Indian independence, partition, and Pakistan has been dominated by Hindu historians, who have inherited the kind of animosity against Muslims usually reserved for their most bitter enemies.

Second, the British historians, who wrote about Jinnah, Pakistan and Muslims, went one better. The British did not write much about him because he stood up to them, because of Jinnah's upright, transparent personality, correct manners, and above all, the way in which he presented his irrefutable arguments. Lord Mountbatten, Britain's last viceroy in India, found him more than his match. Had Jinnah behaved against his conscience, as half-naked, intentionally homeless, starving in public, travelling third class rather than in first as he always did, his value and status in British eyes would have been enhanced. But Jinnah was his own man. He never felt compelled to resort to such a ridiculous position and reduce himself to degrading theatrical acts, as others did. He did not lead a double life. Jinnah's greatness lies in the fact that at all times he presented himself as he really was, irrespective of how others wanted him to behave.

Meanwhile Pakistanis also have not written well about either Jinnah or Pakistan to redress the imbalance. So, the gap was filled by outsiders and foreigners with little sympathy for these subjects.

The result is that Pakistan and Jinnah are universally misunderstood, even by Muslims particularly in the Arab world. His critics' dislike of him also emanates from a misunderstanding that he wanted to divide India to satisfy his own ego. Jinnah denied this time and again. He was determined, though, to fight for the civil and political rights of the Muslims within the union of India. His concentration on this point was unbreakable. His long membership of and active participation in the Indian National Congress Party testify to this.

During his dealings with the Congress, he thought of himself as an Indian nationalist and a believer in Hindu-Muslim unity. After working within the Congress Party for many years he became disillusioned with the machinations of Mohandas Karamchand Gandhi and disgusted with Nehru and other Hindu leaders' prejudices. The Hindus at no time showed any magnanimity towards their Muslim fellow citizens which made it difficult for Jinnah to maintain his faith in the possibility of a permanent amicable relationship between India's two major peoples.

Jinnah's relations with the Congress lasted only long enough for him to discover its true nature, which he found incompatible with the aspirations of the Muslims who longed for their civil and political rights to be protected under constitutional and electoral guarantees. Disillusioned and disappointed, Jinnah finally realised that the parting of ways was unavoidable and made a clean break from the party. These are some of the historical points elaborated in this book which give the reader a greater insight into what really happened and what could have been averted.

Gandhi himself admitted that religion was the inspiration of his politics long before Jinnah started to demand a separate homeland for Muslims. Gandhi frankly declared in his autobiography (1927): 'I can say without the slightest hesitation, and yet in all humility, that those who say that religion has nothing to do with politics do not know what religion means.' In another book, Gandhi is quoted as saying: 'If I seem to take part in politics, it is only because politics today encircles us like the coils of a snake from which one cannot get out no matter how one tries. I wish to wrestle with the snake. I am trying to introduce religion into politics.' Nehru, too, concedes that Gandhi introduced religion into politics. He says in his autobiography, 'Gandhiji, indeed, was continuously laying stress on the religious and spiritual side of the movement. His religion was not dogmatic, but it did mean a definitely religious outlook on life, and the whole movement was strongly influenced by this and took a revivalist character so far as the masses were concerned.'

Jinnah, on the other hand, was convinced that Hindu-Muslim cooperation was a noble and achievable aim provided the political and religious rights of the Muslims could be safeguarded. A united India, free from tensions and social chaos was Jinnah's original dream. But an ideologically united, politically integrated, constitutionally secure India could not be achieved because Gandhi and Nehru never reassured the Muslims that they would be safe in a Hindu-dominated country. The final chance for this was in 1945 when the Cabinet Mission Plan was accepted by Jinnah but rejected out of hand by Nehru. If Gandhi and Nehru had their way, the Muslims would have suffered permanent Hindu majority domination in the name of democracy. A Pakistan, albeit truncated, mutilated or motheaten, was the only option Jinnah could accept. The book is so persuasively written and painstakingly researched that it is difficult to argue with its convincing evidence that Gandhi left no option for Jinnah but to demand a separate State for Muslims.

It is most unfair that Jinnah is often described by Indian and British writers as arrogant and unfriendly. The authors of this book have diligently researched Jinnah's past to discover the sort of person he really was. Their findings after meticulous appraisal belie this description. Even the television footage, shown in Britain on his birth anniversary on December 25 last year, does not support that idea of Jinnah. On the contrary, he is shown smiling at Gandhi, receiving him respectfully at his Bombay residence with good grace. His character assassination may be based on the belief that if enough mud is thrown at him, some is bound to stick.

Had Jinnah been dealing with such Hindu leaders as Bal Gangadhar Tilak, who understood the tears of the Muslims and an accord at the Lucknow Pact of 1916 between the Congress and the Muslim League, or Gopal Krishna Gokhale, another realist who got on well with Jinnah and understood Hindu-Muslim aspirations well, India would be one country today, and a more powerful and prosperous one perhaps. It was after Gokhale's death in 1915, and Tilak's in 1920, that the political atmosphere changed radically. Had either or both lived a bit longer, and Jinnah at the helm of Muslim affairs, not only might India have remained undivided but independence may also have come sooner. The two communities would have had a shared priority: to win freedom for their country. There would have been a will to succeed and a meeting of minds among the leaders of all factions. Instead, the situation rapidly deteriorated into virtual warfare.

Although Gandhi comes in for a great deal of criticism, the authors make it plain at the outset that their 'purpose in discussing the extraordinary aspects of Mahatma Gandhi's philosophy and political tactics is not to question his saintliness nor to deny his status as the most venerated Hindu of modern times. But this book is not on the lofty subjects of religion and ethics. It is on the down-to-earth subject of politics and we needed to explain our view that Gandhi was not a practical politician and that he, and not Jinnah, was really responsible for wrecking the chances of Hindu-Muslim unity.'

A lot of attention is focused on Gandhi's theory of nonviolence by writers and journalists throughout the world. Jinnah's tactics were essentially non-violent too, but nothing is written about this. In fact, one of the greatest violent acts in the history of mankind was committed in India when an approximately two million civilians were murdered under the very noses of Nehru and Gandhi. The authors have undertaken the herculian task of explaining the duplicitous character of Gandhi's political thought, particularly when Jinnah was made to look like a separatist and communal leader while Gandhi cultivated a non-violent, non-sectarian facade. This sham was also promoted, of course, by the Hindu media barons who dominated India's press.

The authors have quoted from some Hindu writers and politicians who did not approve of Gandhi's politics either. For instance, Tilak is quoted as saying, 'I have great respect and admiration for Gandhiji, but I do not like his politics. If he would retire to the Himalayas and give up politics, I would send him fresh flowers from Bombay every day because of my respect for him.'

On May 9, 1933, a joint statement by Subhash Chandra Bose and Vallabhbhai Patel declared: 'We are clearly of the opinion that as a political leader Mahatma Gandhi has failed. The time has, therefore, come for a radical reorganisation of the Congress on a new principle and with a new method. For bringing about this reorganisation a change of leadership is necessary.'

Throughout this book, the writers' experience, knowledge and incisive analysis of the events before, during and after the creation of Pakistan are convincingly explained. There is no confusion or ambiguity as to what they mean. No events of that period are lost in the mist of time or blurred by subsequent developments. The praise it has received is well earned. It is a serious book and can be read by people with all shades of opinion. It is essential reading for historians, teachers and journalists. Having read it, the reader will come to the same conclusion as the authors have reached: that Gandhi was not a practical politician, that he, and not Jinnah, who shattered the unity of India.

JINNAH'S NEW REPUBLIC

Its creator and governor general, M. A. Jinnah, has described Pakistan as "the biggest Moslem state... and the fifth biggest sovereign state in the world." Though the second point might be disputed, Pakistan is unquestionably worthy of attention, for it is situated just where the Anglo-American and Soviet orbits touch in the strategic Central Asian theatre.

Seldom has a new state been created under such contradictory pressures or with such a load of full-grown problems. Control of the government is vested in a few top officials, supported by a powerful bureaucracy, but Britain has a say in matters of defense, finance, and foreign policy. Already the government is shot through with corruption and nepotism. Social life is dominated by Mohammedan concepts, including the subjection of women. The structure of the state, however, has not yet had time to harden, and internal strains may reshape it in another image.

Although Mr. Jinnah exaggerates when he describes his dominion as "blessed with enormous resources and potentialities," Pakistan is undoubtedly "workable" economically. With an: area of 230,000 square miles, one-fourth larger than 1933 Germany, it has a population of 70,000,000, about the same number as 1933 Germany. It produces an agricultural surplus and can export part of its wheat and rice and a good deal of its valuable jute crop. It also has some oil and chromite and considerable potential water power. Industrially it is the most backward part of the whole under-industrialized subcontinent. There are scattered woollen, cement, sugar, and cotton mills, but cloth and most other manufactured goods must be imported; some 85 per cent of the raw jute of all India is grown in Pakistan, but the jute mills are in Calcutta. Pakistan has no known coal or iron and only one modern port, Karachi. The people are largely illiterate; only 4 per cent can read as against 12 per cent in India. Among the well-educated, here as in India, are too many lawyers and too few engineers.

Close and friendly relations with the Indian dominion seem essential to the development of Pakistan's potentialities. The Congress Party, indeed, finally agreed to partition, after years of deadlock, partly in the belief that Pakistan could not exist as a separate state. "Let them have their Pakistan," it was argued, "if they'll take it without the eastern Punjab and without Calcutta and western Bengal. They won't have any coal, capital, or industries, and we can throttle them economically. After a few years they'll come crawling back!" This attitude, although not shared by the entire Congress high command, has certainly pervaded the partition operations. In the division of assets the Moslems have had to make a separate fight for virtually every typewriter and ream of paper. Difficulties have even been raised over the handling of mail.

Pakistan's economic troubles have been immeasurably increased by the bloody communal conflicts and the resulting influx of refugees. Almost every Moslem League leader from Mr. Jinnah down believes that this refugee inundation was part of a plot to swamp the Pakistan government before it could get established. "I'm sure that Nehru isn't a party to this plot," one declared, "but I'm just as sure that it is the backing of Patel [India's Home Minister] and Baldev Singh [the Defense Minister and a Sikh]."

With enormous problems, Pakistan has only a very ordinary set of leaders to cope with them. The brilliant Mr. Jinnah, of course, must be excepted, but he is over seventy and has been in poor health since a severe pneumonia attack two years ago. His voice can barely be heard ten feet away, and he chose to become governor general rather than premier partly because it was an easier post. He has repeatedly told subordinates, "I have done my part of the job; I've given you Pakistan. It is up to you to build it."

Premier Liaqat Ali Khan is a competent administrator with the conservative social views of a typical feudal landlord and a strong belief in a political and economic alliance with Great Britain. He had to chose a man of technical ability for his Finance Minister but the other members of his Cabinet are all mediocrities. So farfetched was the appointment of the Calcutta hide merchant, Faziur Rahman, as Minister of the Interior and Education that an old friend, seeing him in a front seat at the Independence Day celebrations, cried out, "You're in the wrong row; that's for the Cabinet!" Top officials are in the main from the landlord class, with a sprinkling of lawyers and merchants. The sole modern-minded industrialist in the dominion, Hassan Ispahani, is being sent out of the way as ambassador to the United States. Provincial officials are of the same kind: the Punjab Premier is the Khan of Mamdot, the province's largest landholder.

Considerable opposition to this leadership is manifesting itself, although it is still unorganized. After 1944, when the Moslem League became a mass movement, clerks, small shopkeepers, mechanics, and poor peasants thronged to its meetings, and it was they who finally obtained partition. Many of them were recruited through religious appeals; others through the promise of better living conditions. The economic discontent formerly directed against the commercially dominant Hindus and Sikhs—it still provides much of the fuel for the Moslem arson gangs—is gradually being turned against the wealthy Moslem League leaders. The story is told that when Mumtaz Daultana, the brains of the West Punjab ministry, went to his huge Multan estate in August, his Moslem tenants, all staunch League members, congratulated him on the achievement of Pakistan, and landlord and tenants feasted together. But a pall was thrown over the festivities when a peasant asked, "When will the land be given to us?" This question is being asked repeatedly, for agrarian reforms have been promised by the League.

Similar resentment against the rich is voiced in the towns. A Moslem clerk who is the local secretary of the League in his ward is made conscious of social differences when he goes from his filthy, overcrowded tenement home to the palatial residence of the provincial leader. At a recent meeting in Lahore a fervent young Leaguer exclaimed, "The rich are finished! Let us shoot them!"

Some of this radicalism is spontaneous; some of it is the work of the progressives in the League, who are influential throughout Pakistan but especially in the Punjab. These agitators are usually well-educated, modernminded young people with a war-gained knowledge of foreign countries, a strongly nationalist point of view, and a liberal approach to social problems, including the position of women. One of the most prominent is Mian Iftikharud-Din, known as "Ifti," a wealthy, radical Moslem who was formerly president of the Congress Party in the Punjab and twice jailed by the British. Now publisher of the Pakistan *Times* and a member of the Constituent Assembly, he is looked up to by young, progressive Moslems but kept at a distance by League leaders. The tactics of the young progressives have reached a stratum of Moslems never before interested, and at Lahore and Peshawar there have been mass demonstrations of Moslem women clad in the ghostly looking white burqas, a cover-all garment with a net eye-slit which enables orthodox Moslem women to appear in public without being seen. The League leaders welcomed such mass support in fighting for Pakistan—although many had prejudices against women in politics—but now they are embarrassed by the claims of the awakened and demanding millions.

During the Lahore riots some of the inflamed young Moslems asked the League progressives for guidance. "We tried to slow them down," a leftist Moslem leader said, "but we couldn't oppose them openly. The Communists attacked us for this, saying we could not be considered progressive if we did not openly fight Moslem communalism, but we know that would have meant isolating ourselves from our people."

A major conflict is now looming over the question of how closely Pakistan should be tied to Britain. Nationalist-minded Pakistanis, among whom are most of the young people and the new League rank and file, are dismayed by the number of Britons in the administration. Three of the five provincial governors, five of the nine departmental secretaries, and all the high officers of the armed forces are British. Informed nationalists think it necessary to keep certain Britons for their technical skills but do not want this to be carried too far. Army officers do not object to serving under British generals temporarily, but are concerned that the army should continue to be equipped solely with British materiel and indignant that promotions have been left in British hands. Some nationalists charge that when Premier Liaqat Ali Khan was in London a year ago he committed Pakistan to remaining within the British economic sphere.

In the Punjab even the League right-wingers are anti-British, because the British governor there kept the League out of office for over a year and because the boundary award is considered unfair. In consequence a substantial number of Britons have been dismissed, but many of these have turned up with the central government at Karachi. The railway specialist, A. G. Hall, for example, was put out by the Punjab government but is now director general of railways for all Pakistan. To protests about the great number of Britons in the Pakistan service, the Premier is reported to have replied: "Before the transfer of power Lord Mountbatten had both the League and the Congress members of the interim government promise to keep on all British officials who wanted to stay and against whom we could not make a specific case." It is interesting to note that of those who have stayed, the great majority have chosen to serve in Pakistan. While this may be due in part to the fact that opportunities are greater in the less-advanced state, there is certainly a feeling among the British that although

India will probably declare its independence, Pakistan may be kept within the empire. The likelihood is enhanced by the character of the League leaders, almost none of whom are known for militant nationalism.

Since Pakistan's establishment, League officers have been cautious about declaring where they stand with respect to the conflict between Russia and the West. Pakistan is nearer to the Soviet border than to either Britain or the United States, and substantial segments of public opinion show an interest in the U. S. S. R. Even orthodox Moslems are watching developments in the Soviet Moslem areas, such as Bokhara, which are close to Pakistan culturally as well as geographically. Not all the League progressives are pro-Communist, but many seem to feel that some sort of socialism, usually referred to as "Islamic socialism," is necessary to make Pakistan a strong modern state. There would certainly be overwhelming opposition to allowing Britain and the United States to use Pakistan's military strength or strategic position to further their own designs.

The future of the Moslem League is already a subject of dispute. Old League officers, fearing that the impoverished Moslems will follow the progressives if the government does not soon grant their demands, are tending to abandon the organization which brought them to power and to rely increasingly on the bureaucracy which they inherited from the British and on their new powers of bribery through job distribution. Moslem religious leaders are attacking young, modern-minded progressives as "anti-Islamic," and telling the women to forget about politics and go back into *purdah*. But it is not easy to turn back the clock. "We have learned that even women have power, and they can't make us forget it," said a Lahore housewife to me.

LINLITHGOW ASKED JINNAH IF HE SERIOUSLY CONTEMPLATED THAT HIS MAJESTY'S GOVERNMENT

'should now go back to Parliament, after ten years of endeavouring with the help of Indian opinion, and with the utmost publicity, to devise a workable scheme, and after two years experience to suggest that in the Provinces the scheme devised admitted of being worked; say that the idea of the transfer of responsibility to Indian shoulders for which we have been working was all mere nonsense, and that something completely different, on the lines which Jinnah now indicated would have to be devised? Why should we carry that baby?' Jinnah said that was precisely the position. He quite recognised that it was not attractive from the point of view of His Majesty's Government, or to the British in India, but if we carried the advantages we must also carry the burdens, and so long as there was any shadow of authority in India exercised by His Majesty's Government we might be perfectly certain that we should be landed with every possible responsibility by Hindu and Muslim alike.'

The Viceroy found this an extremely informative interview. Even allowing for Jinnah's defensive tendency to exaggerate, his words did link up with the feeling of uncertainty about the future in various quarters...

[*In the spring of 1939*] the chances of a cooperative attitude by Congress toward Federation seemed more promising, [*but*] this was not true of the Muslims. Jinnah had, under threat of resignation, forced the Muslims in the Assembly to abstain in the division of a new trade agreement for India, thus causing an important defeat to the Government. Constitutionally this did not make any difference to the outcome because the Viceroy used his powers of certification to restore the necessary provisions, but tactically the move surprised Linlithgow. It also annoyed many prominent Muslims throughout the country who criticised Jinnah strongly. The Viceroy was told that Jinnah wanted a year in which to try out the policy of supporting neither the Government nor its opponents in the hope that each would be convinced of the value of Muslim support and would bid for it.

Linlithgow reported an hour's discussion which he had with Jinnah, mainly on the subject of Muslim grievances. They talked about the political position generally. Jinnah then turned to the Viceroy and said that he would frankly confess that he saw no solution and that he did not now believe that this country was competent to run a democracy; that he and others who had advocated a reformed system of government had, he felt in the light of practical experience, formed a wrong judgment of the capacity of India to run such a system.

Jinnah thought that propertied Hindus were coming to the same conclusion. Everybody had been carried away by a natural desire for home rule and by an objection to government by aliens, 'but he was satisfied now, he thought, that the present system would not work and that a mistake had been made in going so far. He concluded these observation by reminding me that the country depended on us.'

Linlithgow replied to Jinnah that if this was true he and other Indian political leaders had bluffed His Majesty's Government and the British electorate into thinking that their scheme for self-government under the Act was a good one. In any case to what form of government should they revert? Jinnah did not like this question and made no positive suggestion for carrying on the government of the country if the present scheme broke down.

The Viceroy had no doubt that the Muslims were becoming increasingly uneasy at what Jinnah described as 'Hindu arrogance' and more and more apprehensive of the fate of a minority-even a minority of ninety million people-under the scheme of the Act. He felt there was some foundation for Jinnah's allegations of unfair treatment of Muslims in particular Provinces although investigation had never borne these out.. Zetland's reply was to the point: 'It is at least refreshing to find Jinnah admitting an error of judgment in pressing for parliamentary government for India and saying further that the situation depended upon us. I should however, be not a little surprised if he proved willing to say the same thing in public. Indeed I should be more surprised if, in the event of our even suggesting the possibility of our having to consider the imposition of any restriction on the free play of democratic forces in India, Jinnah did not shout as loudly against us as the most rabid Congressman!'..

Exchanges of view between the Viceroy and Zetland on the Muslim problem continued until well into the summer. Linlithgow traced the course of the argument as it had developed during the three Round Table Conferences and the sittings of the Joint Select Committee which had preceded the 1935 Act. He wrote that neither of them should be surprised that the near approach of Federation had brought Muslim fears to the surface.

During those earlier discussions the Muslims had made demands of the most excessive character but at no stage had the British Government been able to go further than in the scheme of the Act. They had not felt justified in doing so either on the merits of the case or as a matter of practical politics, given the legitimate claims of other communities and the necessity to get them into any workable scheme. The root of Muslim apprehensions, said the Viceroy, lay in any system of responsible central government. [*responsible=responsible to legislature*]. No plan for Federation based upon representative government could be acceptable to those Muslims who contemplated the future course of Indian politics as an unending communal contest. But the Government were agreed that an all-India Federation was the only practical line of constitutional advance as also was it the necessary corollary of provincial autonomy. Linlithgow continued: 'I do not think that the Muslims have it in their power to prevent the attainment of Federation, or to make it unworkable-unless they can discover means to prevent a sufficient number of Rulers from acceding. Indeed I shall be most surprised if, when the test comes, Muslims do not work the federal constitution to the best of their opportunities...I shall be very greatly mistaken if we do not find that the two communities will work much more closely together with the degree of responsibility at the centre which the Federation involves...'

In June there was a meeting of some of the leading Princes and their ministers in Bombay. They resolved that they regarded the terms of the federal offer as fundamentally unsatisfactory and unacceptable in their present form... Linlithgow's dilemma was acute.

He had asked to be allowed to put pressure on the Princes before the Bombay meeting-pressure in their own interests. But Churchill and the diehards were in a determined mood. Having insisted successfully at the outset that the Princes should not be pressed to accept they were not going to draw back now. Their tactical position was strong for they themselves were applying all the pressure they could muster to dissuade the reluctant Princes from acceptance. As Linlithgow pointed out to Zetland, the Government had allowed its hands to be tied....

Whatever the ethics of these Princes' behaviour at Bombay, the main force behind their intransigence lay in the genuine fear activated by the Congress attack on the States the previous winter. Zetland was told this by the Mysore representative at the conference and there can be no doubt of its truth. Congress was reaping where it had so impetuously sown...

On 21st August [the Viceroy] addressed the Standing Committee of the Chamber of Princes at Simla. While he reiterated that the decision was for the Princes to take he told them he thought the federal offer was very favourable to them. They would have one third of the seats in the Lower House and two fifths in the Upper House. This, he told them, had always seemed to him to be a bloc which, if the Princely Order were wise and held together, no political party could afford to ignore...

The Princes must see, as was evident to any skilled observer, how difficult it would be to retain the so-called 'irresponsible Centre' indefinitely... Leading members of the *[Princely]* Order had after all been directly responsible for the emergence of the *[Federal]* ideal as a result of the Round Table Conference... Finally Linlithgow reminded the Princes of all the care which had been taken over many years of deliberation and discussion before the passing of the 1935 Act...

When the outbreak of war put an end to this scheme nearly two-fifths of the States had expressed their readiness to join, some of them making accession conditional upon protection of treaty rights. This represented twenty seats out of fifty-two and a population of eleven millions out of thirty-nine million.. *[When war broke out]* both the Secretary of State and the Viceroy agreed that further steps towards *[Federation]*must now be postponed for the duration. The Hindus, who had so foolishly let slip a golden chance to help in its realisation, now regretted the position. The Muslims were delighted. The Princes felt relieved.

4

Muslim League

The success of Simla Deputation made it imperative for the Muslims of the Sub Continent to have their own political organization. In 1906, the Muslims of India founded a political party of their own known as *"All India Muslim league."*

CAUSES OF MUSLIM LEAGUE'S FOUNDATION

The partition of Bengal by the British Government in 1905 greatly embittered the relations between Hindus and Muslims. The partition ensured a number of political benefits for the Muslim but the Hindus reacted towards the partitions of Bengal in a hostile and violent manner.

This made it clear that the Hindus were not willing to give Muslims their due share. This violent protest of the Hindus convinced the educated Muslims that they could be redeemed only if they created their own political force and their own leadership.

AIMS OF MUSLIM LEAGUE

The aims of Muslim League are given below:

1. To safe guard and protect Muslim interests and to convey their demands to British Government.
2. To create a feeling of respect and good will in Muslim for the British Government.
3. To promote brotherhood between the different nations of India.

Role of Muslim League

The role played by All India Muslim League in the creation of Pakistan is summarized under:

1. *Minto – Morley Reform Act – 1909:* The Muslims under the able leadership of the Muslim league now began to press for the separate electorate for the Muslims. The authorities accepted their demand in an Act, called *"The Minto – Morley Reform Act"*, in 1909.
2. *Lucknow Pack – 1916:* In November 1916, two committees of League and Congress met at Calcutta and drew an agreement draft of political reform for India called *"Lucknow Pact."* Through this pact the Congress recognized the separate status of Muslims.
3. *Simon Commission:* In 1927, Simon Commission was sent to India under the chairmanship of Sir John Simon to settle Muslim Hindu differences. It was rejected because there was no Indian member on the commission.
4. *Jinnah's Fourteen Points – 1929:* The Quaid-e-Azam refused to accept the Nehru – report. In order to protect the Muslim's point of view on the political issues of South Asia, he prepared a draft of guiding principles consisting of 14 points, popularly known as *"Jinnah's Fourteen Points."*
5. *Allama Iqbal's Allahabad Address – 1930:* In 1930, in his presidential address at annual session of League at Allahabad, Iqbal proposed the formation of a separate Muslim State by combining Northern and South-Western Muslim majority region in Sub Continent.
6. *Day of Deliverance:* On 22 December, Muslim League observed *"Deliverance Day"* to thank God for resignation of Congress Ministers.
7. *Pakistan Resolution - 1940:* The attitude of the Hindus made it clear that the Hindus and the Muslims were two separate nations. On March 23, at the annual session of Muslim League at Lahore, the famous resolution, commonly known as the Pakistan Resolution was passed. It was presented by Maulvi Fazlul Haq. Quaid-e-Azam said in his address:

"By all means Muslims are one nation and they need a separate homeland where they could live their spiritual, cultural, economical, social and political lives independently."

8. *Cripps Mission - 1942:* Sir Stafford Cripps was sent by the British Government to India, to discuss with Indian leaders, the future Indian Constitutions. His proposal was rejected by both the Congress and the League. The Congress characterized them as "a postdated cheque on a failing bank." Jinnah said that:

   "If these were accepted "Muslims would become a minority in their majority provinces as well."

9. *Gandhi Jinnah Talks - 1944:* Gandhi held talks with Jinnah to discuss about the future of India, but no fruitful results came out of it because Gandhi did not accept Muslims as a separate nation.

   Louis Feisher wrote:

   "The wall between Jinnah and Gandhi was the Two Nation Theory."

10. *Simla Conference - 1945:* Lord Wavell called a conference at Simla. The conference failed to achieve any purpose due to one sided attitude of Lord Wavell. In this conference, Quaid-e-Azam made it crystal clear that the Muslim League can represent Muslims of India.

11. *General Elections – 1945 -1946:* Elections for the central and provincial assemblies were held in 1945-1946 in which Muslim League won 30 seats of central legislative meant for Muslims and 430 seats out of 495 in the provincial legislative. Quaid-e-Azam said on this occasion:

    "I have no doubt now in the achievement of Pakistan. The Muslims of India told the world what they want. No power of world can topple the opinion of 10 crore Muslims of India."

12. *Cabinet Mission - 1946:* Cabinet Mission visited India in 1946 and submitted its recommendations to the Britishers. As a result Interium Government was formed but Congress and League couldn't cooperate amongst themselves.

13. *Delhi Convention - 1946:* Quaid-e-Azam called a convention of all the Muslim League members at Delhi. At the convention every member took the pledge to under go any danger for the attainment of national goal of Pakistan.
14. *3 June Plan - 1947:* Lord Mount Batten prepared the plan for transference of power according to the wish of people. He emphasized on the partition of the country and told that it was the only solution of the Indian political deadlock. Both League and Congress accepted the plan.

Muslim League thus got its object and Pakistan was created on 14 August 1947. In short we can say that the creation of Pakistan is the result of the ceaseless efforts of the Muslim League and the great heroes which dedicated their lives for the creation of Pakistan. If there were be no Muslim League the fate of the Muslims of the Sub Continent could not be changed.

FOUNDATION OF ALL-INDIA MUSLIM LEAGUE

The year 1324/1906 marks the cleavage and culmination of Muslim politics in the subcontinent, when the Aga Khan III led the Muslim delegation and met Lord Minto (1845-1914), the Viceroy of India from 1905, at Simla to demand the political rights of the Muslims of India. Simla was 1170 miles away from Calcutta, in the hills of northern India, above Delhi. It was the Anglo-Indian Olympus, where the British had been coming every summer since, 1860, and by 1906 there were more than 1400 European dwellings, built on a series of ridges with the native town. At the centre of this was the Viceregal Lodge, five storeys high, furnished by Maples of Tottenham Court Road.

The deputation to the Viceroy consisted of the most influential leaders, such as Mohsin al-Mulk, Hakim Ajmal Khan, Sir Ali Imam, Sir Muzammallah Khan, Sir Rafiquddin Ahmad, Sir Muhammad Shafi, Sir Abdul Rahim, Sir Salimullah, Justice Shah Din, etc. Syed Razi Waste writes in "Lord Minto and the Indian Nationalist Movement 1905-1910" that, "Minto received the Muslim Deputation on October 1, 1906. Thirty-five prominent Muslim leaders from all over India gathered in the Ball Room of the Viceregal Lodge at Simla. Their leader was a young man of twenty-nine years, H.H. Aga Sir Sultan Mohamed Shah Aga Khan from Bombay, who besides being the head of the rich Ismaili sect of Muslims had close and friendly relations with prominent British people." Accordingly, a memorandum was submitted to the Viceroy, insisting that the position accorded to the Muslim community in any kind of representation direct or indirect, and all other ways affecting their status should be commensurate not merely with their numerical strength but also with their political importance.

Lord Minto gave them a patient hearing, assuring that their political rights and interests as a community will be safeguarded in any administrative organisation. The Aga Khan realised that the Muslims should not keep themselves aloof from politics because the Congress was already proving incapable in representing the Indian Muslims. At length, the demands of separate electorate and weightage in number in representation to all elected bodies were accepted by the Viceroy Lord Minto, and incorporated in the Minto-Morley Reforms of 1909.

On October 24, 1906, the Aga Khan wrote a letter to Mohsin al-Mulk regarding a need to form a Muslim organisation what had been achieved at Simla. The letter reads: "It may well be that provincial associations should be formed with the aim of safeguarding the political interests of Muslims in various portions of India and similarly some central organisation for the whole." In the meantime, The All-India Muslim Educational Conference met at Dacca on December 30, 1906 and the letter of the Aga Khan was circulated among the delegates.

The Conference unanimously resolved that a political association styled as the All-India Muslim League be formed to promote among the Muslims the loyalty to the British government, to protect and advance the political rights and interests of Muslims, and to prevent the rise among Muslims of India of any feeling of hostility towards other communities. The Aga Khan III was thus elected permanent President of the All-India Muslim League and Sayed Hussain Bilgrami was made the Honorary Secretary. M. Abdul Aziz writes in "The Crescent in the Land of the Rising Sun" that, "It is well known that His Highness the Aga Khan was the first President of The All-India Moslem League and the way in which he took a keen and sympathetic interest in the organisation and development of the League, is shown from his letter of appreciation in his capacity as its first President."

According to "The Foundations of Pakistan", "In tracing the origins of Pakistan, some commentators give decisive importance to the separate electorates secured by the Muslim Deputation which was received by the Viceroy Lord Minto at Simla on Ocotber 1, 1906. The event has been described in the Diary of Lady Minto as 'an epoch in Indian history.'" According to "The Encyclopaedia Americana", "The delegation established the Muslim League, which carried the seeds of Muslim separation and eventual creation of Pakistan." Aziz Ahmed also writes in "Islamic Modernism in India and Pakistan" that, "One of the chief promoters of this design of Muslim separatism in subcontinent was the Agha Khan."

At the sixth annual session of Muslim League held on March 22-23, 1913 at Lucknow, the Aga Khan resigned from the presidency. He hinted a numerous reasons, but did not propose to cut himself away from the League. "Resignation" he said, "frees me from that necessarily judicial character that attaches to the presidency. The League does not need a leader but leaders." According to "Encyclopaedia of Asian History", "The Ismaili leader, Agha Khan, who presided over the League's destiny from 1906 to 1913, and resigned on November 3, 1913."

On the seventh session of the League at Agra, held on December 30-31, 1913, Sayed Wazir Hasan (1874-1947), the Secretary of League from 1912 to 1929, announced the resignation of the Aga Khan in the meeting, expressing, according to the "Foundations of Pakistan" that, "it would be a calamity for Muslims when His Highness resigned." Sir Ibrahim Rahimtullah appealed to the Aga Khan not to place his resignation in their hands today and to continue as President till the rules of the League were altered. The Aga Khan said that he would remain President for the time suggested.

He said also that in no case, it would severe his connection with the League as Vice-President. In a meeting of the Council of the League, held on February 25, 1914, the Aga Khan was declared the Vice-President of Muslim League, and Sir Ali Muhammad

Khan (1879-1931), the Raja of Mahmudabad was elected as the second President of Muslim League in the eight session at Bombay on December 30, 1915.

JINNAH AND HIS 14 POINTS

Many Muslims were not enthusiastic about the Nehru report. Among them Mohammed Ali Jinnah was a prominent figure. Jinnah felt that Muslims had sacrificed too much in order to reach a compromise the issue of communal representation. As for example, they had allowed congress to go back on concessions granted by the Lucknow pact of 1916. Jinnah declared himself to be anxious for a harmonious settlement. At an 'all-parties' convention held in Calcutta in December, he pleaded for unity. He declared that 'we are sons of this land we have to live together', but at the same time he asked for more safeguards for Muslims. His proposed amendments were rejected and he walked out of the convention.

Jinnah then allied himself with the less progressive Muslims, on whose behalf he drew up a list of principles. These principles are popularly known as the so-called fourteen points. These fourteen points represented the Muslim's minimum demands. These included separate elevates, the reservation of one-third of the seats in the legislative assembly for Muslims although the community accounted for only one-quarter of the ration, and the creation of Muslim majority provinces.

Later the league formally rejected the Nehru report. A brief period of Hindu Muslim co-operation had come to an end. This unfortunate development seemed to be offset for a while by change for the better in the attitude of the British. The labour party had promised so much to Indian nationalism. It came to power in the British elections. The viceroy lord Irwin, went to London, and on his return stated that the government accepted that 'the natural issue of India's constitutional progress' was 'minion status'. He also announced that a round table conference, to which Indian leaders would invited, would be held to work out a constitution for India. In England, there was still considerable opposition to Indian aspirations despite the viceroy's assurances. The labour party did not have a clear majority, and imperialist interests were still powerful. Lord Birkenhead, the former secretary of state, declared 'no one had the right to tell the people of India that they were likely to attain dominion status' but hopes were still high in India. It was stated only two months after Irwin's statement. In the 'Delhi manifesto', Gandhiji, the two Nehru, Tej Bahadur Sapru and others, pledged their co-operation in evolving a dominion constitution. But when Gandhiji, the elder Nehru and others met the viceroy in December, Irwin said that he could not promise that the British government would grant dominion status. This turnabout settled matters for Gandhiji. From this moment he dropped his opposition to complete independence.

LEAGUE'S TRANSFORMATION

The Elections of 1937: The first elections held under the Government of India act 1935 saw Congress emerging as the majority party. It won 711 out of total of 1585 seats, and could form government in 5/11 provinces without the support of any party. Out of these 711 seats only 26 seats were Muslim seats, thereby increasing Congress's reliance on local Hindu leaders, which allowed for their agenda to be imposed on the Congress. Muslim League on the other hand did well on the Muslim seats in the Hindu Majority provinces winning 29 out of 35 seats in the UP. The league however couldn't do well against the regional parties in Muslim Majority areas.

Congress and the League: The Congress refused to come to an arrangement with the Muslim League, choosing instead Jamiat-e-Ulema-Hind for partnership through Azad. This was a death blow to the League and its leadership who were at this point decidedly pro-Congress. On 22nd December 1939, League and its allies, the Scheduled Caste Federation and Justice Party of the Tamil Nadu, celebrated the day of deliverance from Congress rule.

Nehru-Jinnah Correspondence is especially vital in this regard. Nehru had mocked the League as an elitist organization and asked Jinnah to 'depend on the league's inherent strength'. Jinnah had responded in kind informing Nehru that from now on he would only depend on his inherent strength. As a Historian rightly observed: "More than Iqbal, it was Nehru who charted a new mass strategy for the League, prodding and challenging Jinnah to leave the drawing rooms of politics to reach down to the hundred million Muslims... There was ofcourse only one possible way for the league to stir that mass, to awaken it and lure it to march behind Muslim leadership"

Muslim League and the Muslim Majority Areas: The League leadership had realized through experience with Congress, that in order to make good on its claim of representation of South Asian Muslims, it would need to rally the Muslim Majority areas behind it. In order to do that it required a slogan which would be vague enough to bring an overwhelming mass of the Muslim majority areas behind the league.

Jinnah started by luring the regional politicians into his fold. First came Sikandar Hayat of Punjab, and soon to follow him was Fazlul Haq of Bengal. Soon the regional parties who had defeated the league in the elections were ready to come under the league's banner.

The Lahore Resolution: League's transformation was complete in 1940 when it adopted Iqbal's slogan of separate Muslim majority state (s). The two men who moved this resolution were the new entrants into the League, Sikandar Hayat and Fazlul Haq. The Lahore Resolution presented a vague demand which did not specify the nature of the Muslim majority state (s). No references were made to Islam, and the issue presented was a cultural one instead of a religious one. Needless to say this resolution was in contradiction to the stated objective of the league as it did not aspire to solve the problems of League's real constituents, the Muslims in Hindu Majority areas.

The name Pakistan was imposed on the League by the Congress press, and the League leadership after initial protestations accepted it.

League's Rejection of C R's Formula: C R Gopalachari's formula which virtually gave Muslim League Pakistan was rejected by the League leadership. This seemed to suggest that League's interest lay elsewhere, and not in the creation of Pakistan.

RIN MUTINY AND MUSLIM LEAGUE

Sarkar's disapproval of the Congress and the Muslim League's discouragement to the rebels in the Royal Indian Navy (RIN) mutiny is candidly expressed. Gandhi said on February 23, 1946: "A combination between Hindus and Muslims and others for the purpose of violent action is unholy." In his view, it was "a bad and unbecoming example for India". Aruna Asaf Ali disagreed. She said in a rejoinder it would be far easier "to unite Hindus and the Muslims at the barricade than on the constitutional front". Sarkar agrees with this romanticised, thoughtless recipe and wishes we had "radical mass actions forcing an unqualified imperial retreat". Under whose leadership, pray? His view that even in 1946 the British tried to "cling" to power is palpably wrong as Ambedkar realistically noted. The consequence of "mass actions" would have been violence and anarchy.

The effort at documentation is enormous. The documents are grouped under five broad heads – anti-British protests and movements; political organisations; labour and peasants; communalism; economy and society. The section on communalism explains the BJP regime's ire: while not ignoring the Muslim League, the editor exposes the Rashtriya Swayamsewak Sangh (RSS) thoroughly. The volume provides invaluable source material for the events of 1946.

The latest volume of *The Jinnah Papers* includes material from *The Transfer of Power* volumes besides other documents from the archives, which are published in this volume for the first time. There are some very interesting documents. One correspondent, a Delhi lawyer, S.M. Rahman, wrote to Jinnah a year before Partition, on April 5, 1946, a long and angry letter. Parts of it were wild. But in some others he wrote sense.

"...Have you not seen all the Christian people in Europe having the same civilisation, religious faith and social customs, conflicting among themselves and cutting off each other's head? How can you bring the theory of Islamic culture and religion in social unity as an excuse for Muslim separation from political unity? Do you think Muslims of NWFP [North-West Frontier Province] shall tolerate [the] culture of Punjabis or Sindhis or

Bengalis or Assamese? Do you know that a Bengali Muslim shall think a Bengali Hindu nearer to his culture and habits than a Punjabi or Sindhi Muslim? Do you know Pakistan shall have as many nationalities and cultures as you claim about India? Every district of the Punjab has its own culture, customs and even the language that is spoken. Have you ever been to Kangra in the north and D.I. [Dera Ismail] Khan in the west and Ferozepore in the south and Karnal in the east of Punjab? What have you to say about their nationalities and cultures? How can it be possible that Hindus who have lived [for] millions of years in Pakistan-defined area, can ever start thinking that the name of their motherland (place of birth not only of theirs but that of their hundreds of forefathers), is Pakistan when they know well it [is] Bharat or Hindustan or India and they know it long before you got the new invention of Pakistan saying that there are two nations and countries [sic] in India.

"Do you know that Hindus have started now taking very seriously the danger of your political stunt and that underground preparations are going on for a civil war to finish the Muslims? Do you know that so long as there is one Sikh in the Punjab, he will not allow it to be ruled by your majesty? He will take the full toll of yourself and your comrades in arms before you can reach the seat of your fascist govt. in the so-called Pakistan.

"Cannot you think, how foolish it is to assume that the two zones of Pakistan – Eastern and Western – can ever have any connection with each other unless there is a corridor? You might be thinking, let you have the Pakistan conceded, and then you will again put [sic] Islam in danger and demand a corridor. You must know that once Pakistan is conceded, the Hindus are not going to sit calm and digest your Pakistan easily. With the creation of Pakistan there shall be permanent ending of Hindu-Muslim political inter-relationship. Hindus shall be far bitter in their feelings against the Muslims. Their resolve shall be to build military strength far more than that of Pakistan. Their natural development in science and industry shall be a net asset to them in achieving their success. The result will be that when your majesty raises the issue of a corridor, which you will and must, a clash will occur. The result is evident and that is the death of Muslim community." There were not a few thinking Muslims who opposed the partition of India.

Another correspondent from Calcutta (now Kolkata) pointed out that the two wings of Pakistan could not form one state and that Bengal would have to be partitioned into two parts. The Premier of Bengal, H.S. Suhrawardy, introduced the Jharkhand leader Jaipal Singh to Jinnah as "a supporter of the Muslim League".

A brutally frank letter of July 12, 1946, from Syed Ali Bux to Jinnah, after the latter's disastrous meeting with the Nizam of Hyderabad, records Jinnah's clumsy and arrogant behaviour, for which the Nizam duly ticked him off. It also reveals Jinnah's reliance on people in the State who were not worthy of trust. Jinnah indiscreetly discussed matters with two such persons *before* meeting the Nizam. The letter was written while Jinnah was still in Hyderabad. It was a sincere attempt to bring about a compromise. It foreshadowed Jinnah's suicidal policy towards the princely states generally. There are some interesting nuggets; for instance, Ambedkar's request to Jinnah to persuade Ramkrishna Dalmia to donate at least Rs.3 lakh for the college he proposed to set up in Mumbai. The letter was written because Dalmia told Ambedkar that he would have to consult Jinnah in that matter.

The seeds of Jinnah's disastrous policy towards Kashmir were sowed in 1946. On May 23, 1946, Agha Shaukat Ali wrote to Jinnah from Srinagar mentioning Sheikh Abdullah's overtures to the Muslim Conference. The Congress was not pleased with his slogan "Quit Kashmir", which alienated the Maharaja. The Muslim Conference was in a pathetic state. Jinnah simply had no policy worth the name. Pandit Prem Nath Bajaj also sought Jinnah's advice. Ironically, the League press in Lahore supported Sheikh Abdullah while Jinnah did not. In 1947 he expected the Maharaja to accede to Pakistan. Jinnah insisted that the decision on accession belonged to the ruler and not to the people as Nehru rightly asserted.

A long letter by Jinnah's staunch follower Shaukat Hayat Khan, dated July 11, 1947, should serve as an eye opener to Pakistanis. It was written after a trip to Kashmir only a month before

Independence and bears quotation *in extenso*: "I went underground to meet Ghulam Mohiuddin, their [the National Conference's] underground leader. He has achieved considerable amount of popularity.... He is not at all averse to Pakistan but says he is handicapped by our silence. If, he says, a little sympathy was shown to them they would see that Pakistan issue is not decided upon adversely.

They feel that the interests of thirty lakhs of your subjects were being sacrificed at the altar of Hyderabad and Bhopal. Though they understood that your moves have greater strategy in view on account of various repressions, they were impatient of delay and may be reluctant to make greater sacrifices required of them. It was suggested that even a little bit of sympathy from us, in the form of a statement for release of Abbas, Shaukat of the Muslim Conference, and Sheikh Abdullah of the National Conference, in addition to a recommendation for the grant of basic civil rights to the people would give an excuse for them to support Pakistan openly. They discounted the news of Abdullah's assurance to the Maharaja and said that he was in favour of a referendum. My impression was that this party is still most powerful and had the support of the intelligentsia. They had advantage of having a good many honest workers. I did not think that they were in the pay of the Congress....

"*The People:* They are hounded, hunted and hungry. Officials are playing havoc into [*sic*] them. Each day they are being oppressed by illegal arrests and their food is being taken away under a system of most cruel taxation; and worst of all their women-folk every day are being molested with impunity. They are very bitter and look upon you as their saviour and are confident that you will rescue them.

"They are curiously torn between two loyalties, one to Pakistan and the other to Abdullah. They are indeed bewildered. *They pray for Pakistan and for the release of Abdullah in almost the same breath.* If Abdullah fights against Pakistan it would be a very hard test for these poor people and God knows what the result is going to be. My impression, however, is that we will probably win" (emphasis added throughout).

That was not to be. Jinnah rejected Mountbatten's offer, at Lahore on November 1, 1947, of a plebiscite in all the three disputed states – Kashmir, Junagadh and Hyderabad. He wanted Hyderabad excluded, a perverse idea India could not possibly accept. In truth, Jinnah wanted Kashmir and ignored Sheikh Abdullah while Nehru wanted Abdullah but ignored the people of Kashmir. We are paying for their mistakes still.

The documents on Jinnah's parleys with the Cabinet Mission show that on April 16, 1946, he was offered two alternatives – the Pakistan of today and a Centre confined to defence, foreign affairs and communications. He preferred the latter. Jinnah was asked to give his own plan, which he did on May 12. It was for an all-India confederation – not partition. He accepted the Mission's Plan of May 16, 1946, which envisaged a federal India based on groups of provinces. It was wrecked by the Congress at the instance of Gandhi who demurred at the proposals from the very outset. Jinnah said in Nehru's presence on May 11 that "if the Congress would agree to Groups of Provinces as desired by the Muslim League, he would seriously consider a Union".

Peter Clarke's biography of a member of the Mission, Stafford Cripps, narrated the story of the destruction of the last chance for preserving India's unity ("Cripps and India's Partition"; *Frontline*; August 2 and 16, 2002). He has now written a history of the last days of the British Empire as seen from London. The chapters on Palestine and India are particularly useful. Both were partitioned, but with a difference. "One difference was that it was demanded by a religious minority in India with the price to pay of receiving a 'motheaten' Pakistan; whereas partition was demanded by a religious minority in Palestine with the evident ambition of leaving the motheaten fragments to the Arab majority."

At the end of a careful survey, Clarke concludes: "The work of the Cabinet delegation in 1946, which has usually been derided, surely offered the Indian parties independence on the basis of a historic compromise which they would have to make themselves. It was, by definition, hardly the best solution in the eyes of either side; but each side needed to reconcile itself to a second-best solution if hasty partition and predictable bloodshed were to be avoided. Unfortunately, this is not how Gandhi, still the most powerful man in India, looked at the world. His failure to rise to the political challenge in 1946 emerges as the most significant missed opportunity in the whole story... In the final months, Gandhi's response was heroic on a personal moral level, but that need not blind us to the degree of his own responsibility for engendering this situation."

A tell-tale document in Sarkar's collection exposes the Congress' game. It was a letter by Vallabhbhai Patel in reply to Ambedkar's memorandum of demands, which he wrote as a basis for a pact with the Congress. Patel cited difficulties. One of them, incredibly, was the grouping provisions of the Mission's Plan, which he had helped to sabotage. Read this: "For instance, the provincial Constitution will be *settled by the sections* and the Congress will not be in a majority in Sections B (NWFP, Balochistan, Punjab and Sindh) and C (Bengal and Assam)." This was to fob off Ambedkar. For, to the League and the authors of the Plan, the Congress insisted that the provincial Constitution would be drafted *by the province alone*; not by the Section or Group. In December 1946, Gandhi said the Assamese would not be men but mannequins if they joined Section C (with Bengal). Not Nehru alone by his famous outburst in July 1946 but the entire Congress rejected the Plan under Gandhi's determined leadership.

ISLAMIC FUNDAMENTALISM: THE JAMAAT-E-ISLAMI

The Islamic Traditionalism of the Ulema and Islamic Modernism of Sir Syed and Mohammad Iqbal as I have suggested, were each associated with problems and wishes of certain social classes (of Muslims) during the 19th century, whose concerns and aspirations they articulated and expressed. The social roots of the new Islamic Fundamentalism of the Jamaat-e-Islami that was a most insignificant group of Muslim intellectuals at the time of The Partition, but which has gained much notoriety since then, cannot be quite so clearly identified. It originated entirely as an ideological movement and its appeal was initially limited to a small number of dedicated followers whom it offered a dream of an utopian future. It drew to itself a small band of idealists in search of a better society. Many of them were quickly disenchanted and left the Party, often joining left-wing groups and organisations. Their numbers and weight in that party have dwindled steadily. The Jamaat was soon to get generous support from powerful vested interests for whom it began to serve a political purpose. That changed its character radically. The Jamaat-e-Islami was founded in 1941 by Maulana Maududi, a scholar-journalist with a classical education. Maududi was an opponent of Muslim Nationalism and the Pakistan movement. But when Pakistan was created he found it prudent to migrate to Pakistan. With that his political philosophy went through a radical transformation. Maududi's opposition to the Pakistan movement was on the ground that the true vocation of an Islamic militant was a proselytising one, that Islam was a universal religion that knew of no national boundaries. After the creation of Pakistan Maududi revised the conception of his mission and that of the rationale of the Pakistan movement. He now argued that the sole object of the creation of Pakistan was to establish an Islamic State and that it was his Party alone which possessed a true understanding of Islam and commitment to bring that about.

To build an Islamic state the existing state must first be captured and brought under the control of those who, by Maududi's definition, were the only true bearers of militant and authentic Islam, namely himself and his Party. Unlike the Ulema, control of the state apparatus was therefore his first priority. His conception of the ideal Islamic State was a strongly centralised one, run on authoritarian lines, with the help of a strong and effective and dedicated army, under the authority of the Commander of the Faithful. Democracy was despised, for it gave power to the ignorant and those whose commitment, and understanding, of the faith could be doubtful. The onus lay therefore on his Party and on himself as its Guide and Leader, to take Muslim society forward to its true destiny. The Constitution of his Party illustrates this authoritarian philosophy for it demands unquestioning and total obedience from members of the Party to its *Amir*, its Supreme Head, namely himself. His ideas, justifying dictatorship in the name of Islam have, not surprisingly, found much favour with some sections of Pakistan's authoritarian military rulers.

The Jamaat is not a mass Party but one with selected cadre members. Because of its shallow roots in society, the Jamaat has been quite ineffective as a political Party. The full extent of its isolation from popular support was brought home recently to the Jamaat as well as its surprised opponents, by its debacle in the controlled elections staged by the Zia regime in January 1985, for conditions for its electoral success could not have been made more favourable. All opposition Parties were under a ban and their leaders and local activists were in prison or in exile. The field was therefore clear for the Jamaat to make a clean sweep of it. But it was routed completely. The electorate voted negatively, against Jamaat candidates and for non-entities.

The Jamaat's electoral bankruptcy ought not to lead anyone into under estimating its power and influence in today's Pakistan, which are derived primarily from its symbiotic relationship with the ruling regime. It tends to function as a pressure group rather than a political Party and uses its influence with government agencies and power to blackmail and terrorise individuals to achieve its objectives. During the rule of General Zia particularly, the Jamaat acquired a firm grip over the Universities and the entire educational system, its prime objective. It as also acquired a powerful influence on the government owned and control led broadcasting media. Its tentacles extended everywhere so that its opponents lived in fear. The Party, in turn, enjoys enormous capacity of patronage and thereby attracts support from all kinds of opportunists and careerists, which further reinforces its influence within the apparatus of the Government and the army quite apart from its influence directly at the top.

After the Partition the Jamaat attracted a new following among urdu speaking refugees from India, the *muhajirs*, who felt insecure and bitter about India, because of their suffering in the course of their enforced migration. They responded readily to the chauvinistic rhetoric of the Jamaat. But, over the years, this support has been withering away. In part this is because muhajirs who have settled in the interior of Sindh have developed linkages with the Sindhi community, being traders and professionals who serve Sindhi peasants and landlords. They have become the 'New

Sindhis', and sympathise with the Sindhi movement which has got under way quite powerfully in recent years. They dislike the anti-democratic support by the Jamaat of the repression let loose by the military regime against Sindhi nationalism. Even in big cities, like Karachi, where muhajir support for Sindhis is much less, there are elements within the Jamaat, like Prof. Ghafoor Ahmad of Karachi and Jan Mohammad Abbasi, who are critical of their Party's support of the martial law regime because that has been losing the Jamaat popular support.

The leadership of the Jamaat has passed into non-ideologist hands, although exploitation of their ideology remains their principal political weapon. The Party bosses seem to feel that its diminishing support from its meagre popular base, mostly amongst the *Muhajirs* is of less consequence than the support that it is deriving from powerful classes in Pakistan for whom its value lies in its ability to bludgeon radical and left-wing groups, very often quite literally so. The Party receives generous donations from big businessmen and landlords and is believed to be a recipient of generous donations from the Americans and from potentates in the Middle East.

But an excess of money and, for that matter, influence, has also brought problems for the Party. New vested interests have grown up in the Party bureaucracy and the old ideological wing of the Party, in decline, resents that. There is a considerable tension (to say the least) between the ideologists in the Party, mainly Karachi based, and those whose political ambitions lie in what they can get from the military regime. This latter consists mainly of the Punjab based, so-called 'pragmatic' wing of the Jamaat, led by Mian Tufail Mohammed, the Amir of the Jamaat and successor of Maududi. However, to retrieve its standing amongst the people the Party has begun to voice carefully measured criticism of the military regime, to distance itself from it. There is also a third element in the Party namely armed thugs, an element that was reinforced by the repatriation from East Pakistan of members of Al-Badar and As-Shams, its fascist paramilitary organisations, after the liberation of Bangladesh. They go about beating up opponents and breaking up meetings. These elements are associated with, especially, the *Islami-Jamiat-e-Tulaba*, the student organisation of the Jamaat, that maintains an armed presence on University campuses.

To end our account of the Jamaat-e-Islami, we must return to the central doctrinal issue of *ijtihad*, or interpretative development of doctrine, around which the political debate about Islamic State has turned. As it was pointed out above, the Jamaat stands for *ijtihad*, contrary to the position of the Traditionalist Ulema. But at the same time The Jamaat-e-Islami derides the method proposed by the Modernist Iqbal for realising *Ijtihad* under contemporary conditions, through processes of representative democracy, which is represented as the only possible source of *Ijma* modern conditions. Maududi contends against this that this could not lead to a reliable interpretation of Islam, for the voters may not be Muslim and even if they are, they may not have a 'true understanding' of Islam, such as only Maududi and his followers are blessed with. Iqbal's exhortation to educate the people was no solution either. Scholarship was no guarantee, for even the Ulema were misled and ignorant. The logic of that argument, leads Maududi to an authoritarian solution, for by his lights there is only one true and reliable interpretation of Islam and Maududi and his Jamaat are the custodians of that true knowledge. They are a gifted and select elite, and amongst them only its great leader, knows what Islam is.

'According to Maududi', writes K.K. Aziz: 'there is always a person (*Mizaj Shanas-i Rasool*) who alone is competent to decide what the Holy Prophet would have done in a given situation if he were alive. ... He left no doubt in the minds of his followers that he was the only candidate for this supreme pontifical office. And his chief lieutenant, Maulana Islahi declared before the Punjab Disturbances Inquiry Committee that he wholeheartedly and unreservedly accepted Maududi as the *Mizaj Shanas-i Rasool*'.

As far as the Jamaat claims and ideology are concerned, there can be no objective or logical criteria by which their validity can be settled. They can be accepted only as an act of faith, by a religious conversion in effect, to the Maududi sect, which may therefore be properly regarded to be yet another sect of Islam which, like every sect, claims to be the only true one. Paradoxically Maududi's elitism itself militates against a principle which would be regarded as a central tenet of Islam, namely that *ijtihad* by *ijma*, the consensus of the community, has precedence over *ijtihad* by the *alim*, the man of religious learning, because an individual, however learned he may be, is fallible, but Allah in his divine mercy would not allow his community collectively to go in error. This has always been recognised as the principle of democracy in Islam. Maududi's argument contradicts that. The Jamaat-e-Islami ideology while insisting on *ijtihad*, in effect rejects the fundamental notion of *ijma*, and offers little more than a personal charter of authority to the head of the Jamaat-e-Islami to lay down the law in the name of Islam.

It must be said that by virtue of re-interpretation of Islam by Ulema of the 8th and 9th centuries AD, to suit the needs of the feudal Abbasid empire, the concept of *ijma* was itself narrowed down to that of a consensus between 'qualified' scholars, which took away the power from the community that the Prophet Mohammad's Islam had conferred on it. They abolished the right of the community to be represented in the state. Even today such a notion is peddled in Pakistan by the ignorant and to a degree state subsidised *Ulema*. Nevertheless, even this narrowed conception contradicts Maududi's claim. This is quite apart from the impossibility of 'consensus of scholars' in a world in which there are sharp and vicious sectarian differences so that those with differing persuasions call each other *kafirs*, as recorded by the Report of the Court of Inquiry, a high judicial body, that reported in 1954 on sectarian violence that took place in 1953, referred to in footnote no. 12 above. So on doctrinal grounds we can see that there are contradictions underlying every position. There is no way of resolving it except by either imposing one sectarian position over all the others or by accepting a secular conception of the political process and the state so that every individual, whatever his or her religious persuasion may be, would be free to participate in the democratic process, following his or her own private faith and conscience, to shape policies of the state. We will refrain from pursuing this arcane and insoluble debate any further for it cannot be resolved by logic.

5

Beginning of Partition: India and Pakistan

The problem in India is not of an inter-communal character, but manifestly of an international one, and it must be treated as such. Out of this fundamental truth, any constitution that may be built will result in disaster and will prove destructive and harmful not only to the Musalmans, but to the British and Hindus also.

If the British Government, really is earnest and sincere to secure peace and happiness of the people of this subcontinent, the only course open to us all is to allow the major nations separate homelands by dividing India into autonomous national states. There is no reason why these states should be antagonistic to each other.

On the other hand, the rivalry and the natural desire and efforts on the part of one to dominate the social order and establish political supremacy over the other in the government of the country will disappear. It will lead more towards natural goodwill by international pacts between them, and they can live in complete harmony with their neighbours.

This will load further to a friendly settlement all the more easily with regard to minorities by reciprocal arrangements and adjustments between Muslim India and Hindu India, which will far more adequately and effectively safeguard the rights and interests of Muslim and various other minorities. It is extremely difficult appreciate why our Hindu friends fail to understand the real nature of Islam and Hinduism. They are not religions in the strict sense of the word, but are, in fact, different and distinct social orders and it is a dream that the Hindus and Muslim can ever evolve a common nationality, and this misconception of one Indian Nation has gone for beyond the limits and is the cause of most of our troubles and will lead India to destruction if we fail to revise our notion in time.

The Hindus and Muslims belong to two different religious philosophies, social customs, and literature. They neither intermarry nor inter-dying together and, indeed, they belong to two different civilizations, which are based on mainly on conflicting ideas and conceptions. Their expects on life and of life are different. It is quite clear that Hindus and Musalmans derived here inspiration from different sources of history.

They have different epics, different heroes and different episodes. Very often, the hero of one is a foe of the other and, likes wise their victories and defeats overlap. To yoke together two such nations under a single state, one as a numerical minority and the other as a majority, must lead to growing discontent and the final destruction of any fabric that may be so built up for the government of such a state.

Muslim India cannot accept any constitution, which must necessarily result in a Hindu-majority government. Hindus and Muslim brought together under a democratic system forced upon the minorities can only mean Hindu raj. Democracy of the kind with which the congress high command is enamoured would mean the complete destruction what is most precious in Islam. We have had ample experience of the working of the provincial constitution during the last two and a half years and any repetition of such a government must lead to civil war and leasing of private armies as recommended by Mr. Gandhi to Hindus of Sukkur then he said that they must defend them selves violently or nonviolently, blow for blow, and they could not must emigrate.

Musalmans are not a minority as it is commonly known and understood. One has only got to look round. Even today, according to the British map of India out of 11 provinces 4 provinces, where the Muslim dominate more or less, are functioning not withstanding the decision of the Hindu congress high command to non-cooperate and prepare for civil disobedience. Musalmans are a nation according to any definition of a nation and they must have their homeland, their territory and their state. We wish to live in peace and harmony with our neighbours as free and independent people. We wish our people to develop to the fullest our spiritual, cultural, economic, social and political life in a way that we think best and in consonance with our own ideals according to the genius of our people.

Honest demand and vital interest of millions of our people impose a sacred duty upon us to find an honourable and peaceful solution, which could be just and fair to all. But at the same time, we cannot be moved or diverted from our purpose and objectives by threats and intimidations. We must be prepared to face all difficulties and consequences, make all the sacrifices that may be required of us to achieve the goal we have set in front of us...

Resolution of All India Muslim League, Lahore, 23 March 1940 (Pakistan Resolution): While approving and endorsing the action taken by the Council and the Working Committee of the All India Muslim League, as indicated in their resolutions dated the 27th of August, 17th and 18th of September, 22nd of October 1939, and 3rd of February 1940 on the constitutional issue, this session of the All India Muslim League emphatically reiterates that the scheme of federation embodied in the Government of India Act, 1935, is totally unsuited to, and is altogether unacceptable to Muslim India.

It further records its emphatic view that while the declaration dated the 18th of October 1939, made by the Viceroy on behalf of His Majesty's' Government is reassuring in so far as it declares that the policy and plan on which the Government of India Act 1935, is based will reconsidered in consultation with the various parties, interests and communities in India, Muslim India will not be satisfied unless the whole constitutional plan is reconsidered and that no revised plan would be acceptable to the Muslims unless it is framed with their approval and consent. Resolved that it is the considered view of this session of the All India Muslim League that no constitutional plan would be workable in this country or acceptable to the Muslims unless it is designed on the following basic principle—geographically contiguous units are demarcated into regions which should be so constituted, with such territorial re-adjustments as may be necessary, that the areas in which the Muslims are numerically in a majority as in the North-Western and Eastern zones of India should be grouped to constitute Independent States in which the constituent units shall be autonomous and sovereign.

The adequate, effective and mandatory safeguards should be specifically provided in the constitution for minorities in these units and in the regions for the protection of their religious, cultural, economic, political, administrative and other rights and interests in consultation with them and in other parts of India where the Musalmans are in a minority, adequate, effective and mandatory safeguards shall be specifically provided in the constitution for them and other minorities for the protection of their religious, cultural, economic, political, administrative and other rights and interests in consultation with them. This session further authorizes the working committee to frame a scheme of constitution in accordance with these basic principles, providing for the assumption finally by the respective regions of all powers such as defense, external affairs, communications, customs and such other matters as may be necessary.

English Translation of Resolution No. 12, Jamiyat-ul-Ulema Hind, 14th Annual Conference, 4th May 1945 (Original Document):

1. Our object is complete independence.
2. In a free India, Musalmans and their religion and culture will be free. They will not accept a constitution, which does not approve of these freedoms.
3. We stand for the fullest and unrestricted autonomy of the provinces. The centre will enjoy only those powers which the provinces, of their own accord, hand over to it and which concern equally with al provinces.
4. It is our considered opinion that a federation of autonomous provinces of India is essential. But a federation in which 9 crore Muslims with a distinct culture of their own are left at the mercy of a numerical majority, will, in no case,

be acceptable to them; the centre is to be formed on such principles that give a clear guarantee to the Muslims with regard to their religious, cultural and political freedom.

Giving a tentative proposal for the structure of the Federal Government in so far as the cultural, religious and political safeguards for Muslims were concerned, the Jamiyat made the following suggestions:

1. The federal parliament should be composed on the basis of parity between the Hindus and the Muslims.
2. In the federal parliament, if the 2/3 majority of the Muslim members is of the opinion that a particular bill or proposal is prejudicial to their religious, cultural and political interests, then that bill or proposal will not presented before or passed by the house.
3. There should be established a Supreme Court composed of equal number of Muslim and non-Muslim judges who will be appointed by a committee having equal number of representatives from the Muslim and non-Muslim provinces. This Supreme Court should be empowered to give final verdicts on problems arising out of disputes between the centre and the provinces, between one provinces and an other or between two communities in the country. Also if, under the provision No. 2, the majority of the federal parliament differs from the opinion of the 2/3 majority of the Muslim members with regard to a bill being or not being opposed to the interests of the Muslims, the matter will be referred to the Supreme Court.

Did Jinnah renounce the Two Nation Theory towards the end?

In his address to the constituent Assembly of Pakistan on 11th August 1947 Jinnah declared that "everyone of you, no matter to what community you belong, no matter what your colour, caste or creed, is first, second and last a citizen of this state with equal rights, privileges and obligations". Jinnah had added: " you are free: you are free to go your temple, you are free to go to your mosque or to any other places of worship in this state of Pakistan. You may belong to any religion or caste or creed-that has nothing to do with the business of the state.. we are starting in the days when there is no discrimination, no distinction between one community and another, no discrimination between caste or creed. We are starting with this fundamental principle that we are all citizens and this fundamental principle that we are all citizens and equal citizens of one state.. in course of time Hindus would cease to be Hindus and Muslims would cease to be Muslim, not in the religious sense because that is the personal faith of each individual, but in the political sense as citizens of the state".

In this address Jinnah declared that in Pakistan : (a) There would be religious freedom-freedom of religious belief, profession and practice, (b) There would be no discrimination on grounds of religion, caste or creed, (c) All citizens will be equal, irrespective of their personal religion or faith.

This statement of Jinnah has become the matter of debate among scholars-how a person who was a great advocate of religion-based, two nation theory and on these basis, established Pakistan as a homeland for the minority of Muslim Nationals residing in Hindu-majority provinces could, on the eve of his achievement, abandon the two nation theory and proclaim that Pakistan would not be an Islamic State but a secular state. Prior to August 1947, Jinnah had only twice defined the nature of the State of Pakistan. The first was in an interview with the Reuters Correspondent, Doon Campbell, in New Delhi in 1946. Jinnah has said: " The New State would be a modern democratic state with sovereignty resting in the people and members of the new nation having equal rights of citizenship regardless of their religion, caste or creed." Again, on 14th July 1947 Jinnajh explained the rights and status of minorities in Pakistan, which was to come existence in a month's time. Jinnah said: the minorities in Pakistan will enjoy freedom of religion: their religion will be secure and there would be no interference with freedom of worship. Secondly, the members of minority communities would be citizens of Pakistan in all respects". Jinnah said: " I do not know what theocratic state means, Muslims learned democracy thirteen hundred years ago", earlier, he said that non-Muslims would be full citizens in Pakistan.

Jinnah was an eminent lawyer. He could never have made a loose statement. He was addressing the Constituent Assembly of

Pakistan and not making a public speech. He was making a policy statement of fundamental importance for making the Constitution of Pakistan. It shall be presumed that Jinnah had made this statement after due deliberation and there was no looseness in what he said. As early as 1935, Jinnah in his presidential address to the All-India Students Conference at Lucknow, had described the Congress as a Hindu Body and the Muslims as a Separate Entity. When there was an adverse reaction to this observation from the audience, Jinnah had reiterated loudly, " I say, the Congress is a Hindu Body and Muslim League represents the Musalmans".

Again, at the Calcutta session of the All India Muslim Students Federation held in December 1937, Jinnah stressed that the Muslims were "a nation and not a minority". At the Patna session of the Federation held in December 1938, he repeated: "India was not a nation yet, but a counter of nationalities".

Jinnah had declared: Islam and Hinduism "are not religions in the strict sense of the word, but are, in fact, different and distinct social orders. It is a dream that the Hindus and Muslims can evolve a common nationality". "The Hindus and Muslims belong to different religions, philosophies, social customs, and literature. They neither intermarry nor inter-dine together, and indeed, they belong to two different civilizations which are based mainly on conflicting ideas and conceptions".

These characteristics of the two religions and the two societies, Hindu and Muslim, had not undergone any changes after 1940 to explain the change in Jinnah's views that Hindus and Muslims are two nations-nor was Jinnah given to dreaming. In his statement on Partition on the 1st May 1947, barely three months before Partition, Jinnah had observed: "the question of the division of India, as proposed by the Muslim League, is based on the fundamental fact that there are two nations-Hindus and Muslims, and the underlying principle is that we want a national home and a national state in our homeland which are predominantly Muslim..".

" It is obvious that if the Hindu minorities in Pakistan wish to emigrate and go to their homeland of Hindustan, they will be at liberty to do so and vice-versa those Muslims who wish to emigrate from Hindustan can do so and go to Pakistan; and sooner or later exchange of population will have to take place..."

Again, in his concluding speech on 9th June 1947 to the All India Muslim League Council, which endorsed the 3rd June 1947 plan for Partition, Jinnah claimed that he had achieved a separate country for the Muslims of India. Thus, barely two months before Partition, Jinnah was speaking exclusively of Muslims of Pakistan. In 1941 Jinnah defined the ideology of Pakistan with absolute clarity. The Secretary-General of Jama'at-I-Islami met Jinnah to seek his support for the Jama'at's goal of establishing an Islamic State. Jinnah explained to the Jamaat leader that there was no incompatibility between the positions of the Muslim League and the Jamaat and assured the Jamaat leader that, " I will continue to serve for the cause of a separate Muslim State", Jinnah significantly added: " I seek to secure the land for the mosque" and only an Islamic State as distinct from a Muslim majority State, could be the mosque.

For such establishment a separate country or a state was a must. After partition Jinnah had declared, "Let it be clear that Pakistan is going to be a Muslim state based on Islamic ideals. It will not be an ecclesiastical state." "Pakistanwould not be a theocratic state to be ruled by priests with a divine mission and the non-Muslims, Hindus, Christians and Parsis, will enjoy the same rights and privileges as any other citizen but the Constitution will embody the essential principles of Islam."

Role of the British in the Creation of Pakistan: On 18th April 1940 Zetland declared in the House of Lords that England would not force a Constitution for India, which was not acceptable to the Muslims. In august 1940 the British Government in a declaration assured the Muslims of India that power and responsibility would not be transferred to any Government whose authority was not acceptable to large and powerful elements in India's body politic. These declarations vested the Muslim League with veto power on any proposals for constitutional change. The rulers considerably boosted the strength of the Muslim League by recognizing Jinnah and the Muslim League as the sole representative of the Muslims of India. In 1945, Wavell convened a conference of political leaders to consider "proposals designed to ease the present political situations and to advance India towards the goal of full self-government". They were intended to Indianise the Viceroy's Executive Council as a first step towards constitutional changes to be introduced after the Second World War. Only the Congress, Muslim League, Scheduled Caste and the Sikh Political Parties and the European Group in the Central Assembly were invited to attend the conference.

The Hindu Mahasabha, the non-Muslim League Parties like the Jamiat-ul-Ulema-e-Hind, which had been opposing the establishment of Pakistan, as a homeland for Indian Muslims and the Punjab Unionist Party were not invited. However, the Viceroy proposed to reserve one seat in the Executive Council for a Muslim belonging to the Punjab Unionist Party. Jinnah who claimed the exclusive right to nominate all Muslim members of the Executive Council including the Congress Muslims and the Muslim representatives of the Punjab Unionist Party opposed this.

Wavell proposed parity between the number of caste Hindu and Muslim members in the Executive Council. Though the conference failed, it left a profound impact on Indian politics.

1. The British Government virtually recognized the Muslim League as the sole representative of the Muslims; by implication, the Congress would be reduced to a non-Muslim party, essentially a Hindu Party.
2. The Viceroy's capitulation to Jinnah's demand that a Unionist Party Muslim could not be nominated to the Executive Council led to the –destruction of the Unionist Party and paved the way for Partition of Punjab. It deserves to be noted that Punjab was the Heartland of the Pakistan movement. The decimation of the Unionist Party enabled the Muslim League to win the allegiance of the Muslims of Punjab.
3. There were, are, many other religious/ ethnic minorities in India besides the Muslims such as the Christian, Parsis, etc. But parity of representation in the Executive Council was to be between the Muslims (23% of total population) and Hindus (75% of total population). The scheme of parity

thus recognized that the Muslims were not merely a religious or ethnic minority but a separate nation. No other principle could be justified of this parity. At Shimla Conference 1945, Jinnah added a new dimension to the parity doctrine. Jinnah wanted, in the matter of representation, in the interim-Government that Muslim should have-equally with all other communities, Sikhs, Christians, Parsis, etc. taken together with the Hindus in the interim-Government. The Parity Principle was totally undemocratic and could possibly be justified as between two nations working in a joint organization.

4. The failure of the Shimla Conference because of Wavell's unwillingness to reject Jinnah's claim that Muslim League was the sole representative of the Muslim community and that no non-League Muslims could be induced into the Executive Council and his claim for parity with the Hindu Congress, boosted his personal prestige and politics.
5. It was the Simla Conference that helped Muslim League to win in the elections of 1946, all the Muslim League seats in the Central Legislative Assembly and the overwhelming majority of the Muslim seats in the Provincial Assemblies. It was Wavell who helped the Muslim League to become the sole representative of the Muslims of India. The Cabinet Mission Plan of 1945—parity between Hindus including Scheduled Castes and the Muslims in the interim-Government. The Muslim League was also to have the exclusive right to nominate the Muslim members of the Viceroy's Executive Council. On this issue the Shimla Conference had broken up. Wavell did not formally concede to this demand of Jinnah, he also did not reject it. It is the point of understanding, How the Cabinet Mission, after the Shimla fiasco, could put forward such a scheme based on the principles of parity between the Muslims and the Hindus and the Muslim League as a sole representative of the Muslims for formation of interim-Government and expect the Congress to accept it. The British Government considered the Hindus and Muslims as two nations and the Congress as a Hindu Party.

In the early part of August 1946, the Congress alone was asked to form the Interim-Government. The Direct Action in the nature of JEHAD, launched by the Muslim League from the 16th August 1946 and the immense killings that took place in the Calcutta from 16th August to 20th August, Wavell appears to have felt the need to install a coalition government, which would control the communal violence in the country. This is how the British Rulers built up Jinnah and the Muslim League. Simultaneously the rulers supported the demand for Partition through their plans for transfer of power.

Cripps Mission and Pakistan-Under the Cripps Plan, provinces would have the right not to accede to the Central Constitution or the Union Authority that would be established by the new Constitution. It was open to province to retain its existing position in the British Empire. This was the first plan formulated by the British Government for transfer of power or grant of independence, which encouraged the establishment of Pakistan through the device of non-acceding provinces. It also opened the possibility of BALKANIZATION of India especially as the plan also gave Indian States the option to join or not to join India's constitution.

Cabinet Mission Plan and Pakistan – The Cripps Mission Plan of 1942 was followed by the Cabinet Mission Plan of 1946. Cabinet Mission Plan have led to the creation of a bigger Pakistan by including in the Muslim majority groups the undivided provinces of the Punjab and West Bengal and also the non-Muslim majority provinces of Assam. Cripps and the Cabinet Missions could not have been unaware-that none of the Plans would have solved the communal problems arising from the unavoidable co-existence of Muslim and Hindu minorities there would have been large Muslim Minorities in the Hindu majority provinces and large Hindu Minority in the Muslim majority provinces of Punjab and Bengal. On 16th May 1946, the Cabinet recognized in the Para 6 of the statement-that the setting up of a separate sovereign state of Pakistan on the lines claimed by the Muslim League would not solve the communal minority problem.

Further in Para 7 of the statement-neither a larger nor a smaller sovereign state of Pakistan would provide an acceptable solution for the communal problem. By manipulating the induction of the Muslim League into the Interim Government, even though its leaders had publicly declared that the Muslim League would constitutional means to achieve Pakistan, Wavell had driven the last nail in the coffin of a united India.

Mountbatten and Partition of India: The Great Calcutta Killing of August 1946 was a turning point in India's history. It followed Jinnah's Direct Action Day for achievement of Pakistan, which the Government of Bengal, dominated by the Muslim League and headed by Suhrawardy, had encouraged in every way. It brought an immediate violent retaliation by the Hindus of Calcutta and led to a chain reaction in the form of extensive communal disturbances in Noakhali in East Bengal, Bihar and the North West Frontier Provinces and the Punjab.

The Great Calcutta Killing was like a civil war in which the Provincial Government had become partisan. It was now evident that the British Government found itself unable to maintain law and order; India had become a liability to the British. In his report on the Last Viceroyalty to His Majesty's Government in September 1948 Mountbatten states that – the decision to transfer on 15th August was not made hurriedly. An immense amount of thought was given to this part of the problem and the conclusion was reached that the advantage of a yearly transfer of power far outweighed the disadvantages. Ismay in his memories confirms that the date 15th August was settled with the approval of the British Cabinet while Mounbatten was in the U.K. in May 1947. On 3rd June 1947 Mountbatten announced the decision regarding the transfer of power immediately, in 1947. In press conference, 4th June 1947 he announced date of transfer, along with Partition of India, as 15th August 1947. This allowed barely 73 days to complete this complex operation affecting the destinies of millions. Attlee in his statement in the House of Commons on 20th February 1947 had announced that power would be transferred to Indian hands by a date not latter than June 1948. Mountbatten was fully conscious that even this date 30 June 1948 did not allow adequate time both for transfer of power and for partition: he had been emphasizing that it took two years to separate Burma.

After hectic and intensive negotiations from March to May 1947 with different political leaders, Mounbatten came to the conclusion that no agreement between the Congress and Muslim League was possible which would maintain the essential unity of India's, obviate partition, give autonomy to provinces and guarantee protection to religious minorities. He also found that the British, as rulers, were unable to maintain law and order and more especially prevent communal riots as the bureaucracy and the security forces had been considerably enfeebled during the war. Mountbatten was convinced that partition was now the only alternative to anarchy. The parties reached agreement to divide the country on 3rd June 1947. Thereafter, it was the responsibility of the rulers, headed by Mountbatten the Viceroy and Governor-General, to effect the division peacefully and demit and transfer of power smoothly. But that did not happen.

The partition process was accompanied by grave disturbances-violence and mass migration on an unprecedented scale and enormous and extensive loss of life and property. Once the parties had reached a settlement, the division should have been carried out in a peaceful manner especially when the settlement did not envisage transfer of minority populations and the leaders of the divided areas were committed to protect and be just and fair to them.

But it was a bloody partition entirely due to the manner in which Mountbatten carried it out. He advanced the date of partitions and transfer of power from 30th June 1948 to 15th August 1947. Partition of a subcontinent, which was planned originally to be carried out in over 14 months, was eventually carried out in 2 ½ months.

No time was allowed for the communal passions to cool down before effecting the division. The performance of regular duties was neglected. The services of the Central Government and of the divided provinces of Bengal and Punjab were given the option for service, after partition, either in India or in Pakistan. The right of option of service was given, perhaps, in the belief that this would facilitate smooth partition of the country. However this led to communalization of Services. In the result the minorities ceased to receive the protection that they could expect from composite security Services. The search for security against violence and sequestration by miscreants of majority communities provoked the mass migration of minorities.

Option of service meant migration of service personnel from one dominion to another. Though Services were given option with the consent and concurrence of the political leaders, Mountbatten and his seasoned administrators were responsible for this vital and inexcusably wrong step with fatal consequences. Partition tragedy reached its climax when in the final stages of partition; Mountbatten illegally and unjustifiably withheld the publication of Radcliffe Awards till after terminal date of partition, the 15th August 1947. This avoidably caused tremendous loss of life and property in the border areas whose residents were not certain to which Dominion their area would be allocated. Field Marshall Montgomery was very critical of Mountbatten having hustled India into partition.

In Montgomery's judgment "...the fruits of the accelerated rush into independence and partition were potentially catastrophic-the division of India into Pakistan and the Indian Union at such speed raises terrific problems." He also warned: Unless the two new states co-operated, as Mountbatten assumed, there will be the most awful chaos and much bloodshed. Jinnah had fathered Pakistan; the British rulers were the midwife who actively and strenuously worked to convert who should have been a peace full partition into a painful and bloody parturition bringing into existence a Dual Pakistan and a Fragile India. Mountbatten played his cards on his side with such consummate skill that the Congress was driven to accept Dominion Status. First and foremost was the plan of 2 May, 1947-Balkan Plan. It envisaged transfer of power to the provinces. Mounbatten had his responsibility for smooth transfer of power and for maintaining law and order till the power was transferred. The division of the services on communal lines had disastrous and abiding consequences. On 18 June 1947 the civilian officials of the Central government were given the option to select the government they wished to serve. This was later extended to the employees of the Punjab and Bengal provincial governments, which were also to be partitioned. In the case of armed forces, the division was decided upon by the Partition Council on 30 June 1947.

There was a significant difference in the options allowed to the armed forces. They were to be on the basis of domicile, although Muslim personnel of Indian domicile could opt for the Pakistan army and Hindu personnel of Pakistan domicile could opt for the Indian army. As the Muslim component of the armed forces, other than navy, was very largely from West Pakistan areas, especially West Punjab and North West Frontier Province, this effectively ensured that the division of the forces was on communal lines. More importantly, pending combing out of the armed forces units on this basis, it was decided by the Partition Council to effect a rough and ready division of the armed forces on a communal basis, that is, immediate movement to Pakistan of all Muslim-majority units and movement to India of all non-Muslim majority units.

The communal division of the army could only encourage the wavering civilian officials to exercise options on the basis of religion. In the case of civil services, originally it was envisaged that the cadres would be separated according to the options of the officials, but the transfers were to be arranged over a period of time so that organizational efficiency was not impaired. The options were to be effective from 15 August 1947 or a later date dependence on the administrative convenience. But on 11 July 1947 the heads of departments were directed to proceed at once to make arrangements for the transfer of the officers and staff at present located on the wrong side of the new border areas they had elected to serve, with the provision that in the case of certain departments like Railways and Military Accounts Department the transfer were to be staggered if there was a serious imbalance between the number of personnel in different categories opting for India and Pakistan.

Transfer of personnel was to be effected by before 15 August 1947. This, in effect, meant immediate division of the civil services on communal basis. Minorities in certain areas of India and in Pakistan were left without the protection which the armed forces provided in time of disorder and which civil services, the police, provided in normal times. The impact of the communalization of services is brought out by Major-General Rees who was Commander of the Boundary Force, a neutral body of troops to preserve law and order during the process of partition. He recorded in his personal diary on 10 August 1947 that immediately after Kaul replaced Deane, the British Superintendent of Police at Amritsar, he disarmed the predominantly Muslim police of Amritsar City and summoned the rural Muslim police to Amritsar to turn in their arms. This was panic among Muslim populace unrest among Muslim police who wish to take their families away under Military Escort. It is ironical that the instrument that is the administrative machinery, which alone could be used to contain the communal passions, had itself, becomes communalized.

Now the total communalization of services, especially the police and the armed forces, blasted the slender hope of minorities that they might stay on in the areas to which they belonged. This was especially true of the non-Muslim minorities, as Pakistan had avowedly been created as a homeland for the Muslims. It was this act of the communal partition of services, which was to make West Pakistan the Dar-ul-Islam (the land of faithful). The question that naturally arises is, why were the services divided on a communal basis? The decisions and actions of Mountbatten can only be explained in the context of India remaining within the Commonwealth. Since the British were going to quit India in any case, it made no difference to them whether they did so by June 1948 or August 1947.

The communal riots of 1946 and the early part of 1947 had totally shaken the confidence of minorities in the protection of life and property against communal violence. This confidence was fatally undermined when the services, especially the police and the army, were divided on communal lines; the minorities now felt like a flock of sheep without the protecting shepherd. The holocaust that attended partition and the mass migration that took place were not inherent in the partition but were a consequence of the communal division of the services. Each of the two boundary tribunals, one for Punjab and the other for Assam and Bengal, consisted of four judges each, besides the Chairman, representing the major communities. The Chairman's decision was to be final but he did not attend any hearing on the ground that the proceedings of both the tribunals were taking place simultaneously.

The Indian members of the tribunals heard the claims and arguments of the different parties and Radcliffe gave the awards on the basis of the record of the hearings and discussions with the other members of the tribunals. When M.C. Setalved pointed out that this was a strange, almost farcical procedure, Radcliffe's only defense was that the awards had to come before 15 August 1947 and that he did not have the time to hear the parties. Another consequence that flowed from the British bargain to keep India within the British Commonwealth was the delayed publications of Partition Awards. Partition Awards for the Punjab and Bengal were signed by Radcliffe on 12 August 1947 and that for Sylhet the next day, but those were published on 17 August 1947, two days after partition. This delay cost many Hindu and Sikh lives.

There was a widespread belief among the Hindus and Sikhs of the Punjab that, on the ground of the unspecified other factors included in the terms of reference of the Boundary Commissions, certain Muslim Majority areas of the Punjab like Lahore, Montogomery, Lyallpur and Sheikhupura districts, in which non-Muslims, especially Sikhs, had substantial urban and agricultural properties and in which the Sikhs had their religious places, were likely to be awarded to India. Consequently, a large number of Hindus and Sikhs hung on to the areas which were eventually awarded to Pakistan and were shocked to discover on 18 August when the awards appeared in the newspapers, that their hopes had been belied. Many of these Hindus and Sikhs could have made an orderly and safe evacuation from these areas and obtained sanctuary in India, had the award been announced in time. Auckinleck, after a visit to Lahore on the 14th August, had reported on 15th August to Mountbatten-"The delay in announcing the award of the Boundary Commission is having a most disturbing and harmful effect.

It is realized of course, that the announcement may add fresh fuel to the fire, but lacking an announcement, the wildest rumours are current and are being spread by mischief makers of whom there is no lack". The delay was illegal, Mountbatten had no authority to withhold their publication; the two Dominions could not be formed on the 15 August 1947 without boundaries having been precisely defined. Evidently Mountbatten overlooked that the people of the disputed border areas lived in terrible suspense during this week and could not possibly share in the rejoicing at the dawn of independence. Again, while the Independence Day celebration in Calcutta witnessed scenes of Hindu-Muslim fraternization, the situation in the Punjab deteriorated and communal violence reached unprecedented heights.

The real reason for the delay was Mountbatten's apprehension that the adverse reaction of the Indian leaders, which could be easily foreseen, might prejudice them against joining the British Commonwealth. British wanted to prevent the Indian leaders from knowing the details of the award until after the 15 August; and wanted to maintain good Indo-British relations on the day of the transfer of power. The antedating the transfer of power was a bargain to secure India's accession of the British Commonwealth.

The rushed division of the Services and the armed forces on communal basis, the un-judicial procedure adopted by the Chairman of the Boundary Tribunals in making his awards, and the delay in the publications of the awards can all be traced to this bargain and were responsible for the failure to implement the partition agreement in peaceful circumstances. Two steps rendered partition of the Indian subcontinent an entirely unsuccessful exercise in averting this tragedy. First-hurried and premature transfer of power; and second-division of the services, especially the police and the army, on communal lines.

INDIA AND PAKISTAN: PARTITION LESSONS

The sixtieth anniversary of the independence of Pakistan and India on 14-15 August 2007 has prompted official celebration in both countries, as well as an ocean of commemorative coverage in the world's media. The terrible violence that accompanied the birthpangs of the two states from the ashes of empire is an inevitable theme in much commentary. What is being less addressed amid the profusion of human stories - and what this article considers - is whether the problems of communal division in the subcontinent were or are best addressed by the partition of territory.

Ravinder Kaur teaches at the University of Roskilde, Denmark. She is the editor of *Religion, Violence and Political Mobilisation in South Asia* (Sage, 2005) and author of *Since 1947: Partition Narratives among Punjabi Migrants of Delhi* (Oxford University Press, 2007) The bare details of 1947 and its legacy are stark. The territorial partition that created modern India and Pakistan involved the internal division of Punjab and Bengal provinces, which - in unimaginable conditions of collapse of authority, flight, and massacre - resulted in the forced movement of 20 million people (Hindus and Sikhs to India and Muslims to Pakistan) and approximately 1.5 million deaths.

This partition created both a harvest of bitterness and the basis for further conflict. In 1970-71, Pakistan itself was further divided as East Pakistan became the new state of Bangladesh, a process attended by an enormous human tragedy of war and famine. The four armed conflicts between the inheritors of the British Indian partition (1947, 1965, 1971, and 1998) are only the most dangerous moments in a pattern of near-permanent regional hostilities which has also been marked by low-intensity conflict in Kashmir, disputes over terrorism, and an escalating nuclear-weapons rivalry.

The question raised by the "great partition" bridges the divides between 1947 and 2007, and between India-Pakistan and many other global regions - most notably, today, Iraq. In this sense the particular history of the subcontinent is only one stage in a much larger story, one which continues to have potent implications across much of the world.

The Age of Unmixing

The practice of territorial and demographic rearrangements arose in the context of the early-to-mid-20th-century era of world wars and decolonisation in Asia and Africa. As territorial boundaries in Europe were challenged and peoples in other continents began to break free from the European colonial stranglehold, the political map of the world unravelled. In either case, political elites discovered a new solution: amid flux, fix. the best solution found was to fix territorial boundaries of a changing world. Thus the borders of old and new nation-states in Europe were dug deeper, while fresh borders for the emerging nation-states in Asia and Africa were invented to accommodate expressions of national will and demands for self-determination.

Also in open Democracy on India, Pakistan, and history: Maruf Khwaja, "India and Pakistan: states of mind, contests of perception" (23 January 2002)

Rajeev Bhargava, "The political psychology of Hindu nationalism" (5 November 2003)

Maruf Khwaja, "Becoming Pakistani" (19 August 2004)

Rajeev Bhargava, "India's model: faith, secularism and democracy" (3 November 2004)

Muzamil Jaleel, "Kashmir's bus-ride to history" (18 April 2005)

Sadat Hasan Manto, "Toba Tek Singh" (5 January 2007)

Territories had always changed hands, but what was new was the wholesale transfer of populations inhabiting those territories. A growing idea after the "great war" of 1914-18 was that conflicts arise among ethnically heterogeneous populations, and that the best way of resolving and preventing ethnic conflicts was to engineer the "unmixing of populations". The desired unmixing was achieved (for example) in the exchange of population between Greeks and Turks in 1923, and the expulsion of ethnic Germans from east-central Europe in 1944-49.

Behind the aim of achieving an internally homogenous population in a given nation-state was a view of peoples as a national collective whose membership was defined by ethnic-religious affiliation. This implied less tolerance to ethnic-religious groups that did not fit easily into the national imaginary: only when the defined communities could be fixed in their own territories would violence cease.

The Fruit of Division

It was against this background, when international opinion was already in favour of territorial rearrangements and population transfers, that the partition of British India took place in 1947. As the tripartite negotiations over power- sharing between the Indian National Congress, the Muslim League and the British colonial government began to fail, partition came to be seen as the most realistic option. At the same time, outside leading circles "partition" was little more than a vague, unfathomable - even harmless - word that cropped up occasionally in the speeches of political leadership. That they would be forced one day to leave their homes and livelihoods amidst raging violence, was yet inconceivable to millions of ordinary people.

This feeling of disbelief is best summarised in the words of an officer in charge of refugee rehabilitation in Punjab, who said: "we in India were only vaguely familiar with the word 'refugee' and used to wonder why people should be compelled to leave homes. Even *our* refugees [my italics] expressed surprise at the strange phenomenon of exchange of population and were heard saying we used to hear about the change of rulers but for the first time the ruled are also changing places".

The partition of 1947 was far more than an abstract line across administrative maps; it sought to create separate enclaves for different religious communities. In August 1947, when the "Radcliffe award" partitioning Punjab and Bengal was announced, millions of Hindus, Muslims and Sikhs now found that they no longer "belonged" to the place they were born in and had lived in forever. The advocates of territorial separation (most prominently according to the "two-nation theory" of Pakistan's founder, Muhammad Ali Jinnah) saw borders as the natural, physical expression of communal differences: that the new borders would exacerbate and reinforce these perceived differences was not considered.

Since the early summer of 1947, the abstract notion of "not-belonging" had become real when private armies belonging to the Muslim League's national guard), the Sikh *Akal Fauj* and the Hindu-nationalist *Rashtriya Swayamsevak Sangh* (RSS) began orchestrating major attacks on minority groups in their area of influence. The formal creation of borders in August meant that what was considered a temporary movement by many people to avoid violence months before had now became absolute and permanent.

From that point, the trickle of refugee movement turned into a deluge as millions began seeking safety in areas across the border where their community was in a majority. Hindus and Sikhs now "belonged" to India, and Muslims to Pakistan. The chaos of the early days abated as the two states began a planned exchange of population amidst continuing violence.

This period in Indian-Pakistani history is often visualised through archival photos of packed "refugee special" trains with people clambered on the rooftops, epic refugee walking-caravans, and women and children in bullock-carts escaping to safety with their meagre belongings. The personal memories of those affected, especially those who witnessed mass violence, are often saturated by scattered limbs, the inescapable stench of dead bodies, extreme sexual violence against women, and of people who took their own lives amid unbearable grief.

Such heartbreaking memories and images are testimony to the unconsolable pain of partition. They also contrast vividly with the single most striking image I encountered during six years of research into violence and identity in the region for my book *Since 1947: Partition Narratives among Punjabi Migrants of Delhi* (Oxford University Press, 2007). It was a photo published in several Delhi newspapers during the nuclear stand-off of 1998, when popular media discourse was spiced with comment about how the Indian nuclear-tipped warheads could reach all the way to Lahore and Islamabad. Hindus and Sikhs dancing in patriotic celebration of India's momentary advantage over Pakistan in the race for regional military supremacy. What intrigued me was that the revellers were the descendants of Hindu and Sikh refugees from Pakistan; in hard logic, they were cheering the capacity to annihilate the land of their parents and grandparents. Such nationalist intoxication too is the fruit of partition.

The Echo of History

The enduring hostility between India and Pakistan at official level - notwithstanding the efforts of many to seek to cross the divide - is at the very least a warning to those who argue for territorial partition as a solvent of violent antagonism. Iraq is the foremost contemporary example. Since 2005, the idea of partitioning Iraq into three regions - *Shia, Sunni* and Kurdish - has gained momentum in direct proportion to the intensification of sectarian violence. A number of policy-makers and commentators in the United States and Britain - among them Peter Galbraith, Joseph Biden, Leslie H Gelb, Richard Betts and Simon Jenkins - have endorsed this idea in one form or another (other analysts, such as **open Democracy** authors Zaid Al-Ali and Reidar Visser, have argued powerfully against it). The general notion is that the internecine violence between *Shia, Sunni* and Kurds would cease once each group has gained political control and territorial sovereignty in a tripartite Iraq; partition is regrettable but inevitable, and the earlier the world accepts it, the better.

The idea of partition may in large part emanate from the good intention of seeking to end violence and chaos in Iraq - though in some cases, a post-imperial "divide and rule" instinct may also be at work. But what is more important than the motive is the logic and the human implications of the proposal to divide people according to an accident of birth. The lesson of India-Pakistan in 1947 for the world is: don't make new borders between people, but work to make borders irrelevant.

Indian Muslim leader and Pakistan's first governor-general. Mohammed Ali Jinnah, a Muslim Indian politician, played the leading role in the formation of the nation of Pakistan. Born in Karachi, Jinnah initially pursued a business career in London but soon switched to studying law at Lincoln's Inn and eventually became a barrister in Mumbai (then Bombay). Hiscareer in politics began when he helped Parsi Dadabhai Naoroji win a seat in the Indian legislature. He joined the Indian National Congress in 1906 and in 1913 became a member of the Muslim League, working to increase cooperation between Hindus and Muslims. Jinnah contributed significantly to drafting the Congress-League Lucknow Pact of 1916.

PARTITION AND PRECEDING EVENTS

After World War II the British were in a hurry to leave India. The elections of winter 1945-46 were thus in point of fact about the future political shape of an independent subcontinent. Congress sought a mandate to keep India united while the Muslim League stood for a separate Pakistan. Emotive and sensationalist slogans such as 'Pakistan Ka Naara Kaya? La Illaha Il Lillah (What is the Slogan of Pakistan? It is that there is no God but Allah)' and 'Muslim Hai to League Mein Aa' (if you are a Muslim then join the Muslim League) were raised. Hindus and Sikhs were demonised as infidels and exploiters. Muslims who opposed the Muslim League were portrayed as renegades to Islam. In some cases fatwas (religious rulings) were issued to the effect that such persons should be denied a proper Islamic burial. On the other hand, support was solicited from Sunnis, Shias, the Ahmadis, Muslim Communists and anyone who was registered in the census records as a Muslim. The election results vindicated the contradictory claims of both parties. Congress secured 905 general seats out of a total of 1,585 while the gains of the Muslim League were even more impressive. It won 440 seats out of a total of 495 reserved for Muslims. It is to be noted that Muslims in the Hindu-majority provinces also voted massively in favour of the Muslim League.

The Cabinet Mission of 1946 sent by the post-war Labour Government of Clement Atlee failed to convince the two rival parties to agree upon a formula of power sharing within a united India. The factor that sealed the fate of unity was the eruption of large-scale communal violence following Jawaharlal Nehru's ill-considered press statement of 10 July 1946 in Bombay declaring that Congress would enter the Constituent Assembly' completely unfettered by agreements and free to meet all situations as they arise'.

On 29 July 1946, Jinnah gave the call to direct action to Muslims to protest the alleged anti-minority attitude of Nehru. On 16 August 1946, communal massacres, initiated by hotheads despatched by the Muslim League chief minister of Bengal, Hussain Shaheed Suhrawardy, took place in Calcutta, which left thousands of people, mostly Hindus, dead and homeless. The Hindus retaliated with great ferocity. More Muslims died in the counter-attack. The Calcutta killings proved a contagion, and communal riots broke out in many parts of India. The real explosion, however, originated a few months later in the key Punjab province, where the Muslim (57.1 per cent), Hindu (27.8 per cent) and Sikh (13.2 per cent) groups maintained an uneasy peace until the beginning of 1947. In the third week of January 1947, the Muslim League started its 'direct action' in Punjab against the non-Muslim League government of Khizr Hayat Tiwana.

On 3 March, the Sikh Akali Dal leader, Master Tara Singh, gave what in effect was a call for an all-out confrontation with Muslims. It resulted in immediate clashes between Hindu-Sikh and Muslim demonstrators. The first large-scale, organised communal clashes took place in the Rawalpindi area. On the night of 6-7 March, Muslim gangs attacked a number of Sikh and Hindu villages, the campaign continuing until 13 March. It left more than 2000 mainly Sikh and Hindu men, women and children dead. Muslim League cadres were identified as the culprits behind it.

At that point, the Sikh leaders demanded that Punjab be also divided on communal lines if Pakistan was granted to the Muslims. On 6-8 March, the All-India National Congress Committee passed a resolution demanding the division of Punjab into two provinces so that 'the predominantly Muslim part may be separated from the predominantly non-Muslim part'. Congress also demanded the partition of Bengal. The British Government announced the partitions of India, Bengal and Punjab on 3 June 1947. Congress, the Muslim League, representatives of the Sikhs and the various other minor religious and caste groups negotiated the actual demarcation of the Pakistan-India border before the Bengal and Punjab Boundary Commissions.

These deliberations served as the basis for the Radcliffe Award of 17 August 1947 (Pakistan and India had already become independent on 14 and 15 August, respectively). The Radcliffe Award did not satisfy any of the major contestants, and has subsequently been criticised and even condemned by various disgruntled actors.

The riots and pogroms, which accompanied Partition, were most harrowing in the Punjab and effectively led to the first successful post-war experiment in massive ethnic cleansing in the world. At that critical moment Muslim League, the Sikh Akali Dal,

RSS and Congress cadres became vicious killers. However, some 30-35 million Muslims stayed on in other parts of India while in East Pakistan some 23 per cent of the population continued to be Hindu. Some half million Hindus stayed behind in Sindh in West Pakistan (since December 1971 the only part which constitutes Pakistan).

INDIA

The failure to keep India united left the Congress ideal of a composite Indian nation in shambles. Millions of Hindu and Sikh refugees were devastated by that traumatic experience. Many objected to the Muslim presence and wanted Muslims driven away to Pakistan. At that critical movement, Gandhi, Nehru and many other stalwarts of the freedom struggle became a bulwark against the forces of reaction and revenge, and although attacks on Muslims continued for some time in many parts of India, they were small-scale occurrences. When discussion began on the constitution, the notion of a modern individual-rights-oriented civic and composite nation prevailed. The Hindu ethno-nationalist lobby argued in favour of a Hindu cultural hegemony in terms of national identity, but was overruled. It can be asserted, however, that the trauma of Partition made everybody in the Congress High Command overly sensitive to the question of unity.

The Constitution and Education System

The high point of the Nehruvian model was the enshrinement of universal values and norms in the Indian Constitution, which came into force on 26 January 1950. Its declarations on human rights and freedoms were quite radical. Universal citizenship was granted. Public office was open to all citizens. Some 23 percent of jobs (i.e. the ratio of those groups in the Hindu population) were later reserved by law for the so-called untouchable castes and tribes. In 1955 the Untouchability (Offences) Act, was passed. It criminalised the practice of untouchability. The constitution therefore clearly sanctioned a secular-democratic model of the polity. Although various amendments were subsequently made, the basic structure has remained unchanged.

The rational-modernising elite chose the educational system to gradually foster a democratic national identity. Liberal and Marxist scholars (many of Muslim origin) dominated until recently prestigious Indian social science and humanities university faculties and institutes. Their interpretation of the freedom movement was largely imbued with the emancipatory ethos of the European Enlightenment. Not surprisingly, the Hindu communal organisations and parties were very critical of such a foundation of Indian nationalism. The current BJP-led government seems to have decided to promote an educational agenda that will project a pro-Hindu bias in the production of knowledge and education. At the provincial level, such changes have already been introduced, typically identifying former Muslim rulers as responsible for all the ills of society.

Hindu Nationalism and the Growth of Hostility to Minorities

Congress had completely sidelined rightwing Hindu ethno-nationalists during the freedom struggle and alienated them from the state in the early years. Consequently they had to devise strategies to advance the project of Hindutva from outside the state. The loss of life and property and expulsion from their ancestral homes left in Pakistan were blamed on the Congress's willingness to concede Partition. Muslims as a whole were held responsible for the vivisection of the motherland. Such propaganda did boost the fortunes of the rightwing parties somewhat. For example, in 1943 the total membership of the RSS was only 76,000. In 1948 it had soared to 600,000. In electoral terms, however, such gains did not mean that a major challenge to Congress could be mounted. Rather, initially a major set back resulted from the involvement of the RSS in the assassination of Gandhi. The Hindu ethno-nationalists were infuriated over Gandhi's insistence that the Indian government pay 550 million rupees to Pakistan as compensation for losses incurred during Partition. Accordingly, he began a fast unto death to put pressure on the government. On 31 January Nathu Ram Godse, a member of the RSS, murdered Gandhi. Nehru decided to deal firmly with the Hindu ethno-nationalists. The RSS was banned, although it reappeared in 1952 in the form of Jana Sangha.

In the 1960s some other avenues for a Hindu political revival were tried. The Vishwa Hindu Parishad (VHP) was founded in 1964 ostensibly as a cultural movement purporting to inculcate pride among Hindus in their great culture and civilisation. Initially the VHP identified the proselytising activities of Christian missionaries as a major threat. It is intriguing to note that the VHP movement was sustained with considerable assistance from the Hindu diaspora, especially the large Indian/Hindu population of North America consisting of successful professionals and other upwardly mobile groups. Support from the UK has also been significant. The VHP and its various student and labour affiliates have been able to acquire political clout and infiltrate the state machinery and important cultural and media institutions. However, the most significant boost to Hindu great nation chauvinism came initially from another quarter: the Congress government led by Mrs Indira Gandhi. In December 1971 India defeated Pakistan in the latter's eastern wing, where a rebellion had been going on since March of that year. In 1974 India exploded a nuclear device. Mrs Gandhi began to be hailed as a great stateswoman. Sycophants began to raise slogans such as 'India is Indira and Indira is India'. However, in 1974 popular strikes, demonstrations and agitations broke out in protest against price rises, unemployment and bad government. The government retaliated by suspending many of the normal parliamentary practices and civil liberties. The Hindu ethno-nationalists made capital out of the situation by joining the democratic opposition. On 5 April 1980, some of them came together and founded the Bharatiya Janata Party (BJP).

A shift in the Congress electoral strategy could also be noticed. Instead of relying upon its traditional supporters, the so-called vote-banks comprising the various social and religious minorities such as the Dalits and Muslims, Mrs Gandhi began to cultivate the more traditional upper caste voters. In the 1980s, the BJP, RSS, and the rabidly anti-Muslim Shiv Sena in Mahrashtra and several other such parties and organisations began to evolve a martial discourse based on the mythical Mahabharta Epic and other heroic tales with a view to instilling militancy and a sense of collective nationalism. The idea of Hindutva or Hindu nation, first propounded by Sarvarkar in the 1920s, was revived. It asserted that only Hindus were trustworthy and loyal citizens of India; and further, that Nehruvian secularism had been harmful to Hindus, while it pampered the minorities. In particular, hostility was directed against the Muslims, who constitute some 13 per cent of the total Indian population.

It is important to note that the vast majority of Indian Muslims are converts from the poorest sections of Hindu society. They have been the main sufferers of the Partition Syndrome. They are grossly underrepresented in education and employment. Discrimination is therefore institutionalised in practice if not in theory.

It is, however, their portrayal as a fifth column and therefore a security threat that makes them most vulnerable to hostile propaganda. Thus, even the liberal mass media gave sensational coverage to a report that some Dalits had converted to Islam in Tamil Nadu in 1981. Exaggerated reports of Arab money donated to Islamic organisations and the alleged rapid growth rate of the Muslim population also figured prominently in media discussions.

The galloping Hindu cultural revival struck terror among the minorities. Anti-Muslim attacks became larger, more frequent, and more gruesome. The xenophobia and paranoia, which typifies such a pathological frame of mind, proved to be a self-fulfilling prophecy. However, Muslims did not mount the first challenge. It was the Sikhs of Punjab who were attracted to the idea of a separate Sikh state, Khalistan.

The Khalistanis argued that Partition gave India to the Hindus and Pakistan to the Muslims therefore Sikhs should be given Khalistan. The Khalistan conflict came to a head in June 1984 when Mrs Gandhi ordered the Indian army to flush out the Sikh leader Sant Jarnail Singh Bhindranwale and his militants who had been occupying the holiest Sikh shrine, the Golden Temple at Amritsar since 1982. The military action was successful but it cost a great deal in human lives. On 31 October 1984, Mrs Gandhi was assassinated by two of her Sikh bodyguards. Immediately Hindu gangs began to hunt down Sikhs all over India. In the capital Delhi alone at least 3,000 Sikhs were butchered.

The Sikhs had barely been crushed when another major separatist movement emerged in the predominantly Muslim-majority Indian-administered Kashmir. India and Pakistan had inherited the Kashmir dispute at the time of Partition. Its resurgence proved even more difficult for India to bring under control.

The Kashmir conflict continues to claim lives almost every day and India has not been able to bring the situation under control despite extreme repression and the deployment of hundreds of thousands of soldiers and security forces. India's worries have been compounded further by the re-emergence of separatist insurgency among a number of different Christian tribal peoples in the smaller north-eastern border states (provinces of India). The Indian government and mass media have been alleging that the Pakistani secret services, especially the Inter-Services-Intelligence (ISI) help the Sikh, Kashmiri and other separatist movements in India with training, arms and other facilities. From time to time some Indian Muslim is arrested on charges of working for the ISI. This undoubtedly helps portray all Muslims as pro-Pakistan and a subversive factor in Indian society.

While the anti-minority polices of the Hindu right have been steadily growing, a major worry for the BJP, which seeks power through the electoral process, has been the alienation of a significant number of Dalits and the so-called Other Backward Castes (OBCs), a rather large segment of peasant and other castes, which occupy a position between the upper castes and Dalits. The BJP had been seeking ways and means of enveloping such social strata into its fold of Hindu cultural nationalism. An emotive cause or symbol was found in the long, drawn out dispute between Hindus and Muslims over the site of the Babri mosque in Ayodhya. It was alleged that the god Rama had been born there and a temple existed on that spot before the mosque was built in 1528.

Consequently in the 1980s the BJP, VHP and other communal entities launched a campaign to dismantle the mosque. The Bajrang Dal (established in 1984), a youth wing of the VHP, employed mainly for agitation purposes and demonstrations, played the leading role in mobilising mass action and other activities in favour of the campaign. In early December 1992, the BJP and its supporters the VHP, Bajrang Dal, Shiv Sena and other fanatical groups finally arrived in Ayodhya after a long countrywide march in which thousands of people joined, including OBCs and other traditionally alienated sections of Hindu society.

The mob easily overpowered the rather small police force, climbed onto the top of the mosque and demolished it in a few hours. The Congress government under Narashima Rao seemed to have let the event take place mainly for opportunistic electoral reasons. The demolition of the mosque was accompanied by mob attacks on Muslims all over India and several thousand were killed. Suddenly India was in the midst of perhaps the most serious communal conflict since the partition. There was a fierce reaction in Pakistan and the old temples in Punjab were razed and some Hindus were also killed. The Hindu ethno-nationalists have plans to destroy some 3000 other mosques built allegedly on Hindu temples and holy places. Building the Ram Mandir is part of the BJP's election manifesto. The BJP has subsequently been increasing its electoral support and is currently the biggest party in a coalition government of 25 parties. Thus far it lacks parliamentary support for realising such a project. In fact moderate sections of the BJP have been trying to woo the Muslim vote bank and have made some gains. However, the Shiv Sena leader, Bal Thackerey, has recently demanded that Muslims should be disenfranchised.

The 20 million-strong Christian community had most of the time escaped the type of animosity faced by Muslims since they had played no role in bringing about the division of India. Some conversions to Christianity had continued to take place, mainly among the aborigines. Attacks upon churches and mission-run schools had been taking place, but after Sonia Gandhi (Italian-Catholic by birth) became the leader of the Congress Party in the late 1990s, the Hindu Right has been peddling a Christian conspiracy to annexe India. The last couple of years have witnessed a dramatic increase in church burning, killing of Christians and a countrywide campaign against missionaries. Thus on the night of 22 and 23 January 1999, the Australian missionary Graham Stuart Staines and his two sons were burnt alive in Monouharpur in Orrissa. Finally, the most enduring cleavages in Hindu society remain as deep as before: those between the twice-born upper castes, the assertive OBC groups and the Dalits. Attacks against Dalits continue to take place frequently all over India.

PAKISTAN

A notorious ambiguity about the purposes for which Pakistan was created was it to be simply a national state of Muslims or a theocratic Islamic state based on Sharia (dogmatic Islamic law)? characterises its travails with national identity. Jinnah had never provided any clear answer to this question. Pakistan can therefore be described as an unimagined nation. The elite that came to power in Pakistan lacked political vision and preparedness. It did not allow democracy to be institutionalised. Recurrent military-bureaucratic take-overs and a host of bizarre decisions contributed to the fostering of a pathological political culture at all levels of state and society. Such a tendency was aggravated by the traumatic loss of East Pakistan in late 1971 through a popular local rebellion backed by an Indian military intervention.

The Constitutional and Legal Structure

However, the first authoritative statement made on 11 August 1947, that is only three days before independence, in the Pakistan Constituent Assembly by Jinnah deviated from the main thrust of the Muslim League's propaganda in favour of cultural nationalism. To the utter surprise of many, he made the following observation in a long address:

> You are free, you are free to go to your temples, you are free to go to your mosques or to any other place of worship in this State of Pakistan. You may belong to any religion or caste or creed that has nothing to do with the business of the States. We are starting with this fundamental principle that we are all citizens and equal citizens of one States I think we should keep that in front of us as our ideal and you will find that in due course Hindus would cease to be Hindus and Muslims would cease to be Muslims, not in the religious sense, because that is the personal faith of each individual, but in the political sense as citizens of the State.

This patently secular and territorial idea of nation contradicted the rationale for the creation of Pakistan as a state for a cultural nation. The controversy that it caused has been generating ever more confusion as time goes by. While the fundamentalists usually dismiss it as irrelevant and an aberration, mainstream Muslim modernists argue that he was actually operating within an ideal Islamic framework of tolerance and justice for non-Muslims within an Islamic state. Marginalised secularists, leftists and oppressed minorities, however, raise it to the level of a sacred covenant that his successors have allegedly broken.

It seems that Jinnah's wording reflected his usual political sagacity rather than a firm ideological position. Communal violence was at its worst at that time. The Radcliffe Award was about to be announced and one could guess that it would result in population movement on a gigantic scale. The speech probably purported to discourage mass migration, uprooting and further communal violence. However, it is doubtful whether in the wake of the communal riots such a prescription enjoyed any real credibility in Muslim-Pakistani society, Jinnah's prestige and authority notwithstanding. In this regard, it is significant to bear in mind that Jinnah never again reiterated such a commitment although he lived for another year. After his death on 11 September 1948, the idea of a secular state never again received much attention in mainstream Pakistani politics. Rather, Islamic idiom became a central feature of official rhetoric.

One can even argue that once the initial euphoria was over and a framework for national identity and nation building had to be found, the Pakistani leadership felt constrained to distinguish itself from India. There were undoubtedly other issues to be dealt with by the government of Prime Minister Liaqat Ali Khan (d. 1951) but maintaining distinctiveness from Congress and secular India must have been an important consideration. Thus the Objectives Resolution moved in the Pakistan Constituent Assembly by Prime Minister Liaqat Ali Khan on 7 March 1949 proclaimed the novel idea that sovereignty over the entire universe belonged to God. Democracy was to be practised, but within 'Islamic limits'. The minorities were assured that their legitimate interests would be safeguarded, and that provisions would be made for them in accordance with Islam freely to profess and practise their religions and cultures. Although such proclamations sounded like innocuous 'boasts', in the longer run they proved to be constraints that facilitated the politics of exclusion of different religious minorities and deviant sects from the category of nation.

Thus the first constitution of Pakistan adopted in 1956 contained a commitment to bringing all laws into conformity with Islam. In 1973 the third constitution was adopted. Unlike the first two constitutions that only required the president of the republic to be a Muslim, the third also required the prime minister to be a Muslim. It further obliged them to take an oath testifying their belief in the finality of Prophet Muhammad's mission.

The Educational System

The invention of a distinct historical past for the so-called Muslim nation of India justifying its separate existence within the boundaries of Pakistan has been felt to be necessary for conferring legitimacy and authenticity on it. Attempts to imagine such a nation have unsurprisingly resulted in distortion and exaggeration of facts on a massive scale, resulting in mythogenesis.

The main concern has been to foster a Pakistani-Islamic identity defined negatively, as a contrast to India. In his book The Murder of History a leading Pakistani educationalist and historian Prof. K.K. Aziz has scrutinised 66 textbooks used for teaching history, Pakistan studies and social studies in Pakistani schools, colleges and universities. Pakistan studies deal largely with the Muslim nationalist/separatist movement. It is a compulsory subject from 1st grade up to university and not only all students of humanities and social sciences but also scientists, doctors and engineers must gain a pass.

The author alleges that Islamisation by the government of General Zia-ul-Haq vitiated the general academic environment in Pakistan. He cites extensively factual errors, logical fallacies, inconsistencies, falsifications, mythologisations and crass propaganda from books used both in the Urdu and English-medium schools and colleges.

The military and the long military rules are presented in positive terms while hostility towards India, Hinduism and Hindus is their hallmark. For example, Congress is described as a Hindu party. That there were many Muslims among its members and that some held leading positions is not reported. India is described as the state of Hindus, although there are as many Muslims or more living in India as in Pakistan.

Furthermore, a grossly exaggerated role is assigned to Muslims in the anti-colonial struggle. The Muslim League is declared as the party of the Muslim masses that successfully resisted both British colonialism and Hindu domination. Only Muslims are mentioned as victims of the partition riots and massacres, which are alleged to have been begun by Hindus and Sikhs. Any comment on the loss of lives among Hindus and Sikhs during that period is conspicuous by its absence. He sums up this approach in the following words:

It is declared that the Muslims of India made 'tremendous' sacrifices to win their freedom. The fact is that, apart from the brief years of 1858-60 and 1920-22, Muslims suffered little hardship between 1857-1947. It is forgotten by everyone that the Muslim League's search for protection and safeguards (in the early years) and its struggle for an independent state (in the later years) were strictly constitutional efforts, peaceful campaigns and political fights, conducted through parliamentary debates and negotiations No Muslim League leaders languished in prisons. No Muslim masses faced British bullets. The many people who died or suffered horribly in 1947 were running away from their homes because their life was in danger, not because they were fighting for the creation of Pakistan. They were casualties of communal riots, not of anti-British warfare.

He comments further, 'A sane educational system does not train students in hate. Whatever the justification for it or the compulsions of patriotism, hatred corrupts the mind, more so if it is still tender, and retards its healthy growth'.

Islamisation, Confessionalism and Hostility to Minorities

States founded on religious and ethnic nationalism invariably discriminate against atypical minorities. Ethnocracies can be a more apt description of such states, even when they practice democracy. Israel is a case in point. However, Pakistan has the rather unenviable distinction of extending the logic of confessionalism to its ultimate limits. In Pakistan, not only non-Muslims but also deviant sects within the broader category of Muslims who were mobilised in support of the 1945-46 elections have been alienated over time. Also, women as a whole have been victims of the so-called Islamisation process.

In 1953, violent anti-Ahmadiyya riots took place in Punjab in which several hundred lives were lost and considerable Ahmadiyya property was destroyed. The masterminds behind those riots were politicians from the ruling Muslim League seeking to challenge the ruling faction within the party. In 1974, the Islamic socialist Zulfikar Ali Bhutto played the anti-Ahmadiyya card again in the hope of extending his populist constituency into the stronghold of the doctrinal-minded Islamic parties of Pakistan. Consequently, when General Muhammad Zia-ul-Haq seized the reigns of power in July 1977 by toppling Zulfikar Ali Bhutto in a bloodless coup, a long tradition of relying on Islam to define national identity and the rights of citizens was already in place.

Upon coming to power in 1977, General Zia announced an ambitious programme to Islamise Pakistan. He expressed his political philosophy in a succinct manner : 'I have a mission, given by God, to bring Islamic order to Pakistan'. His main source of inspiration for an Islamic order was the ideas of the arch fundamentalist Abul Ala Maududi. The latter had set up headquarters in Lahore after Partition, from where he had been propagating his idea of a totalitarian Islamic state. The pre-Partition tradition of exploiting Islamic slogans to rouse Muslim fears against Hindus had been converted into a Machiavellian art by Pakistani politicians that involved damning their opponents as renegades to Islam and enemies of Pakistan. The various governments used it to slur the opposition's call for democracy and elections, while the various fundamentalist parties and factions pushed all governments into a corner with allegations of insincerity in their commitment to Islam. An Islamist political discourse evolved incrementally, each addition supplanting modernistic vagaries with puritan certainty. It bore the hallmarks of Maududism.

Thus in 1979, the government announced the imposition of the Hudud Ordinance, i.e. traditional Islamic punishments for the offences of adultery, false accusation of adultery, drinking alcohol, theft, and highway robbery. In 1984, a new Law of Evidence was adopted which reduced the worth of the evidence give by a female witness in a court of law to half the value of that given by a male witness. It was also a period when Islamic scholars notorious for their misogynist views appeared on television to advocate strict segregation between men and women and the confinement of the latter to the private sphere. In subsequent years the incidence of 'honour killings' has increased sharply. The victims are wives and daughters killed by their own families for allegedly defiling the family honour by demanding divorce or refusing to marry a man chosen for them by their elders. The courts have generally been very lenient to the culprits.

Also in 1984, many new restrictions were imposed on the Ahmadiyya group. They were prohibited from using Islamic nomenclature in their religious and social activities and may no longer call their places of worship mosques. In 1985, separate electorates were reintroduced (they were abolished in 1956), whereby non-Muslims were to constitute a separate body of voters, being thus entitled only to elect non-Muslim legislators to the various assemblies. Consequently their right to take part in normal law-making is severely restricted. It was followed by the adoption of the Blasphemy Law in 1986. It reads as follows:

Use of derogatory remarks etc. in respect of the Holy Prophet: Whether by words, either spoken or written, or by visible representations, or by any imputation, innuendo or insinuation, directly or indirectly, defiles the sacred name of the Holy Prophet (peace by upon him) shall be punishable with death, or imprisonment for life, and shall be liable to fine.

General Zia died in a plane crash in August 1988. The elected governments of Benazir Bhutto (1988-90, 1994-96) and Nawaz Sharif (1990-93; 1997-99) did not dare question the validity of the laws passed during the time of General Zia. It seems that once a law has been adopted in the name of Islam no politician is willing to attempt to rescind it. In October 1997 retired Lahore High Court judge Arif Iqbal Bhatti was shot down by unidentified members of extremist religious groups. His death was believed to be linked to his role in the acquittal in 1995 of two Christians, Salamat Masih and Rehman Masih, charged with blasphemy. The Pakistan Human Rights Commission has been providing details of the increasing terrorisation of minorities. Charges of blasphemy have been framed against many Ahmadis and Christians. Forced conversions of Hindus have also been reported. The military government of General Pervez Musharraf, which came to power through a coup d'état on 12 October 1999, initially presented a progressive position on Islam, but it had quickly to withdraw from such a position under pressure from the extremists.

Shia-Sunni Terrorism and the Emergence of the Jihadis

During Gen. Zia's regime Sunni-Shia doctrinal differences erupted into open conflict. The difficulties were compounded further when in the late 1980s powerful external actors began to cultivate their lobbies in Pakistan. Thus Saudi Arabia and Iran were believed to be sending large sums of money, books, leaflets, audio and video cassette-tapes and other propaganda material to Pakistan. Such propaganda offensives were backed by the inflow of firearms and other weapons. Sunni and Shia militias began to menace and terrorise society; the assassinations of several rival Sunni and Shia ulama and regular gun battles and bomb explosions have been taking place in Pakistan in recent years.

An international Islamic guerrilla movement comprising Sunni militants, aptly described as Jihadis (holy warriors), has been establishing its headquarters in the northern Pakistani city of Peshawar in recent years. The Jihadis have declared war on India and want to liberate Kashmir through violent means.

The United States is another enemy, as are Israel, secular Turkey and the central Asian republics. In some pronouncements, all non-Muslims have been declared enemies of Islam. The coming into power of the arch-fundamentalist Talebans in neighbouring Afghanistan has once again revived the old pan-Islamic project of Chowdhary Rahmat Ali. In a recent interview, a leading American South-Asia expert Selig Harrison claimed that General Zia's involvement in Afghanistan was meant to promote a pan-Islamic superstate in the region. He also alleged that such a scheme has powerful backers in the Pakistani military establishment. It can be assumed that Iran (because of its deviant Shia Islam), Turkey (secular) and the central Asian republics (also secular) will have no interest in such a project. Instead what is more likely is that the totalitarian, obscurantist, anti-modernist, medieval type of state and society created in Afghanistan could envelope Pakistan.

Separatist Movements

Although the Muslim League was successful in presenting a broad Muslim unity against Congress, after Partition it quickly dissipated and the centre became a stronghold of mainly Punjabi-Urdu-speaking groups. Recently the equation has been changed and it is a Punjabi-Pukhtun ruling axis which dominates Pakistan. Separatist movements have emerged several times. The Pukhtun nationalists seeking to create a separate Pukhtunistan in the north-western province of Pakistan were contained by a policy of carrot and stick during the 1950s and 1960s. The people of the former East Pakistan seceded to form their independent state of Bangladesh in 1971. It cost, however, between 1.5 and 3 million lives. The Pakistan army especially targeted the Hindus. A bloody guerrilla war raged in Baluchistan during the early 1970s, which was defeated by forceful military action. However, a virulent ethnic conflict that has claimed several thousand lives has been going on in the Sindh province, mainly as a confrontation between the native Sindhi-speakers and the Urdu-speaking refugees (both primarily Sunni Muslims) who settled in the urban areas of that province after Partition. Military action has been undertaken several times to restore law and order. In addition, hundreds of thousands of Afghan refugees have settled in Karachi, where armed militias run lucrative businesses in drugs and arms smuggling.

ALTERNATIVES TO PARTITION IN 1947

The idea of separate Hindu and Muslim interests in India was a commonplace for years before the eventual break-up of the British raj. Indeed, British policy-makers had taken it for granted that Muslim and Hindu interests could never be coalesced - this was the lesson of the Mutiny in 1857. Even when the Indian National Congress arose to agitate for the rights of Indians, this too never had a great appeal to the Muslim populations of India, except on rare occasions such as the Calcutta Congress of 1920 when it provided cross-community backing for the Khilafat movement.

In terms of membership the Congress was a predominantly Hindu body, and Muslim membership had never risen to more than 15 per cent (or to more than 10 per cent of the Congress Committee) moreover, Gandhi's doctrine of nonviolence carried a decidedly Hindu flavour. Yet the Muslim element in the Congress was consistently more numerous than in the Muslim political parties proper, and to the Congress leaders the claim to be fully representative of all communities in India seemed unchallengeable. In the 1936 elections, more Muslim members of the legislative assemblies were members of Congress than any other single Muslim party.

Yet Muslims also failed to take part in many of the Congress activities, such as the Civil Disobedience movement of 1930-1. This proved to be a difficult problem for an Indian National Congress which sought to claim rights to represent the whole of Indian society, fighting not communal rivalries but the appalling poverty, unemployment and indebtedness of the peasantry. 'The contest' said Nehru, 'lies between. .. the British and the Congress... All third parties and middle and undecided groups have no real importance.'

Indeed, Nehru's careless attitude was shared by many of the secular leaders of the nationalist movement, who simply could not conceive the fears of the Muslim minority that democracy would see their particular interests consistently outvoted. As late as February 1938 he was still publicly complaining to Jinnah: 'I am afraid I must confess that I do not yet know what the fundamental points of dispute are.' To reinforce the Muslim minorities fears about unitary democracy, they only needed to look at the rhetoric of the Hindu revivalist leaders, such as V D. Savarkar, who castigated Congress in his Presidential Address to the Hindu Mahasabha in 1938: 'They call themselves Indian Nationalists! But every step they take is communal. They have guaranteed special protection to minorities - Muslims, Christians, Europeans etc. Is this Indian Nationalism? A true Indian Nationalist must know nothing of Muslims and Hindus, minorities and majorities. To him all must be Indians only.'

This British were endlessly creative at allowing Muslim autonomy without breaking up India. For a long time, the separate electorates guaranteed by the Montagu-Chelmsford reforms following the First World War eased Muslim tensions - but the bodies that were being elected were relatively powerless. When the British attempted a more powerful federal solution, with the Government of India Act, a continued problem of representation was proved.

A pre-electoral deal in 1936 between Congress and the Muslim League offered mutual cooperation in the legislatures and coalition governments; but the Congress's strong showing meant that they were not dependent on the League for support outside the UP. Even in the UP, the terms did not amount to a coalition: the Muslim League was to cease to function in the assembly as a separate group, its members were to become part of the Congress party and to share fully its privileges and obligations; the League parliamentary board was to be dissolved in UP, and no candidates were to be put up by it at any by-elections.

The style of Congress government in the provinces also gave causes for concern.

The 1935 Act not only extended the franchise to a very large population but also failed to provide that preferential treatment for the zamindars which they had hitherto been used to.' Nationalist policies aimed to build on this, and as Nehru said, 'economically and socially it must mean the ending of special class privileges and vested interests.'

One of the first acts of the Congress ministry in the UP was to bring in the UP Tenancy Act which provided for greater security of tenure - a deliberate attack on the landlords, who sought the protection of political parties opposed to the Congress. Thus the Hindu landlords turned to the Hindu Mahasabha, and the Muslim landlords to the League. Gandhi's Wardha system ordered that primary education 'should centre round some form of manual and productive work, and that all the other abilities to be developed or training to be given should, as far as possibly be integrally related to the central handicraft chosen with due regard to the environment of the child.' Clearly this offended large swathes of Western-educated opinion, and especially among Muslims, who claimed that the study of the Quran, and therefore the sanctity of Islam would be endangered.

Indeed, Jinnah commented on the whole raft of Congress governmental policies by saying, 'Is there any doubt now in the mind of anyone that the whole scheme of Hindi-Hindustani is intended to stifle and suppress Urdu? Take next the Wardha scheme of education. Were the Muslims taken into confidence when the scheme was under preparation?

The whole scheme was conceived and its details worked out behind the back of the Muslims?... I have no hesitation in saying that it is Mr Gandhi who is destroying the ideal with which the Congress was started. He is the one man responsible for turning the Congress into an instrument for the revival of Hinduism. His ideal is to revive Hindu religion and establish Hindu raj in this country.'

The experience of Congress rule convinced Jinnah that separation and partition were the only ways to further Muslim interests. Before the 1937 election he had repeatedly asserted that 'Hindus and Muslims could join hands and form one party', but after the election he concluded that 'Honourable settlements can only be achieved between equals, and unless the two parties learn to respect and fear each other, there is no solid ground for any settlement.' This mistrust only increased as time went on.

In 1939, he urged 'Musalmans all over India to observe Friday the 22nd December as the 'Day of Deliverance' and thanksgiving as a mark of relief that the Congress regime has at last ceased to function.' More condemnations of Congress rule followed in 1940: 'Democracy of the kind with which the Congress High Command is enamoured would mean the complete destruction of what is most precious in Islam. We have had ample experience of the working of the provincial constitutions during the last two and a half years and any repetition of such government must lead to civil war.' Jinnah's only solution to this was to reinforce the idea of fundamental separate Muslim identity against the Hindu *kafirs*. In 1940, he urged the League in Lahore that 'The Musalmans are a nation by any definition with the need for a homeland, territory and state if we are to develop to the fullest our spiritual, cultural, economic, social and political life.'

Later on in that session, the League passed the famous 'Pakistan' Resolution which resolved 'that no constitutional plan would be workable in this country or acceptable to the Muslims unless it is designed on the following basic principle, viz that geographically-contiguous units are demarcated into regions which should be so constituted with such territorial readjustments as may be necessary that the areas in which the Muslims are numerically in a majority, as in the northwestern and eastern zones of India, should be grouped so to constituted 'independent states' in which the constituent units shall be autonomous and sovereign.'

The League's resolution was put forward on behalf of 'Muslim India'; but at that time it was entirely unclear whether the demand for partition was actually supported by the Muslims. The results of the 1936 elections showed that the League at that time had only a small following among the Muslim masses: only a quarter of Muslim votes were cast for them - even before the Pakistan demand was articulated. Muslim opinion was also deeply divided about the meaning of 'Pakistan'.

As Jinnah had expressed it, it had no decided territorial integrity, no proposed form of government, no policy on the role of Islam in the State, no policy regarding the position of Muslims in other provinces or of the position of non- Muslims in Pakistan. Even if answers to this were clear, which they were not, there was still a significant proportion of Muslim opinion which was definitely against.

The dominant party of NWF Province, *Khudai Khidmatgar,* was a Pathan nationalist movement, allied with Congress. The Jamiyat-ul-Ulema-i-Hind never accepted the doctrine of the two nations as propounded by the League. The Ahrar Party in the Punjab had refused to join the League and declared its determination to 'crush it because it is a party of reactionaries' - accepting instead the political and economic objectives of the Congress.

In Bihar, the Momin Ansar Conference (party of Muslim weavers) remained opposed to the League. Baluchistani nationalists, organized by Allama Mashriqui, were also opposed to the division of the country.

Furthermore there were in the Congress itself a large number of nationalist Muslims who were opposed to the League. Many organizations with Muslim members, such as the Shia Conference, the States Peoples Conference, Trade Unions, and Kisan Sabhas had adopted the same political platform as the Congress had done. Even in the Muslim majority provinces, the League initially found little support for its policies. In the Punjab, the Unionist Party was outside its control, and the Punjabi premier from 1937-42, Sir Sikander Hyat Khan, continued to voice his opposition to 'Pakistan' - as did Allah Buksh, the Prime Minister of Sind. The successful coalition governments in Punjab and NWFP demonstrated an admirable alternative to Partition - though not as electorally-popular.

However, the 1940s saw the Muslim League expand until virtually all Muslim interests were expressed through Jinnah. After the arrest of the Congress leaders in August 1942, Jinnah, he made the best political use of it in strengthening the hold of his party over the Muslim masses.

He denounced the 'Quit India' movement as an attempt to establish the 'Hindu Raj, and to 'deal a death blow to the Muslim goal of Pakistan'. Between the years 1937 and 1943 the Muslim League grew strength to strength. Towards the end of 1938 the Madras Muslim League claimed a membership of 43,920; in 1940 it rose to 88,833.18 In the Central Provinces the membership increased from 23,000 in 1938 to 56,541 in 1943. In Sind the membership rose to over 300,000 in 1944, while in Bengal the League reached 550,000 members. The upsurge in the League's numerical strength was matched in its electoral strength. Sixty-one by-elections were held for Muslim seats in the legislatures during 1937-43, and of those 47 were won by the League, 10 by independent Muslims, and only 4 by the Congress. In the provincial elections of 1945-6 it took nearly 90% of the Muslim seats and - even more impressively - all of the Muslim places for the Central Legislature. The Pakistan policy and the effects of war had transformed the Muslim League from an elitist body into a mass gathering - it could not be taken off the agenda after this. To some extent this massive growth in the League's fortunes came about due to their clear support from the British rulers - a *quid pro quo* for Jinnah's support for the war effort.

The rebellious actions of the Congress encouraged the British to view the Muslim League as being a counterweight and rival of the Congress on the all India political scene.' 'That such divisions and conflicts should be used as practical aids to practical government was only to be expected', admits Linlithgow's constitutional adviser, 'for who with the daunting task of governing, with absurdly small force, an Indian district or province or all India would not use such useful means as lay to hand'? In reply to the Congress's demand for a definition of war aims, Linlithgow implicitly accepted the League's claim to speak for all the Muslims of India, while the Congress was dubbed a Hindu body.

However, the latest election results from 1936 had shown this to be untrue - the League had won only 105 out of 489 Muslim seats and did not control a singe government in any of the Muslim majority provinces, while the Congress formed governments in eight provinces, including the NWFP with its 95 per cent Muslim population. Jinnah was not slow to recognize the changed situation. He remarked: 'after the war began, I was treated on the same basis as Mr Gandhi.

I was wonder-struck why all of a sudden I was promoted and given a place side by side with Mr Gandhi.' From this moment onwards, Jinnah's negotiations with the Congress and British became more forceful and less flexible. From this time on, possible solution after possible solution was offered - and spurned by both sides. Jinnah concluded in January 1940 that 'a constitution must be evolved that recognises that there are in India two nations who both must share the governance of their common motherland'. - but the actions the League performed were bitter sectarianism, such as the observance of 'Deliverance Day' 22 December 1939.

Wartime negotiations between the Muslim and Hindu communities saw petty wranglings over semantics, such as the exchanges in which Jinnah rejected Gandhi's offer for a plebiscite to be held in Muslim areas since 'the right of self-determination shall not be exercised by the Muslims but by the inhabitants of these areas so demarcated.'

Both parties rejected the Cripps Offer of 1942 which offered an Indian Union which the Muslim areas may or may not join. When in 1946 the British offered a *de facto* responsible interim government and a constituent assembly, in which both sides were invited to share, Jinnah demanded long-term protection from Congress for Muslim and minority interests, leading Nehru to exclaim 'when India is free, India wild do just what she likes. It is quite absurd and foolish to lay down now what she is going to do a few years hence'.

It had also always been a item of British faith that any solution to the communal problem could be achieved within the integral borders of British India without the need for a division of the country into two sovereign states - and certainly not a division of existing provinces. This remained the case even as far as Mountbatten's Viceroyalty. It also remained the position of Congress, who had consistently called for a unitary India when freed from colonial control.

As late as 1942, they resolved that 'any proposal to disintegrate India by giving liberty to any component state or territorial unit to secede from the Indian Union or Federation will be detrimental to the best interests of the people of the different states, and provinces, and the country as a whole, and the Congress, therefore cannot agree to any such proposal'. However, the sovereignty of Pakistan remained an immovable bargaining position for Jinnah, who on the contrary increased the stakes by demanding the total separation in the name of Pakistan of almost the entire areas of Assam, Bengal, the Punjab, Sind, NWFP, and Balochistan.

By this point, Partition of India was inevitable - though partition of individual provinces was not. In fact, these areas were precisely the areas which had given very little support to the Muslim League in the previous election campaigns. Punjab and NWFP had formed coalition governments very happily with the Hindus of the province, even in coalition with Congress.

The Muslim peasants of Bengal were still the group which offered the least support to the League programme, and saw little interest in furthering the sectarian aims of the League's leaders. The same applied to the Hindus of Bengal with regard to the Congress High Command.

As the bhadralok Hindus had formed the most Westernised and educated sections of the Hindu population, they had been the early luminaries of Congress when it was set up. However, the rise in Hindu politics and radicalism had seen leadership pass elsewhere, while the bhadralok busied themselves in local government according to the provisions of the 1935 Act.

Separate electorates did not apply to districts and localities, where elections to local institutions - Local and District Boards, School Boards and Committees - continued to be held on the basis of joint electorates. Local politics more accurately reflected social relations of a minority but wealthy Hindu population, since the electorates for local elections, perhaps 15 per cent of the adult population, was not defined by community but by wealth and education.

For bhadralok Hindus, denied an effective role in provincial politics by the provisions of the Communal Award, local and district institutions remained one area where they could continue to exercise influence. Until the outbreak of communal violence in Calcutta city in 1946, there had been no serious consideration of a partition of Bengal - and in most of Bengal there remained little reason to arbitrarily demand partition.

A panicked reaction to urban violence, the constraints of timepressure set by the British, and an unsympathetic treatment from Hindu and Muslim leaders from elsewhere in India, forged a division which was to many eyes made more ironic due to the nationalist efforts to unify Bengal in 1906. In Punjab, the provincial government had also been one which had seen a successful effort to maintain intercommunality up until 1946 - crucially again, it did not rely on the Muslim League or Congress until the elections of December 1946.

Even then, the Muslim League did not gain a majority of the seats, and for a short while a coalition government was possible - it was outside and all-India pressure which encouraged the communal violence while spread across the province in 1946, not a hardening of local political willingness to compromise. In both cases, partition was a solution formed at great speed, in order to prevent a civil war that had been urged by the national parties themselves. That it failed to prevent this civil war as well showed the intransigence which both sides had so assiduously cultivated over the previous few years.

6

Role of Nehru, Patel and Jinnah in Partition

ROLE OF SARDAR PATEL

Some critic say that Sardar Vallabhabhai Patel was the founder of Indian Partition, according to them, Jinnah may have raised the flag of partition but now the real flag bearer was Patel, according to Maulana Azad, the two nation theory of Jinnah and demand for Pakistan were only a slogan, a bargaining counter, but Patel was an even greater supporter of the two-nation theory than Jinnah. The views of Azad may be of great importance because he was one of the leading politicians who actively participated in the freedom movement and held negotiations with the Viceroys of India from time to time, with the Cripps Mission 1942 and the Cabinet Mission 1946.

As he was a leading nationalist Muslim Leader in the Congress, later historians and scholars have accepted his view uncritically in responsibility for Partition of India. Tayebullah a Congressman from Assam, hold Patel and also Nehru were as authors of Partition of India. Asghar Ali Engineer say-it would also be wrong to entirely blame on Jinnah and the Muslim League for Partition. Certain Congress Leaders including J L Nehru and Sadar Vallabhbhai Patel were also responsible for the Partition. According to Zakaria-neither Nehru nor Jinnah wanted Partition but accepted it because of the failure of Nehru and Patel to control the forces that Jinnah had unleashed.

In making Sardar Patel as the author of Partition and as creator of Pakistan, Maulana Azad disregards the facts that Sardar Patel never accepted the two-nation theory of Jinnah nor did he support the demand for a homeland for the Muslims of the provinces in which they were in minority.

Patel may have eventually conceded the demand for Pakistan, more precisely he was driven to agree to partition to avoid further bloodshed due to riots between the two communities, almost verging one civil war-Calcutta Killing of 16 August 1946, large scale riots in Noakhali in Bengal, in Bihar Sharif and in Bombay in 1946, in Rawalpindi in Punjab in 1947. India was heading towards total breakdown and anarchy. Conceding the demand for Partition and creating Pakistan are entirely two different things. It appears that Maulana Azad had forgotten the facts of history when he held Sardar Patel as the author of Partition.

In the words of Percival Spear, the hope of a united independent India was extinguished in the blood and monsoon passion of 1946. Partition was now the only possible solution though it took another nine months to convince all parties of this fact. To the specter of civil war in British India was added the grave danger of India being splintered by the British officials of the political department manipulating the princes to become independent through the mischievous device of lapse of paramount. Thus the British would not transfer power and quit unless there was an agreement between the Congress and Muslim

League: In the absence of such an agreement, there was grave danger of civil war. At the same time if the British continued to govern India, there was the grave risk of India being splintered into numerous princely states. Partition was thus the only key to independence, and partitioned British India and princely states forming a united India.

These Political Compulsions and prudence drove Patel to discard United India and accept Partition. This finds confirmation in his speech at Nagpur 1947 when Patel disclosed that the British officials of the Political Department were arranging secretly to lease out the native state of Bastar to the Nizam of Hyderabad. The Sardar came to the conclusion that the best course was to hasten the departure of the foreigners even at the cost of partition of the country. By April-May 1947 the Sardar felt that acceptance of Dominion Status had another tactical advantage.

In 1947, the policy of the British Government was to avoid a formal partition, to keep India united with a congenitally frail federal government and autonomous provinces grouped into Muslim and Hindu majority areas in fact a bigger, autonomous Pakistan within the Indian Union, and princes becoming independent through lapse of paramount. Jinnah and the Muslim League were working for partition and the establishment of Pakistan at any cost with inflexible determination and for independent princely states banding themselves into a third India-Princesstan.

With his experience that the interim-Government had been paralyzed by the Congress-League squabbles, Sadar Patel realized that Gandhiji's stipulation to agree to Partition only after the departure of the third party, the British, would only prolong the British rule and would therefore, be self-destructive.

Political prudence demanded that the Congress should agree to immediate transfer of power by accepting Dominion Status and to a government for partitioned India that was constitutionally the same as before, that is, as powerful as the British Government. This also enabled the Sardar to curb the mischief of lapse of paramount by securing peaceful accession of the states to the Indian Union, which more than offset the areas hived by Partition. Thus the Congress, and Sardar Patel in particular, outmaneuvered both Mountbatten and the British officials, and Jinnah, and established a strong and united India rid of a separatist and disruptive lobby.

ROLE OF NEHRU

Some eminent scholars are of view that Nehru committed some grave blunders in 1937 and 1946, which created conditions which led to the partition of India.

a. 1937: Nehru and failure to forge a Congress-League alliance in the U.P.

b. Shimla Conference of 1945

c. The Cabinet Mission Plan of 1946 and role of Nehru

(a). In the provincial legislative elections held in the U.P., under the Govt. of India Act, 1935, the Congress won an overwhelming majority of the general or non-Muslim seats. So far as the seats reserved for the Muslims were concerned, there was an understanding between the Congress and the Muslim League before the elections, under which the Congress put up their candidate only in 7 reserved seats leaving 57 to the Muslim League. The Muslim League won 27 out of 64 Muslim seats. In a Cabinet of six, the Muslim League sought two seats for Khaliquazzaman and Nawab Ismail khan. They were said to have assured Azad that they would cooperate with the Congress and fully support the Congress programme. But Nehru informed the League MLAs that only one of them could be taken in the Ministry, so none joined. If the League's offer of cooperation had been accepted, the Muslim League party would, for all practical purpose, merge with the Congress, Jawaharlal's action gave the Muslim League in the U.P. a new lease of life. All students of Indian politics know that it was from U.P. that the League was organized. Mr. Jinnah took full advantage of the situation and started an offensive, which ultimately led to Pakistan.

Jinnah's ego was hurt by the manner in which the National Congress dealt with him. He became bitter when, after the 1937 elections, the Congress refused to have an understanding with the League in U.P. and called the Congress an enemy of the Muslims. Jinnah wanted to be treated as an equal and as the sole spokesman of the Muslims that the Congress consistently refused. While the Muslim League and Jinnah wanted to share power with the Congress on impossible terms, Maulana Azad, as a member of the Congress Parliamentary sub-committee, shut the door for any possible coalition by imposing equally impossible conditions for a Congress-League coalition in July 1937. The failure of the Congress to accommodate the League was one of the first seed of Pakistan. Exclusion of the League from the Congress Ministries after the elections of 1937 was the last point that swept off the concept of United India. On the 7th May 1937 the Muslim League

Parliamentary Board reiterated, " The Muslim League Party in the Legislature can not and should not join the Congress in its policy and programme of wrecking the Constitution." We do not find any evidence whatsoever of the Congress spurring the hand of friendship of the Muslim League or the Muslim League wanting to form an alliance or coalition Government except on its own terms.

There is also conclusive evidence of Azad's active role in the formulation of the terms for an alliance between the Congress and the League in U.P. Maulana Azad had appended a note to the proposed terms which stated: " ...if these terms were agreed to and the Muslim League group of Members joined the Congress Party as full members, that group would cease to exist as a separate group...". We should keep in our minds these facts also, as Maulana had criticized Nehru as being responsible for the alienation of the Muslims in U.P. in 1937. Maulana Azad had also shut the door on any negotiations for a coalition with League. Maulana Azad was responsible for the failure to forge an alliance between the Congress and the Muslim League in 1937 in as much as Maulana Azad had engineered a spilt between the Muslim League and the Jamait-ul-Ulema.

Nehru's greatest mistake was to reject in 1937 Jinnah's offer to form coalition Congress-Muslim League Government in provinces. This may appear to be so in the light of-after events, but in the context of the man, the time and the circumstances, Nehru acted correctly.

(b). In June, July 1945, Wavell convened a conference of leaders of political parties at Shimla for the purpose of forming an interim-Government of Indians by inducting representatives of political parties in Viceroy's Executive Council. The Conference, however, failed because Jinnah made impossible demands for the Muslim League joining the interim-Government. Wavell called off the Conference, on the ground that his list of nominees to the Executive Council was not acceptable to the Muslim League.

The Conference had failed but it produced far-reaching effects. Patel observed: " we were called all, the way to Shimla. What for?

Just, to be told that nothing could be achieved without Jinnah's cooperation!." The abortive Shimla Conference was a major milestone in the Pakistan movement.

(c). Azad and others had blamed Nehru for repudiating on the 10th July 1946 the earlier acceptance by the Congress of the Cabinet Mission Plan of the 10th May 1946. According to Azad, Nehru had declared that the Congress would completely unfetter by agreements and would be free to modify the Cabinet Mission Plan. This reopened the whole question of political and communal settlement. Jinnah took full advantage of this mistake and withdrew the League's earlier acceptance of the Cabinet Mission Plan. The mistake in 1937 was bad; the mistake in 1946 was more costly. The Shimla Conference of 1945 wherein Wavell had made an abortive effort to bring about a settlement between the Congress and the League. Both sides adopted rigid stands striking a further blow to the forces of unity, Wovell could have managed to bring Jinnah round if Nehru and Patel were more flexible. Their dislike and distrust of Jinnah, prevented a workable solution. The rejection of the 1946 Cabinet Mission proposals, destroyed the unity of India, this refusal forced the Muslim to Partition.

C. ***Jinnah:*** Jinnah was the true architect of Pakistan. But there have been laboured efforts to play down the role of Jinnah in Partition thereby subtly shifting the blame on to the opposing actors-Nehru and Patel, apart from the British Government and Viceroys.

According to Maulana Azad, " till perhaps the very end Pakistan was for Jinnah a bargaining counter..." Since Partition would not solve the communal problem, Jinnah had raised the slogan of the two nations. Kanji Dwarakadas, a friend of Jinnah, wrote, " I do not think Jinnah wanted Pakistan. Right till 1946 he was prepared to work for one united India. So, all the time he was talking in terms of Pakistan, this was a bargaining point for him. Not only Jinnah and the other Muslim Leaders were responsible for the Partition of India and creation of Pakistan, Maulana Azad, J.L. Nehru and Saradar Patel were also responsible for Partition.

Zakaria wrote-I am convinced that Jinnah was never really serious about Pakistan. One of close friend of Jinnah told Zakaria, that if India had not been divided, the Muslims would have had to face either abject-poverty or complete-annihilation at the hands of Hindus. Jinnah's theme was in his public meetings in Muslim majority areas that if Muslims did not vote for League candidates, the Muslims would be reduced to the status of SHUDRAS and Islam would be vanquished. And yet, Maulana Azad and Zakaria consider that the demand for Pakistan was only a bargaining point. Asghar Ali Engineer says: neither Islam nor Muslim was responsible for the creation of Pakistan. Pakistan was the result of a very complex inter-play of forces. If we can say anything with certainty, it is that vested interests on both sides played a crucial role in bringing about vivisection of the country...

Ayesha Jalal strongly suggests that Jinnah did not want Partition. He was primarily interested in autonomous provinces within a federation. She stresses that Pakistan resolution of 1940, made no mention of Partition, certainly, none of Pakistan. Jinnah in 1943 stressed that Pakistan with its connotation of partition, was not the League's idea but a caricature-thrust upon it by the Hindu Press: They Fathered this word upon us. Salman Khurshid says: Partition was the result of inconsiderateness on both sides. Not of intransigence of one and the timorousness of the other; not the communal politics of one and secular principles of the other. Partition came because little things had shattered faith.

According to S.R. Khairi: Jinnah resisted for a long time the proposal to partition the subcontinent. Jinnah, as President of the Muslim League, issued a Memorandum of its Minimum Demands on 12th May 1946 in the wake of the Conference with the Cabinet Mission and further explained them in his statement of 22nd May 1946.

According to these Minimum Demands:

1. The six Muslim provinces of the Punjab, N.W.F.P., Balochistan and Sindh in the North-West and Bengal and Assam in the East and North-East will be grouped together to form the Pakistan Zone; the remaining provinces will be grouped together to form the Hindustan Zone;

2. Each of the groups will frame their own Zonal Constitution for the provinces and the Zonal federations;
3. The two Zonal federations will form a Union which will deal with three subjects only *viz.*, Foreign Affairs, Defense and Communications necessary for defense but the Union will have no powers of taxation.
4. The Zonal federations will be sovereign and independent states, as residuary sovereign powers will vest in the provinces.
5. There should be parity of representation between the two groups of Provinces in the Union Executive and the Legislature, if any.

This Memorandum provides conclusive evidence that Jinnah was absolutely determined to divide India and established sovereign and independent Pakistan. At best he was prepared to establish a Confederation with India to deal with the foreign affairs and defense of the two states and the Confederation was to be provided funds by the federating states.

The role of Jinnah and the Muslim League in Partition of the country with enormous loss of life and property and suffering and with successor states being perpetually in a state of hot or cold war.

IDEOLOGY OF MUSLIM SEPARATISM

A Historical-cum-Sociological Study Pakistan was not the product of the conduct or misconduct of Hindus. It had always been there, only they were not conscious of it. Hindus and Muslims, though living in the same towns and villages had never been blended into a nation, they were always two entities. The foundation of Pakistan started the moment the first Hindu was converted to Islam in India, long before the Muslim established their rule as Pakistan. As soon as a Hindu embraced Islam he was outcast not only religiously but also socially, culturally and economically. As for Muslim, it was a duty imposed on him by Islam not to merge his identity and individuality in any alien society. Throughout the ages Hindus had remained Hindus and Muslims had remained Muslims, and they had not merged their entities, this was the basis for Pakistan.— — —Speech Delivered by M.A. Jinnah at A.M.U. 08 March 1944.

The roots of the ideology of separatism of the Muslim community, the two-nation theory, cause in the Partition of India, can be traced in the Mughal Period of Indian history. During the Sultanate period, there was a conflict within the Islamic community, between ULEMAS & SUFIS.

The ULEMAS represented the orthodox institutes of Islam, rigid of the Shariah, the Islamic code of conduct, especially the rituals and the personal law, the law relating to marriage, divorce, dissolution, inheritance and the Islamic code of conduct, especially, the rituals and the personal law, Shariah was the highest virtue.

The Sufis laid emphasis on TARIQA instead of on Shariah; tariqa was on good conduct, practice of devotion, asceticism, instead of performance of rituals. Sufism of this period was accommodative, even respectful of non-Muslim beliefs and practices.

In the Mughal Period, the Muslim community became more fundamentalist. The ULEMA opposed to Akbar's policy of SULH-I-KUL-peace with all religions-which could lead to the evolution of composite culture and harmony between religious communities. Later Akbar attempted to establish DIN-I-ILAHI, a faith to which a member of any religion could subscribe without having to renounce his own.

Fundamentalist maintained that Shariah is the true religious way. In the Indian context this preached that Islam and Hinduism were two opposites that could never integrate. The fundamentalists were fighting the subtle Indianization of Islam in the countryside due to creeping Hinduism.

The ULEMA were determined that Indian Muslims must purge themselves of un-Islamic beliefs and practices. They powerfully boosted the ideology of separatism.

To sustain the Shariah institute and the dominance of its ideology among the Muslims, the leaders of the ULEMA established MADARSAS, where students could be imparted the doctrines and philosophy of Islam in general, and the ideology of the Shariah in particular.

ULEMA, QAZI and MUFTI are the products of MADARSAS. Notable among such MADARSAS were the Nizamiya MADARSAS of Firangi Mahal in Lucknow, was established in the time of Aurengzeb in 1694.

The MADARSAS of Barelvis at Patna was established in the first quarter of the 18th century and the MADARSAS of Deoband in 1867 and Nadwat-al-Ulema Lucknow in 1891.

Islamic fundamentalism also thwarted the growth of composite culture. Aurengzeb's life and activity was the starting point in the growth of Muslim nationality in India is a statement of profound historical truth. The seed of the ideology of social separatism was sown by Sheikh Ahmad Sirhind and nurtured and propagated by his successors-ULEMA, MADARSAS nurtured separatism and smothered composite culture; the seed of two nation theory-separatism at political plane-was sown by Aurengzeb and nourished in the communal and finally flourished in the hot house of communal politics of the nineteen forties to spilt the country.

MADARSAS, Islamic seminaries, produced a class of ULEMA steeped in orthodox Islam who subscribe, as a class, to the theory and belief that Muslims and non-Muslims in general and the Hindus in particular, are different communities-two nations and have opposed/ discouraged any attempts towards integration of religious communities. The ULEMA of Barelvi institute were staunch supporters of Pakistan though their MADARSA is situated at Patna, Bihar.

ULEMA of the MADARSA of Firangi Mahal in Lucknow likewise subscribed to the two-nation theory and fully supported the Pakistan movement.

Of all the Muslim MADARSAS, that of Deoband is world famous. It is ranked next only to the Al-Azhar Muslim seminary of Egypt. It is an orthodox institute, which seeks to reform Islam by ridding it of non-Islamic beliefs and practices.

ULEMA of this MADARSA had dominated the Jamiat-ul-Ulema-I-Hind, a powerful political organization of the Deobandi Ulema, which played a prominent role in India's freedom movement. The dominant group of the Deoband ULEMA in the

Jamiat-ul-Ulema Hind did oppose the demand for Pakistan. They emphasized that India was "the common homeland of all citizens, irrespective of race or religion..." and that " from the national point of view every Muslim is an Indian".

However, one of the reasons for their opposition of the demand for Pakistan was that the establishment of Pakistan would considerably reduce the field of missionary activities of the Muslims. Another ground for opposing the Pakistan movement was that it had created an atmosphere of hatred and antagonism between the Hindus and Muslims, which was likely to hamper the progress of Islam in India and its goal of absorbing non-Muslim.

It is clear that the nationalist Muslims represented by the Jamiat-ul-Ulema Hind, wanted the Muslim community to have the right of veto over any legislation of purely political character and which did not affect the cultural and religious rights of minorities. They also wanted the majority of judges in the Supreme Court to be Muslims. These ULEMA were divided in two groups; one was in favour of Pakistan.

In a multi-religious society, adoption and commitment to secularism is an essential pre-requisite to making ineffective the sentiments of religious separatism and to the evolution of an integrated society.

Again a secular state alone can ensure that a religious minority is not unfairly treated by the dominant religious majority and that the minority enjoys full freedom to practice its religion and to preserve its culture. However, secularism as a creed was/is not acceptable to Muslims as a religious community.

Was Partition Unavoidable?

Pakistan was, however, conceived as an Islamic MILLAT nation; the Punjabis, Sindhis, Pathans, Balochis were different racial and linguistic groups to be united in one sub-state, west Pakistan, on the basis of territorial integrity and one religion; the second sub-state, East Pakistan was to be formed on the basis of territorial integrity, linguistic homogeneity and one religion. But the two sub-states were to be conjoined into Pakistan on the basis of their belonging to the Islamic

MILLAT, Muslim brotherhood. Jinnah's demand virtually amounted to repudiation of the two-nation theory and of his thesis that the two communities could not co-exist in peace. Jinnah had come to believe that all Hindus were sub-human creatures with which it was impossible for the Muslims to live.

Jinnah had all along maintained that there was no solution to India's problems arising from the termination of the British rule in India and the consequent transfer of power to India except through the establishment of Pakistan as a homeland for the Muslims of India.

In his speech at public meeting in Bombay on 12th august 1947 Sardar Patel delivered, " Under the prevailing conditions in the country.... It was impossible to do anything constructive with the Muslim League. The League representatives during their continuance in office did nothing but create deadlocks and their role was entirely obstructionist....the rot, could not be permitted to prolong any longer except at the risk of disaster for the whole country....,...the economic life of the country was paralyzed and there was little security of life and property....,... to prevent the slaughter of innocent peoples, the Congress decided to agree to the division of the country."

In his speech at the Banaras Hindu University on 25th November 1948, Sardar Patel explained, "I felt that if we did not accept partition, India would be split into many bits and would be completely ruined. My experience of office for one year had convinced me that the way we had been preceding would lead us to disaster. We would not then have one Pakistan but several." In November 1949 in Constituent Assembly, Patel said, "I agreed to Partition as a last resort when we had reached a stage when we would have lost all".

Mahatma Gandhi had been opposed to Partition while India was still being governed by the British. By the first work of April 1947, however, he had come to accept that Partition was totally unavoidable and this could no longer await the transfer of power by the British rulers.

On 31st March 1947, in a discussion with Azad Gandhiji said that Nehru and Patel had agreed to the country being partitioned, and declared: " if the Congress wishes to accept partition, it will be over my dead body. So long as I am alive I will never agree to the partition of India. Nor will I ...allow Congress to accept it.". But after his meeting with Mountbatten on 2nd April 1947 Azad found that Gandhi, " had changed. He was still not openly in favour of partition but he no longer spoke so vehemently against it....the situation was such that partition appeared, to Gandhi, inevitable". On 1st June 1947, Gandhiji explained by citing a worldly-wise Gujrati saying: Independence –cum-Partition was like a WOODEN-LOAF. " if the Congress leaders eat it, they die of colic: if they leave it, they starve".

Partition was based on four fundamental premises, were basically fallacious:

1. The Hindus and Muslims are two different nations who cannot co-exist peacefully.
2. In a democratic setup in India, the Hindus (KAFIRs), will always be the rulers and Muslims will be slaves of KAFIRs because the Hindus are in overwhelming majority.
3. During 1937-39, Muslim were persecuted, free profession of religion and practice of religious rite was curbed, they were denied their due share in services, URDU deemed to be the language of Muslim, was displaced by Hindi as the language of administration besides English.
4. The Congress Governments had imposed un-Islamic practices on Muslims, especially school children, such as singing the VANDE MATRAM, the national song, showing respect to the Congress flag, called the national flag, dancing and music as subjects of study for the Muslim school children.

All the propositions and assumptions, on which Pakistan was created, were fallacious. It was totally untrue that Hindus and Muslims were two different nations merely because their religions are different. Religion is not the determinant of nationality, Arabs, Turks, Iranians, Afgans, Uzbeks, Bangladeshis, Indonesians, Malays etc., are all Muslims but belong to different nationalities based on territorial integrity and linguistic and racial affinity. The Arabs are divided into different nations; Saudis, Iraqis, Jordanians, Egyptians,

Morroccans, Palestinians, etc. even though they are of Semitic race, speak Arabic or a variant thereof and are all Muslim by faith. Partition became unavoidable when in 1946, the Muslim League members of Interim-Government openly declared that they would wreck the Interim-Government from within and would continue Direct Action for achieving Pakistan even though they would be in the Interim-Government. The need for an immediate settlement further became imperative due to potential danger of BALKANIZATION of divided India from the mischief of the device of Lapse of Paramount that facilitated the princely States becoming independent.

To sum up, by the middle of 1946 the country had reached a stage where:

1. There was grave danger of civil war.
2. The Viceroy's Executive Council was not a Cabinet but had become a cockpit for fights between the Congress and League members.
3. The danger of disintegration of the country in the wake of Lapse of Paramount, to the princely States was real.
4. Unwillingness of the British Government to relinquish and transfer power till there was agreement among the political parties about the constitutional set-up in the country made it imperative that, under no circumstances, the political deadlock be allowed to be prolonged.

So the Congress was driven to Surrender to the Muslim League and opt for the lesser evil of the two alternatives: a confederal India with built-in potentialities for paralysis and disintegration or dividing India and thereafter uniting the divided country consisting of British Indian provinces and the princely states. Thus, the Partition was the only way out of the political impasse.

NEHRU AND JINNAH

This volume appeared just about the time the Government of India decided to allow the Indian Council of Cultural Relations to occupy the magnificent Jinnah House at Mount Pleasant Road in Mumbai. A few years after Partition, the British Deputy High Commissioner (DHC) began to reside there. The most senior information officials at the DHC occupied the first floor. Both moved out in the early 1980s. Around this time India agreed to Pakistan's request that it be allowed to buy or use Jinnah House to house its Consul-General and his offices, only to change its mind. For well over a decade no one lived there. The place went to seed; but never faded away from public memory or of those interested in the history of Partition and its aftermath.

For one thing, it was of undoubted historic significance. The Gandhi-Jinnah talks were held at this bungalow in September 1944. So were Jinnah's talks with Subhash Chandra Bose and Jawaharlal Nehru who met him there last; ironically, on August 15, 1946, exactly a year before India became independent and was partitioned. The host became Governor-General of Pakistan and the visitor, Prime Minister of India. Astrologers might ponder over the fact that Jinnah's only child, his daughter Dina, was also born on August 15, 1919.

Less famous was Jinnah's house at 10 Aurangzeb Road in New Delhi where the Ambassador of the Netherlands now resides. Jinnah bought it, he did not build it, unlike the Bombay house. The house at 10 Aurangzeb Road was sold to Ramkrishna Dalmia for Rs.3 lakhs shortly before Partition. In contrast, Liaquat Ali Khan did not sell his house. He gave it to his country. "Pakistan House" at Tilak Marg, formerly Hardinge Road, is now the residence of Pakistan's High Commissioner. Liaquat, born to wealth, died an impoverished man.

But it is not these "small" houses that we are here concerned with. *Sunday Standard* of June 14, 1981, had a detailed account of all that from one Adil Dastoor. Of greater relevance is Jinnah's concept of the greater house he built, Pakistan, and of its relations with India. Pakistanis little realise that his dream was shattered with the exodus of non-Muslims from West Pakistan. For reasons more than one, not least the character of the state, he wanted them to live there. Events overwhelmed him. He had, obviously, not quite reckoned with the rancorous atmosphere to which he himself had made no small a contribution with his abrasive rhetoric, arrogance and, of course, the poisonous two-nation theory. Most in the Congress did not lag behind in this, either.

Partition was not a parting in amity, but in bitterness. How then does one explain Jinnah's financial dealings on the eve of Partition and immediately thereafter? He prided himself on his sense of realism and rightly so. But hubris is a cruel master to those it possesses. It robbed Jinnah of that gift. Jinnah, it seems, thought that there would be no barriers between India and Pakistan.

His colossal fortune was not built up only from earnings from his lucrative practice at the Bar and the high fees he charged. He was a careful and persistent investor in shares and landed estates. By March 1947, both the Congress and the Muslim League were agreed that India would be partitioned. How then is one to explain Jinnah writing to share brokers and estate agents that very month buying 500 shares in Air India Ltd. And showing keen interest in the purchase of "Sandow Castle", described as "a large property near Bombay with 18 acres of land and with an unrestricted view of the sea". Its price was advertised at Rs.5 lakhs. He could have easily afforded to give 10 Aurangzeb Road in New Delhi to his country instead of selling it for Rs.3 lakhs.

Therein lies the relevance of this volume. A couple of documents it publishes would suggest that Jinnah liked to return to Bombay (as it was known then) and spend his last days in the house he had so fondly built. It confirms the account which India's first High Commissioner to Pakistan, Sri Prakasa, gave in his memoirs *Pakistan. Birth and Last Days* (Meenakshi Prakashan; Meerut, 1965).

Nehru left the Bombay house undisturbed out of courtesy. But there was a shortage of accommodation and questions were asked. Sri Prakasa was directed to consult Jinnah's wishes and the rent he wanted for letting it out. It may be recalled that the Administration of Evacuee Property Ordinance was promulgated in 1949 with retrospective application from March 1947. Travel restrictions (passports and visas) were imposed abruptly in 1948. Many were stranded on the wrong side of the frontier.

Jinnah was completely taken aback by Sri Prakasa's inquiry "and almost pleadingly said to me: `Sri Prakasa, don't break my heart. Tell Jawaharlal not to break my heart. I have built it brick by brick. Who can live in a house like that? What fine verandahs?

It is a small house fit only for a small European family or a refined Indian prince. You do not know how I love Bombay. I still look forward to going back there.'

"`Really Mr. Jinnah!' I said. `You desire to go back to Bombay. I know how much Bombay owes to you and your great services to the city. May I tell the Prime Minister that you want to go back there?' He replied: `Yes, you may'."

Sri Prakasa recalled this talk in a letter to Jinnah dated July 30, 1948. It bears quotation *in extenso* for it reveals a lot of Jinnah's and Nehru's civility. "You will perhaps remember the interview that you were good enough to grant me on May 14, when I asked for your permission, on behalf of the Government of India, to requisition your Bombay house, in view of the acute shortage of accommodation, particularly when the house was vacant for the preceding many months.

"Besides the consideration of sentiments which we all understand, and the Government of India appreciate, you particularly mentioned that a house like that could only be occupied by either a prince or a multi-millionaire of very refined tastes, and that if it were given to all sorts of persons they would only destroy the house. You were also pleased to add that it would be difficult for anyone to imagine how much you loved Bombay and hoped, when things were settled, to go back there some day. You asked me to help in saving the house and I promised to do my best.

"I immediately sent a long telegram to Jawaharlal, conveying to him your sentiments and your desires. In deference to your wishes, he advised the Government of Bombay accordingly, and your house was not touched. I have now heard from him again; and I have to write to say that owing to the acute shortage of housing in Bombay, the Government of Bombay are being considerably embarrassed by permitting this big house remaining unoccupied, particularly when they have introduced a very rigorous housing control in that city. I have, therefore, once more to approach you with the request that you may be pleased to permit the Government of Bombay to allot your house to one of the principal foreign consulates stationed there...

"The Government of India also assured me that when the house is allotted to the consulate, a condition will be imposed that whenever it should be required for your personal use, it will be vacated by them on the expiry of a suitable period of notice. I may be permitted to add that it was a matter of great gratification to me when I learnt you were expecting to be able to go back to the city, which owes so much to you...

"If I may suggest, it would, indeed, be gracious on your part if you could yourself offer the house, in view of the conditions in Bombay, for the use of a foreign consulate. This will eliminate the fear that you expressed that the requisitioning of your house would create bitterness in the mind of Indian Muslims who may interpret the action of [the] government in a very different light; when they know that you are voluntarily making the offer in order to meet legitimate requirements, no hostile feeling will be roused, and the act will naturally and rightly be regarded as a most gracious gesture on your part."

Jinnah replied on August 16: "Thank you for your letter dated the 30th of July and for all the trouble that you have taken, and to Jawaharlal for giving careful considerations to this case. I am quite willing, as suggested by him, to let this house on the terms mentioned in your letter to a foreign consulate, not because of any racial feeling but (because) the house is built entirely in European style and for the use of a small European family.

"As regards the rent, I was offered some time ago Rs.3,000 per month, but it does not lie in my mouth to fix the rent. As it is requisitioned by [the] government, I leave it to the government to make fullest inquiries and fix such rent as they may think reasonable.

"I would prefer the American Consulate to occupy it because they would be really in a position to keep the amenities, and the very large and pretty garden which is very essential, in good condition. Thanking you for all that you have done, and looking forward to meeting you when I return to Karachi." That was not to be. Jinnah was then in Quetta, a dying man. He breathed his last on his arrival at Karachi on September 11, 1948.

BUT Jinnah House did not cease to invite attention. In a note to the Cabinet on March 7, 1955, Nehru recalled the relief in Pakistan at the decision not to auction it as evacuee property. "I think we should further be prepared to make a gift of it to the Pakistan government, should they desire to use it as a memorial. I should like the Cabinet to consider the matter... " (*Selected Works of Jawaharlal Nehru*, Second Series, Volume 28; Oxford University Press; page 595). On January 13, 1956, India's High Commissioner to Pakistan C.C. Desai suggested to Nehru that Jinnah House be preserved "as a relic of Jinnah" (as the editors put it in their footnote). Thereupon Nehru wrote to the Ministry of External Affairs (MEA) in January 1956 recalling that as the Cabinet did not give his suggestion a "whole hearted welcome... There was no decision."

His colleagues objected to India, rather than Pakistan, putting up "a Jinnah memorial in Bombay". Nehru felt that in the "disturbed conditions" in the city, owing to the Maharashtra movement, the idea was "impracticable". S. Dutt, Foreign Secretary, minuted on January 20, 1956, that a Jinnah memorial by India would be inappropriate; but if the Pakistan government wanted to buy the house and preserve it as a memorial to Jinnah, "we certainly should raise no objection" (*Selected Works of Jawaharlal Nehru*, Volume 31; pages 375-6).

It reflects the pettiness in some other quarters that in New Delhi the tax authorities began a probe "to find from which income" 10 Aurangzeb Road had been bought by Jinnah. This to a man who paid advance income tax in July 1947, knowing that he would soon be leaving India for good and acquire immunity as head of a foreign state. Jinnah sent a polite reply to the Income Tax Officer in New Delhi on April 6, 1948. It read: "With regard to the 10 Aurangzeb Road property, it was purchased by me from the funds that became available to me by selling my securities. The property was purchased, as far as I remember, in 1938 from Mr. Bisakha Singh of New Delhi, and as to further particulars that you require, all the Title Deeds are now handed over to Seth Jaidayal Dalmia (Dalmia Jain Niwas, New Delhi) and you can inspect them all. The income from the property was nil as it was never let, hence I have not been able to include this in my return for the year 1947-48. The position was the same in 1946-47. I am glad to note that you will now complete the assessment at your earliest convenience." He was willing to pay his taxes even after Partition.

SO much for matters of human interest. Some documents record events that were to loom large decades later. Sindh Chief Minister M.A. Khuhro wrote to Jinnah on January 13, 1948, complaining of the refugee influx from India. "Unless we take some prompt and energetic action, we would some day find ourselves completely overwhelmed by the problem." To this day they are dubbed *mohajirs* (refugees). The Mohajir Qaumi Movement began in Karachi in the early 1980s.

The seeds of East Bengal's secession were also sown in 1948. Or, were they always present in its soil? M.A. Rahim wrote to Jinnah on March 10: "You are expected to visit Dacca shortly. The Bengalis are pretentiously (sic) against the Urdu language. They are afraid of the Punjabi element permeating in (sic) the local administration. In your awaited speech at Dacca, you may say out openly (that) if that be their fear they may reserve reasonably a certain number of posts to be held by the Bengalis (say 60 per cent) and the rest by the non-Bengalis... " Attached was a note by Abdul Matin Chaudhury, a veteran politician, who said: "Fuel was added to the smouldering fire by the controversy as to what should be the state language of Eastern Pakistan, Urdu or Bengali. In Dacca, the student community, which dominates the political landscape, is amongst the most vehement protagonists of Bengali, while a section of public men, the Jamiyyat Ulema-i-Islam, Bengal, with its branches in different districts are championing the cause of Urdu. But in this controversy the target of the wrath of the champions of Bengali happens to be those whose mother tongue is not Bengali." This rift persists still between the two major parties in Bangladesh.

The United States Consulate in Calcutta reported to the Secretary of State on March 6: "The newcomer has... procured almost all of the government jobs, even those in post offices, railroads and district administration. The Bengali Muslims had expected that the Eastern Pakistan government would be manned by its Provincial Muslims and this development has created among them a very strong resentment. This resentment is not local; it was evident in Chittagong and reports from various districts indicate that the feeling is quite general.

"The political sign-post that displays most forcibly this resentment is the Urdu question. The Bengali Muslim speaks Bengali which has distinct political, cultural and provincial values that are traditional.

All Bengalis, either Muslim or Hindu, have been proud of their language and literature. During the late months of 1947, widespread dissatisfaction was manifest when there was talk of making Urdu the *lingua franca* of all Pakistan. Attempts to change from Bengali to Urdu in the schools have failed; the President (Vice-Chancellor) of the University of Dacca-a prominent Muslim-has stated openly to the writer that Urdu is impossible as a replacement for Bengali; the great majority of Muslim Bengalis know no other language than Bengali.

"Ministers of the Central government, when speaking to Bengalis, have been forced to speak either in Bengali or English, and students repeatedly have staged protest meetings against the introduction of Urdu. The question was considered almost settled in East Bengal when its people were surprised to hear that their Prime Minister, Mr. Nazimuddin, had declared in Karachi, on February 25, that `the feeling of the majority of the people in Eastern Pakistan was that Urdu was the only language that could be adopted as the *lingua franca* of all Pakistan'."

Jinnah's speech in Dacca on March 21 made matters worse. It revealed how far removed he was from the realities: "Let me tell you in the clearest language that there is no truth that your normal life is going to be touched or disturbed so far as your Bengali language is concerned. But ultimately it is for you, the people of this province, to decide what shall be the language of your Province. But let me make it very clear to you that the state language of Pakistan is going to be Urdu and no other language. Any one who tries to mislead you is really the enemy of Pakistan. Without one state language, no nation can remain tied up solidly together and function. Look at the history of other countries. Therefore, so far as the state language is concerned, Pakistan's language shall be Urdu. But as I have said, it will come in time."

That very day the Deputy Leader of the East Bengal Congress Assembly party, Dhirendranath Datta, reminded Jinnah: "Your Excellency's statement at the opening session of the Pakistan Constituent Assembly to the effect that Pakistan would be a democratic secular state and that Hindus and Muslims in Pakistan would cease to be Hindus and Muslims in political and economic sphere created a very good impression in the Dominion and was very heartening to the minority communities. But the subsequent statements of different high functionaries of the state that Pakistan is a Muslim state and the Constitution would be framed according to the Shariat has created confusion and grave misgivings in the minds of the non-Muslims is greatly contributing to produce a sense of insecurity in their minds. A statement from your Excellency will go a long way to clarify the position."

A letter from Khan Abdul Ghaffar Khan dated April 18 promised full cooperation. "The nature of my talk with you has been placed by me before the representatives of the Khudai Khidmatgar organisation. They have unanimously decided that they shall spare no efforts in strengthening and safeguarding the interests of Pakistan and they shall be prepared to make every sacrifice for this cause. And they have also agreed that they shall do nothing which may tend to obstruct the work of the government, but will indulge in legitimate criticism."

Jinnah was a stickler for propriety, in most matters. He was against holders of public office occupying posts in the party. But he flouted propriety by presiding over the Cabinet and holding some ministerial portfolios himself though he was Governor-General. This was utterly unprecedented and wrong. He laid the foundations of autocracy. In a speech to Officers of the Staff College at Quetta on June 14, he reminded them of their oath and said meaningfully:

"I want you to remember, and if you have time enough, you should study the Government of India Act, as adapted for use in Pakistan, who is the Governor-General and, therefore, any command or orders that may come to you cannot come without the sanction of the Executive Head. This is the legal position." He overlooked the fact that he had to act on the advice of Prime Minister Liaquat Ali Khan. But in Pakistan the roles were reversed by Jinnah.

Thus in 1947-48 itself were sown the seeds of the four disasters that overcame Pakistan later-autocracy, secession of East Pakistan, Islamisation and the Mohajir movement. Jinnah himself sowed the seeds of autocracy and East Pakistan's alienation.

Documents of real value are few and far between. The vast majority of the documents in the volume cover trivia-applications for jobs, for work, including one from Beverly Nichols, published speeches and the like. The editor tells us that "material of repetitive character, such as requests for photographs... congratulatory letters have not been included". There are, however, very many of them. To cite a few, on pages 132, 151, 163 and 621. Included are papers which are not "Jinnah Papers" at all and do not even refer to him; such as state papers of no relevance to his life.

Included are some which make one wonder why the editor included them. Sample this from an English businessman who had come to Bombay: "I have been in India since October, charged by my firm Messrs Johnson and Johnson (Gt. Britain) Ltd. of Slough, Buckinghamshire, England, a subsidiary company of Messrs Johnson & Johnson of New Brunswick, USA, medical supply manufacturers and distributors-primarily of Baby Powder of worldwide fame-to report on the possible extension of our trading activities in the Dominion of Pakistan. It is my company's intention to seek to combine with the Government of Pakistan in such an extension." Would he have dared to write thus to the Governor-General of Canada or Australia?

There is no annotation, as is required in such a work. We are not told who the writer of a letter is. When we are, it is of someone known to all. Page 164 has 6 footnotes enlightening us who Churchill and other famous ones were. The same page, like most others, has another letter. But we are not told who the writer was. Poems of poor quality by obscure rhymesters are included.

The test is: Does the volume help one the better to understand Jinnah's record during this period? Publication of the papers is a government project. "The Cabinet decision of December 1996 regarding conversion of the project into an autonomous body has not been implemented even more than five years on."

Jinnah was one of the truly great men of our times. Detractors in India and adulators in Pakistan alike obscure his greatness, as do those of his contemporaries in India-Gandhi, Nehru, Azad and Patel.

We are told that "documents relating to the princely states have been grouped into two separate volumes, the 8th and 9th, which should be out in the near future". Dare one hope that they will shed at least as much light on Jinnah's policies on Kashmir, Hyderabad and Junagadh as the Nehru and Patel Papers do?

The series began in 1993 with a volume that covered events since February 20, 1947, the day the British government announced its plans to quit by June 30, 1948. A mass of material before that yet awaits publication. The printing and get-up have maintained high standards over the decade. Oxford University Press has ensured a wide distribution of these fascinating volumes which no student of history can afford to ignore.

At the historic conference in New Delhi on June 7, 1947, at which Lord Mountbatten disclosed Britain's "partition" plan for India. (From left) Jawaharlal Nehru, Lord Ismay, Adviser to the Viceroy, Lord Louis Mountbatten and Muhammad Ali Jinnah, president of the All-India Muslim League. There is an aspect to L.K. Advani's comments on Jinnah at Karachi which has been overlooked. A month or so earlier, Qazi Hussain Ahmed, the rabid Jamaat-e-Islami leader of Pakistan, had denounced Jinnah's famous presidential speech to Pakistan's Constituent Assembly on August 11, 1947. Advani's praise and quotation from the speech has boosted the morale of Pakistan's secularists who always cited it.

The speech has been quoted in bits and pieces; never analysed as a whole. Nor for that matter the entire and considerable corpus of Jinnah's record from 1906 to 1948. There is no single complete series of his *Collected Works*. One such effort ended in 1931. Historians in India, Pakistan and abroad propound fanciful theories from their own standpoints; never mind the record. The speech was neither an act of contrition or repentance nor a reflection of two Jinnahs. He had unwisely used the poisonous two-nation theory to promote under the slogan of Pakistan, his real objective-a power-sharing accord. Gandhi, Nehru and Patel sabotaged the Cabinet Mission's Plan of May 16, 1946, for United India which was done in complicity with Stafford Cripps (vide "Cripps and India's Partition", *Frontline,* August 2, 2002).

Opinion

Jinnah's speech was a *crie de coeur.* He had not changed his outlook. In 1919 he gave evidence before the Joint Select Committee of the British Parliament on the Government of India Bill. His answers to questions by one of its members, Major Ormsby-Gore, bear recalling today.

Q: *You said you spoke from the point of view of India. You speak really as an Indian nationalist?*-I do.

Q: *Holding that view, do you contemplate the early disappearance of separate communal representation of the Mohammedan community?*-I think so.

Q: *That is to say, at the earliest possible moment you wish to do away in political life with any distinction between Mohammedans and Hindus?*-Yes. Nothing will please me more than when that day comes.

Q: *I am only referring to them, of course?*-And therefore that is why I really hope and expect that the day is not very far distant when these separate electorates will disappear.

Jinnah was then a member of the Congress, a president of the Muslim League, and architect, along with Tilak, of the Pact between the two bodies at their sessions in Lucknow in 1916.

It was the same Jinnah who famously declared on August 11, 1947: "Now, if we want to make this great state of Pakistan happy and prosperous we should wholly and solely concentrate on the well-being of the people, and especially of the masses and the poor. If you will work in cooperation, forgetting the past, burying the hatchet, you are bound to succeed. If you change your past and work together in a spirit that everyone of you, no matter to what community he belongs, no matter what relations he had with you in the past, no matter what is his colour, caste or creed, is first, second and last a citizen of this state with equal rights, privileges and obligations, there will be no end to the progress you will make."

He did not stop there. What is little recalled is that he proceeded to put *intra-Muslim differences on a par with Hindu-Muslim differences*: "I cannot emphasise it too much. We should begin to work in that spirit and in course of time all these angularities of the majority and minority communities-the Hindu community and the Muslim community because even as regards Muslims you have Pathans, Punjabis, Shias, Sunnis and so on, and among the Hindus you have Brahmins, Vashnavas, Khatris, also Bengalis, Madrasis, and so on-will vanish. Indeed, if you ask me this has been the biggest hindrance in the way of India to attain freedom and independence and but for this we would have been free peoples long ago. No power can hold another nation, and specially *a nation of 400 million* souls in subjection; nobody could have conquered you, and even if had happened nobody could have continued its hold on you for any length of time but for this."

Jinnah's reference to "*a nation of 400 million*" rather than the "*Muslim nation of 100 million*" implied rejection of the two-nation theory. He concluded: "Now, I think we should keep that in front of us as our ideal and you will find that in course of time Hindus would cease to be Hindus and Muslims would cease to be Muslims, not in the religious sense because that is the personal faith of each individual, but in the political sense as citizens of the state."

These extracts read together reveal that the man's outlook on nationalism and secularism had not changed since 1919. *It was an extempore speech.* Few care to study it carefully. He said that their *first* duty was "to maintain law and order"; that is, protect minorities. The next duty? Combat "bribery and corruption. That really is a poison. We must put that down with an iron hand". Thirdly, "black-marketing is another curse". Fourthly, "the evil of nepotism and jobbery. This evil must be crushed relentlessly."

It was *after* these four points that he went on to dilate, first, on the partition and, next, on secularism: "I know there are people who do not quite agree with the division of India and the partition of the Punjab and Bengal." He was reaching out to them. He then went on to say the things quoted above. *It was straight from his heart: "I cannot make any well-considered pronouncement, at this moment."*

He made another pronouncement in 1925, which provides a clue. When discussing the Indian Finance Bill (1925), he stated on the Legislative Assembly floor: "I Sir, stand here with a clear conscience and I say that I am a nationalist first, a nationalist second and nationalist last... I once more appeal to this House. Whether you are a Musalman or a Hindu, for God's sake do not import the discussion of communal matters into this House, and degrade this Assembly, which we desire should become a real National Parliament. Set an example to the outside world and our people."

Few people have cared to study Jinnah's pronouncements on secularism as a whole. One of the few is Dr. Awajeet Jawed. Her father Dr. Balwant Singh was a Congressman and freedom-fighter. Jawed's book *Secular and Nationalist Jinnah* is based on solid research (Kitab Publishing House, Jhandewalan, New Delhi; pages 318, Rs. 400).

How many know that Jinnah was once president of the Postal Union, which had 70,000 members, or that the Governor of Bombay, George Lloyd, included his name in a list of eight for deportation to Myanmar?

His vision of Pakistan was of a democratic secular state based on the rule of law. Cordial relations with India were crucial for its fulfilment. He told the communist lawyer, A.S.R. Chari, who then represented *Daily Worker* (London, October 5, 1944): "We will say `hands off India' to all outsiders." Eric Streiff of *New Zurcher Zeitung* was told (March 11, 1948) that the paramount interests of India and Pakistan demanded that they "should coordinate for the purpose of playing their part in international affairs... and jointly... defend their frontiers... but this depends entirely on whether Pakistan and India can resolve their own differences."

He had a curious notion of an India which comprised two member states-Pakistan and "Hindustan". He angrily wrote to Mountbatten on August 26: "It is a pity that for some mysterious reason Hindustan have adopted the word 'India' which is certainly misleading and is intended to create confusion."

If Jinnah, the partitionist, had a latent sense of an India above the two states, Jawaharlal Nehru, the ardent Unionist, not only contributed to the collapse of the 1946 plan but adopted a policy that would congeal the partition: Congress leaders demonised him systematically. So did Indian academics and the press. Jinnah yet awaits a fair assessment, warts and all. That must include his own mistakes and grave lapses as well. The Congress spurned him in 1937-39. But he went overboard and did much harm by his miscalculations. Indians and Pakistanis must reflect on all aspects of his life, not selectively as they do.

By any test Muhammad Ali Jinnah was a truly great man. In personal integrity this tragic figure had no peers. His political record from 1906 to 1939 reveals a spirit of conciliation and statesmanship, which Congress leaders did not reciprocate. Indians must begin to acknowledge his greatness and the grave injustice the Congress leaders did to him. Pakistanis must begin to acknowledge the ones he did not only to himself but to the infant state he founded.

7

Creation of Pakistan

Jinnah had originally been dubious about the practicability of Pakistan, an idea that Sir Muhammad Iqbal had propounded to the Muslim League conference of 1930; but before long he became convinced that a Muslim homeland on the Indian subcontinent was the only way of safeguarding Muslim interests and the Muslim way of life. It was not religious persecution that he feared so much as the future exclusion of Muslims from all prospects of advancement within India as soon as power became vested in the close-knit structure of Hindu social organization. To guard against this danger he carried on a nationwide campaign to warn his coreligionists of the perils of their position, and he converted the Muslim League into a powerful instrument for unifying the Muslims into a nation.

At this point, Jinnah emerged as the leader of a renascent Muslim nation. Events began to move fast. On March 22-23, 1940, in Lahore, the league adopted a resolution to form a separate Muslim state, Pakistan. The Pakistan idea was first ridiculed and then tenaciously opposed by the Congress. But it captured the imagination of the Muslims. Pitted against Jinnah were men of the stature of Gandhi and Jawaharlal Nehru. And the British government seemed to be intent on maintaining the political unity of the Indian subcontinent. But Jinnah led his movement with such skill and tenacity that ultimately both the Congress and the British government had no option but to agree to the partitioning of India. Pakistan thus emerged as an independent state in 1947.

Jinnah became the first head of the new state. Faced with the serious problems of a young nation, he tackled Pakistan's problems with authority. He was not regarded as merely the governor-general; he was revered as the father of the nation. He worked hard until overpowered by age and disease in Karachi, the place of his birth, in 1948.

HISTORY OF CREATION PAKISTAN

The visible trend of the two major communities going in opposite directions caused deep concern to leaders of all-India stature. They struggled to bring the Congress and the Muslim League on one platform. Quaid-i-Azam Muhammad Ali Jinnah (1876-1948) was the leading figure among them. After the annulment of the partition of Bengal and the European powers' aggressive designs against the Ottoman empire and North Africa, the Muslims were receptive to the idea of collaboration with the Hindus. The Congress-Muslim League rapprochement was achieved at the Lucknow session of the two parties in 1916 and a joint scheme of reforms was adopted. In the Lucknow Pact, the Congress accepted the principle of separate electorates and the Muslims in return for 'weightage' to the Muslims of the Muslim minority provinces agreed to surrender their slim majorities in the Punjab and Bengal. The post-Lucknow Pact period witnessed Hindu-Muslim amity and the two parties came to hold their annual sessions in the same city and passed resolutions of similar content.

The Hindu-Muslim unity reached its climax during the Khilafat and the Noncooperation Movements. The Muslims of South Asia, under the leadership of Ali Brothers, Maulana Muhammad Ali and Maulana Shaukat Ali, launched the historic Khilafat Movement after the First World War to protect the Ottoman empire from dismemberment. Mohandas Karamchand Gandhi (1869-1948) linked the issue of swaraj (or self-government) with the Khilafat issue to associate the Hindus with the Movement. The ensuing Movement was the first countrywide popular movement. Although the movement failed in its objectives, it had far-reaching impact on the Muslims of South Asia. After a long time they forged a united action on a purely Islamic issue which created momentarily solidarity among them. It also produced a class of Muslim leaders experienced in organizing and mobilizing the public. This experience was of immense value to the Muslims during the Pakistan Movement.

The collapse of the Khilafat Movement was followed by the period of bitter Hindu-Muslim antagonism. The Hindus organized two highly anti-Muslim movements, the Shudhi and the Sangathan. The former movement was designed to convert Muslims to Hinduism and the latter was meant to create solidarity among the Hindus in the event of communal conflict. In retaliation, the Muslims sponsored the Tabligh and Tanzim organizations.

In the 1920s the frequency of communal riots was unprecedented. In the light of this situation, the Muslims revised their constitutional demands. They now wanted preservation of their numerical majorities in the Punjab and Bengal; separation of Sind from Bombay; constitution of Balochistan as a separate province and introduction of constitutional reforms in the North-West Frontier Province. It was partly to press these demands that one section of the All-India Muslim League cooperated with the Statutory Commission sent by the British Government, under the chairmanship of Sir John Simon in 1927. The other section of the League boycotted the Simon Commission for its all-white character and cooperated with the Nehru Committee to draft a constitution for India. The Nehru Report had an extremely anti-Muslim bias and the Congress leadership's refusal to amend it disillusioned even the moderate Muslims.

Several leaders and thinkers having insight into the Hindu-Muslim question proposed separation of Muslim India. However, the most lucid exposition of the inner feelings of the Muslim community was given by Allama Muhammad Iqbal (1877-1938) in his presidential address to the All-India Muslim League at Allahabad in 1930. He proposed a separate Muslim state at least in the Muslim majority regions of the northwest. Later on, in his correspondence with Quaid-i-Azam Muhammad Ali Jinnah, he included the Muslim majority areas in the northeast also in his proposed Muslim state. Three years after his Allahabad address, a group of Muslim students at Cambridge, headed by Chaudhry Rahmat Ali, issued a pamphlet Now or Never in which, drawing letters from the names of the Muslim majority regions they gave the nomenclature of Pakistan to the proposed state.

Meanwhile, three Round Table Conferences was convened in London during the period 1930-32, to resolve the Indian constitutional problem. The Hindu and Muslim leaders could not draw up an agreed formula and the British Government had to announce a 'Communal Award' which was incorporated in the Government of India Act of 1935. Before the elections under this Act, the All-India Muslin League, which had remained dormant for some time, was reorganized by Muhammad Ali Jinnah, who had returned to India in 1935 after a self imposed exile of nearly five years in England. The Muslim League could not win a majority of Muslims seats since it had not yet been effectively reorganized. However, it had the satisfaction that the performance of the Indian National Congress in the Muslim constituencies was bad. After the elections, the attitude of the Congress leadership was arrogant and domineering. The classic example was its refusal to form a coalition government with the Muslim League in the United Provinces. Instead it asked the League leaders to dissolve their parliamentary party in the Provincial Assembly and join the Congress. Another important Congress move after the 1937 elections was its Muslim mass contact movement to persuade the Muslims to join the Congress and not the Muslim League. One of its leaders, Jawaharlal Nehru, even declared that there were only two forces in India, the British and the Congress. All this did not go unchallenged. Quaid-i-Azam countered that there was a third force in South Asia constituting the Muslims. The All-India Muslim League, under his gifted leadership, gradually and skilfully started to consolidate the Muslims on one platform. It did not miss to exploit even small Congress mistakes in its favour.

The 1930s saw realization among the Muslims of their separate identity and their anxiety to preserve it within separate territorial boundaries. An important element that brought this simmering Muslim nationalism in the open was the charter of the Congress rule in the Muslim minority provinces during 1937-39. The Congress policies in these provinces hurt Muslim susceptibilities. These were calculated aims to obliterate the Muslims as a separate cultural unity. The Muslims now abandoned to think in terms of seeking safeguards and began to consider seriously the demand for a separate Muslim state. During 1937-1939, several Muslim leaders and thinkers inspired by Allama Iqbal's ideas, presented elaborate schemes of partitioning the subcontinent on communal lines. The All-India Muslim League on March 23, 1940, in a resolution at its Lahore session, demanded separate homeland for the Muslims in the Muslim majority regions of the subcontinent. The resolution was commonly referred to as the Pakistan Resolution.

The British Government recognized the genuineness of the Pakistan demand indirectly in the proposals for the transfer of power which, Sir Stafford Cripps brought to India in 1942. Both the Congress and the All-India Muslim League rejected these proposals for different reasons. The principle of secession of Muslim India as a separate dominion was, however, conceded in these proposals. After the failure, a prominent Congress leader, C. Rajagopalachari, suggested a formula for a separate Muslim state in the Working Committee of the Indian National Congress, which was rejected at the time but later on, in 1944, formed the basis of the Gandhi-Jinnah talks.

The Pakistan demand was popularized during the Second World War. Every section of the Muslim community - women, students, Ulema and businessmen - was organized under the banner of the All-India Muslim League. Branches of the party were opened in the remote corners on the subcontinent. Literature in the form of pamphlets, books, magazines and newspapers was produced to explain the Pakistan demand and distributed largely.

The support gained by the All-India Muslim League and its demand for Pakistan was tested after the failure of the Simla Conference 1945. Elections were called to determine the respective strength of the political parties. The Muslim League swept all the thirty seats in the central legislature and in the provincial elections also its victory was outstanding. After the elections, on April 8-9, 1946, the All-India Muslim League called a convention of the newly elected League members in the central and provincial legislatures at Dehli. This convention which constituted virtually a representative assembly of the Muslims of South Asia, on a motion by the Chief Minister of Bengal, Hussein Shaheed Suhrawardy, reiterated the Pakistan demand in clearer terms.

In early 1946, the British Government sent a Cabinet Mission to the subcontinent to resolve the constitutional deadlock. The Mission conducted negotiations with various political parties but failed to evolve an agreed formula. Finally, Cabinet Mission announced its own plan which, among other provisions, envisaged three federal groupings, two of them comprising the Muslim majority provinces, linked at the Centre in a loose federation with three subjects. The Muslim League accepted the Plan, as a strategic move, expecting to achieve its objective in a not-too-distant future. The Congress also agreed to the Plan but soon realizing its implications to the Congress, its leaders began to interpret in a way not visualized by the authors of the Plan. This provided the All-India Muslim League an excuse to withdraw its acceptance of the Plan and the party observed August 16 as a 'Direct Action Day' to show Muslim solidarity in support of the Pakistan demand.

In October 1946, an Interim Government was formed. The Muslim League sent its representatives under the leadership of its General Secretary, Mr. Liaquat Ali Khan, with the aim to fight for the party objective from within the Interim Government. After a short time the situation inside the Interim Government and outside convinced the Congress leadership to accept Pakistan as the only solution of the communal problem. The British Government, after a last attempt to save the Cabinet Mission Plan in December 1946, also moved toward a plan for the partition of India.

The last British Viceroy, Lord Louis Mountbatten, came with a clear mandate to draft a plan for the transfer of power. After holding talks with political leaders and parties, he prepared a Partition Plan for the transfer of power which, after its approval by the British Government, was announced on June 3, 1947. Both the Congress and the Muslim League accepted the plan. Two largest Muslim Majority provinces, Bengal and Punjab was partitioned. The assemblies of west Punjab, East Bengal, and Sind; and in Balochistan, the Quetta Municipality and the Shahi Jirga voted for Pakistan. Referenda were held in the North-West Frontier

Province and the District of Sylhet in Assam which resulted in an overwhelming vote for Pakistan. On August 14, 1947, the new state of Pakistan came into existence.

The Islamic Republic of Pakistan emerged as an independent state on 14 August 1947. It has its roots into the remote past. Its establishment was the culmination of the long struggle by Muslims of the South-Asian subcontinent for a separate homeland of their own. Its foundation was laid when Muhammad bin Qasim subdued Sindh in 711 AD as a reprisal against sea pirates that had taken refuge in Raja Dahir's kingdom. The advent of Islam further strengthened the historical individuality in the areas now constituting and further beyond its boundaries.

The historic origins of the land stretch far back into time. Some of the earliest relics of Stone Age man have been unearthed in the Potohar region near Rawalpindi and, in the Indus valley more than four millennia ago, a mature and sophisticated civilization flourished around the twin cities of Harappa and Mohenjodaro. With the arrival of Muslim military led by Muhammad bin Qasim and trading expeditions from Arabia, the subcontinent began to emerge as a unified and exemplary Islamic state - a trend that reached its full swing under the Mughal dynasty in the sixteenth and seventeenth centuries AD. The names of the great emperors of this period - Babur, Humayun, Akbar, Jehangir, Shah Jehan and Aurengzeb - ring with splendour and power.

The impact of Islam on the South-Asian subcontinent was deep and far-reaching. Islam introduced not only a new religion, but also a new civilization, a new way of life and new set of values. Islamic traditions of art and literature, of culture and refinement, of social and welfare institutions were established by Muslim rulers throughout the subcontinent. A new language URDU, derived mainly from Arabic and Persian vocabulary and adapting indigenous words and idioms, came into existence.

With the decline of Muslim power during 16th and 17th centuries the British (starting with the East India Company) began to emerge as the dominant force in South Asia. Their rise to power was gradual, extending over a period of 100 years. They replaced the *Shariah* by what they termed as Anglo-Muhammadan law whereas Urdu was replaced by English as the official language. These and many other developments had great social, economic, and political impact especially on the Muslims of subcontinent. The uprising of 1857, termed as the Indian Mutiny by the British and the War of Independence by the Muslims, was a desperate attempt to reverse the adverse course of events.

The failure of the 1857 War of Independence had disastrous consequences for the Muslims as the British placed all the responsibility for this event on them. Determined to stop such a recurrence in future, the British followed a repressive policy against the Muslims. Properties and estates of those even remotely associated with the freedom fighters were confiscated and efforts were made to close all avenues of honest living for them. The Muslim response to these situations also aggravated their plight. While this repression was going on, the Muslims kept themselves aloof from modern education as well as government service. But, their compatriots, the Hindus, did not do so and accepted the new rulers without reservation. They acquired modern western education, imbibed new culture and captured position hitherto filled in by the Muslims.

At the dawn of the 20th century, a number of factors convinced the Muslims of the need to have an effective political organization. Therefore, in October 1906, a deputation comprising 35 Muslim leaders met the Viceroy of the British at Simla and demanded separate electorates. Three months later, the All-India Muslim League was founded by Nawab Salimullah Khan at Dhaka, mainly with the objective of safeguarding the political rights and interest of the Muslims. The British conceded separate electorates in the Government of India Act of 1909, which confirmed the Muslim League's position as an All-India party.

Several leaders and thinkers, having insight into the Hindu-Muslim question proposed separation of Muslim India. However, the most lucid exposition of the inner feeling of the Muslim community was given by Allama Muhammad Iqbal in his Presidential Address at the All India Muslim League Session at Allahabad in 1930. He suggested that for the healthy development of Islam in South Asia, it was essential to have a separate Muslim state in the Muslim majority regions of Indian subcontinent. Three years after his Allahabad Address, a group of Muslim students at Cambridge, headed by Chaudhry Rehmat Ali, issued a pamphlet, *Now or Never*, in which drawing letters from the names of the Muslim majority regions, they gave the nomenclature of **"PAKISTAN"** to the proposed state.

Meanwhile, three Round Table Conferences were convened in London during 1930-32, to resolve the Indian constitutional problems. The Indian National Congress and All India Muslim League leaders, who were invited to these conferences, could not draw up an agreed formula and the British Government had to announce a *"Communal award"* which was incorporated in the Government of India Act of 1935. Before the elections under this Act, the All India Muslim League, which had remained dormant for some time, was reorganized by **Quaid-i-Azam Muhammad Ali Jinnah** who had returned from England in 1934, after an absence of nearly five years. The Muslim League could not win a majority of Muslim seats since it had not yet been effectively reorganized.

After the elections, the attitude of the Congress leadership was arrogant and domineering. The classic example was its refusal to form a coalition government with the Muslim League in the United Provinces. Instead, it asked the League leaders to dissolve their parliamentary party in the Provincial Assembly and join the Congress. They also began mass contact movement to persuade the Muslims to join the Congress and not the Muslim League. One of its leaders, Jawaharlal Nehru, even declared that there were only two forces in India, the British and the Congress. Quaid-i-Azam Muhammad Ali Jinnah challenged and countered that there was a third force in South Asia constituting the Muslims. The All India Muslim League, under his gifted leadership, gradually and skilfully started organizing the Muslims on one platform.

During 1937-39, several Muslim leaders and thinkers, inspired by Allama Iqbal's ideas, presented elaborate schemes for partitioning the subcontinent according to two-nation theory. The All India Muslim League effectively took these schemes into consideration and finally, on 23 March 1940, the All India Muslim

League, in a resolution, at its historic Lahore Session, demanded a separate homeland for the Muslims in the Muslim majority regions of subcontinent. The resolution was commonly referred as the **"PAKISTAN RESOLUTION"**. The demand for a separate homeland had a great appeal for the Muslims of every persuasion. It revived memories of their past greatness and future glory. They, therefore, responded to this demand immediately. This demand became very popular among the masses.

In 1945, after the failure of the Simla Conference, convened by the Viceroy, Lord Wavell, the elections were called to determine the respective strength of political parties. All India Muslim League election campaign was based on the Pakistan demand. The Muslim community responded to this call in an unprecedented way. The Muslim League's victory was outstanding. After the elections All India Muslim League called a convention of the newly elected League members in the Central and Provincial Legislatures at Delhi. This convention, which constituted virtually a representative assembly of the Muslims of South-Asia, on a motion by the Chief Minister of Bengal, Hussain Shaheed Suharwardy, reiterated the Pakistan demand in clearer terms.

In October 1946, an Interim Government was formed. The Muslim League sent its General Secretary Mr. Liaqat Ali Khan with the aim to fight for the party objective from within the Interim Government. After a short time, the situation inside the Interim Government and outside convinced the Congress leadership to accept Pakistan as the only solution of the communal problem. The British Government, after its last attempt to save the Cabinet Mission Plan in December 1946, also moved towards a scheme for the partition of India. The last British Viceroy, Lord Louis Mountbatten, came with a clear mandate to draft a plan for the transfer of power.

After holding talks with political leaders and parties, he presented a Partition Plan for the transfer of power, which after approval of the British Government was announced on June 3, 1947. Both the Congress and Muslim League accepted the plan. Two largest Muslim majority provinces, Bengal and Punjab, were partitioned. The Assemblies of West Punjab, East Bengal, Sindh,

Balochistan, the Quetta Municipality, and the Shahi Jirga voted for Pakistan. Referenda were held in the Northwest Frontier Province (NWFP) and District of Sylhet in Assam, which resulted in an overwhelming vote for Pakistan. As a result on August 14, 1947 a new Ideological Islamic State "Pakistan" came into existence.

FREEDOM OF ISLAM

"....We are ready to sacrifice everything for the freedom of Islam and the Muslim nation. We are determined to regain our past glory and honour and for that purpose the hundred million Musalmans of India must be free and powerful, but we cannot be powerful unless we have our own free Muslim state in our homelands. We must have it and, God willing, we will have it by our unity, faith and discipline."

Advice on the Occasion of a Visit to a Local Intermediate College, Quetta, on 6th July, 1943

"Concentrate on your studies" and "equip yourselves for the future"

> *[In his reply, the Quaid advised the students not to take an active part in politics but at the same time to remain well informed about India and the world events. He said:] "Equip yourself for the future because you have a mighty part to play. Concentrate on your study and try to make education common in your province which is lying far behind other provinces in this respect."*

Address to Balochistan Muslim Student's Federation, on 7th July, 1943

"Idea of Pakistan had been nourished since long, Muslim League gave it definite shape only"

"Do you now realize that due to your constant organizational works for the last 10 days Balochistan has now secured a place on the map of India? Not only that it has now a foot on the world map. Even the foreign radio stations are now quoting your activities".

"You have seen the result of your works and will see more. Balochistan is going to play a very important part in India in near future. Give up your lethargy, apply your mind readily, be steady and work hard for industry and labour are essential for success and steadfastness and toleration are essential for missionaries. I assure you it will be a great strength for not only yourself but for the whole of India."

Address at Prize Distribution Ceremony at Anjuman-i-Islam Janmahomed Cassam Commercial School, Bombay, on 28th January, 1944.

"Commercial Education is most essential for Muslims" – "Without Education, we can achieve nothing"

"Musalmans do not want to work. Sustained effort is an impossibility with them. They want best things of the life without work. Change this mentality. Only hard work, energy and working together like an army will enable you to get all what you want".

War has created the need of such institution. To show distinct results, spadework is necessary. It requires activity and energy. We should have more institutions... Commercial education is most essential for Muslims. After years of study in our universities, what field is open to them. What is the use if they do not get more than Rs. 60 (then basic pay scale of a clerk). There is a lot of field in the world of business. Give up crowded professions and devote your energies to more useful channels with hard work and sustained effort. With study you can climb the highest rung of the ladder. Without education, we can achieve nothing in life and even if we achieve, it will not be possible to retain

Address at a Meeting of the Bombay District Muslim Students' Federation, Bombay, on 2nd February, 1944.

Pakistan's "Pillars were educational, economic, social and political"- Hardwork, industry and perseverance should be the Keynote of Muslim Youths"

"Emphasizing the determination of the Muslims to achieve their goal of Pakistan, the Quaid appealed to Muslim youth to give their best in the building up of the pillars upon which, he said, would rest the edifice of Pakistan. *The pillars were educational, economic, social and political uplift of their people and in their construction the first three should have a priority before they could tackle the political problem. Hard*

work, industry, and perseverance should be the key note of Muslim youth in their task ahead...and advised the students to take a deep interest in not only what was happening to the Muslims but what was happening throughout India and all over the world. He was glad that the Federation had opened a library but warned them that education should not mean that they should be book worms or get through examinations by cramming. They must acquire a general knowledge... He urged that students should do some concrete work which would have definite results in the social, educational and economic spheres of the life of Muslims."

Pillars

"In order to make the Muslims a strong and solid nation they must find out and acquire the necessary ingredients that went to the building up of a strong nation.

The pillars upon which they should build up their structure were educational, economic, social and political uplift. ...No nation, could ever successfully struggle while they were being economically dominated by another nation... Hard work and industry were essential, and it would do good not only to the individual but to the community at large. No nation had ever achieved anything without a struggle."

"If you want to accelerate your progress then build up these pillars,"... "The Muslim demand for Pakistan, meant nothing more than that each community should manage their own homelands."

Address on the Occasion of Opening Ceremony of Students' Jinnah Library, Bombay, on 2nd February, 1944

"Education meant acquisition of Knowledge" not merely "passing of Examination"

The Quaid said that Unity in action was now the foremost and first task of Muslims to achieve their goal. Education did not mean the passing of examinations or getting employment. It really meant acquisition of knowledge about what was going all over India and beyond. He emphasized that students should study politics and have press of their own. They should understand current political problems. He said:

"Ninety per cent of Muslims, are now in the League and everybody knows that it is their only representative organization. We have so far established unity in thought and one ideal. Now our task is to establish unity in action and consolidate Muslim India into one. To achieve unity in action, we will have to lay its foundation right now and build some pillars. They are educational, social and economic. Only after building these three pillars, we shall be able to place the last pillar and that will be the political pillar. We have been forced by circumstances to come to the conclusion that it is impossible for us to live unitedly in India and it is therefore we [sic] say 'divide and live'. There can never be Pakistan without a free India. Hindus know better than ourselves that we are two brothers in a joint family – a system obtaining in India – our home. When one brother is not treated properly, he is given his share and let alone. So, why should not we, the Hindus and Muslims, do likewise?"

Address at Strachey Hall, Aligarh Muslim University, on 9th March, 1944

"You must now concentrate more on social, educational and economic uplift of our Great Nation"

"The address of the Viceroy was provocative and thoughtless of the Muslim position as he was anxious to throw a bait to the Congress and to Mr. Gandhi to secure their good behaviour during his period. No doubt, Lord Wavell, like his predecessors, has started fishing in the Congress waters."

"His conception of unity can only be interpreted a clear indication how best to maintain and continue the British occupation and its imperialist stranglehold over India. Of course he has disregarded the demands of the Muslim India- nay he has gone out of his way to placate the Pundits of Akhand Hindustan..." "The futile bait to the Congress would not lead India any where and it is my firm opinion it is a dangerous game to play and might lead to very serious consequences. The surest way to win the war which the Viceroy considers his first job is to concede the Pakistan demand which means freedom both for Hindus and Muslims." "division of India is inevitable. Blending two nations – Hindus and Musalmans – is an impossibility and Pakistan is a certainty.

It is futile and unwise now to obstruct or delay its establishment."

[In reply to an Address of Welcome by the Students the Quaid while eulogizing the hard work of the Muslim Youth for the cause of Pakistan gave a resume of the happening during his last visit to the University, He said]: "During the first three years there were no tangible results to show. Some people treated us with indifference, some laughed at us and some actively opposed us, but we kept on struggling against all odds and handicaps. But now, he could say without exaggeration that they had reached a stage through patience, perseverance, determination and sustained effort on which they could congratulate themselves. In all great movements a good deal of spadework had to be done. You cannot remould and remake millions of people in a day, a week, a month or even a year."

Our Claim

"We claim that the Muslim League is the authoritative and representative organization of Muslim India. This claim imposed on them a sacred obligation to make the Muslims of India as great a nation in the future as they were in the past. What was our condition seven years ago? Hundred million souls were for all practical purposes dead. In fact, Mr. Gandhi and Lord Linlithgow were preparing to perform the funeral of the Muslims of India, but thank God we are saved." "We now have a platform and a goal of our own. I said some time ago in this very Hall that we had already forged our own charter of Pakistan and we did not need any other charter. We do not want any lessons in geography or in history. The Muslim League has secured for the Muslims a status not only in this country but even abroad. Five years ago did anybody talk about us or did anybody care to know who we were and what we wanted? But a great change had come about during the last few years. There is now not a day when every newspaper, friendly or unfriendly, does not talk about the Muslim League; if they were not friendly to us they abused us, and people do not abuse anybody, if he is nobody.

"Flattering references are often made to me that the key to the situation lies in my hands and that I can resolve the deadlock.

Indeed, our friends went so far as to offer me the crown of the Premier of this great united India. It is all very complimentary, but we stand by our convictions and neither flattery nor coercion can divert us from our determined purpose. The League today occupies a powerful position in the life of this country. You must now concentrate more attention on social, educational and economic uplift of our great nation. Now that we have attained unity of the thought and purpose we must take the next but you must have patience. You cannot have tangible results all at once. It will require all the patience, energy, discipline and solid work that we can put forth."

Committee of Action

"We now have a Committee of Action whose function it would be to further and better organize the Muslim League all over India.

"Secondly, we have a Parliamentary Board. The third thing is the Planning Committee whose personnel I have not yet been able to announce. People have very vague ideas about it but it is difficult to find suitable and qualified men for this Committee. It is no use having merely politicians or lawyers on this Committee. We cannot, however, wait too long. It will be too late. What we want from the Planning Committee is that it should make us ready before the occasion arises to make the fullest use of the potentialities of Pakistan areas.

"Here we must look to the example of the Hindu community. They were always prepared in advance to utilize any opportunity that may come their way. For instance, what have we done in Commerce? Commerce does not merely mean the business of a shopkeeper or the exporter or importer. It means heavy industries and the scientific means of trade and industry. If you look at the list of Joint Stock Companies, you will find that the Musalman is nowhere. When this war broke out the Hindus were ready and prepared to utilize all the opportunities of expanding trade and commerce that the war created; the Musalmans being unprepared were again left behind. It was no use to complain when we lost the chances due to our own negligence. We have merely been producing B.As. and M.As., who look for a government job carrying a salary of Rs. 50 or Rs. 60. Temperamentally the Musalman spends more than he earns. This is a very unsatisfactory state of affairs. I say to you and to all our leaders that we must now take immediate steps to train our youth in a manner that they may be diverted to other useful channels where they have better prospects; but the channels will also have to be created. All Hindu commercial concerns are closed to Muslims; no Hindu firm would employ any Muslim. Therefore, you must have your own commerce and your own industries in which you will be able to give employment not only to thousands of workers and labourers but also to the educated youth who will have infinitely better prospects and will be in a position to do better work in these lines than government service.

IQBAL & JINNAH VS REHMAT ALI IN PAKISTAN'S CREATION

First published in *Dawn* (Karachi) *Encounter* September 3 2005. Muhammad Iqbal (1877-193 was the poetic and spiritual genius who (at least in the 20th Century) inspired the notion of a Muslim homeland in northwestern India. His seminal 1930 presidential speech to the Muslim League in Allahabad laid the foundation stone of the new country that was yet to be. He said "I would like to see the Punjab, Northwest Frontier Province, Sind and Balochistan amalgamated into a single state. Self-government within the British Empire or without the British Empire, the formation of a consolidated North West Indian Muslim state appears to me to be the final destiny of the Muslims at least of Northwest India...".

Iqbal did not see such a Muslim state being theocratic and certainly not one filled with anti-Hindu bigotry: "A community which is inspired by feelings of ill-will towards other communities is low and ignoble. I entertain the highest respect for the customs, laws, religious and social institutions of other communities... Yet I love the communal group which is the source of my life and my behaviour... Nor should the Hindus fear that the creation of autonomous Muslim states will mean the introduction of a kind of religious rule in such states... I therefore demand the formation of a consolidated Muslim state in the best interests of India and Islam. For India it means security and peace resulting from an internal balance of power, for Islam an opportunity to rid itself of the stamp that Arabian Imperialism was forced to give it, to mobilise its law, its education, its culture, and to bring them into closer contact with its own original spirit and the spirit of modern times".

Now such a Muslim country as conceived by Muhammad Iqbal — and which, as it happens, constitutes more or less the territory of present-day Pakistan other than East Punjab— did not necessarily have to receive the name it did come to receive. It might have been named "Dar-e-Islami-Hind" or the "Indus Islamic Republic" or "Indic Islamabad" or "The Republic of North-Western India" or some other such appropriate appellation — even "Iqbalistan" perhaps or some name deriving from Iqbal's notion of "khudi" which he had developed from his admiration as a young man for the philosophy of Friedrich Nietzsche.

Nor did Muhammad Ali Jinnah (1876-194 himself, the explicit and acknowledged political founder of the new country, use the appellation that it did come to have, not even when he introduced the Lahore Resolution in the 1940 meeting of the Muslim League which aimed to implement Iqbal's idea. It was Iqbal who persuaded Jinnah to return to India from England, where Jinnah had settled in a law practice again after his first stint in Indian politics, and in 1934 Jinnah had done so when elected to the Central Legislative Assembly in a reserved seat for Bombay Muslims.

By 1938 Jinnah had declared his permanent opinion: "Congress leaders may shout as much as they like that the Congress is a national body. But ... (the) Congress is nothing but a Hindu body". Finally, at the Lahore session of the Muslim League in 1940, Jinnah introduced the idea: "That geographically contiguous units are demarcated into regions which should be so constituted, with such territorial readjustments as may be necessary, that the areas in which the Muslims are numerically in a majority, as in the North-Western and Eastern zones of India should be grouped to constitute Independent States in which the constituent units shall be autonomous and sovereign".

Who had seconded Jinnah's Lahore Resolution? It had been Sikander Hyat Khan, leader of the Punjab Muslims, and Fazlul

Haq, leader of the Bengal Muslim peasantry. Jinnah as of 1940 had been most conspicuously a leader of Muslims only in the Muslim-minority provinces of British India, and clearly had felt it necessary to demonstrate that in proposing the Lahore Resolution he had the support of the two leaders of the two largest Muslim-majority provinces, Punjab and Bengal.

Sikander Hyat Khan had been due to become Deputy Governor of the Reserve Bank of India in Bombay in 1936 when instead he returned to Punjab to lead the Unionist Party of Muslim, Sikh and Hindu landlords in 1937. "The Sikander-Jinnah pact stipulated that the Unionist Party of the Punjab, led by Sikander, would retain full autonomy of the affairs of the province." Fazlul Haq would later conceive with Sarat Bose (elder brother of Subhash Bose) of a Muslim majority "United Bengal" in an attempt to keep Calcutta out of the new India, a notion which would have Jinnah's backing but otherwise would not get anywhere. Support for the Lahore Resolution among the Muslims of the princely states like Jammu and Kashmir or Hyderabad was conspicuous by its absence. Neither were they mentioned in Iqbal's seminal 1930 speech nor in Jinnah's 1940 Lahore Resolution backed by Sikander Hyat Khan and Fazlul Haq. What has been called the "Paradox of Kashmir" is that prior to 1947 Jammu and Kashmir did not seem to appear in any discussion whatsoever, and yet it has consumed almost all discussion ever since.

To this must be added now another newly understood dimension having to do with the conceptualization and foundation of the new country not only by Iqbal the poet and Jinnah the politician, but by the third and upstart founder of Pakistan: its young radical Islamist ideologue, Choudhry Rahmat Ali (1895-1951).

Official Pakistan has venerated Iqbal and accorded Jinnah due honour and respect but has apparently treated Rahmat Ali as the lunatic uncle who has needed to be locked up secretly in the attic. Yet Rehmat Ali's impact on the creation of Pakistan and events in the subcontinent equalled those of his two better educated, more respectable and eminent compatriots — and may yet come to exceed them (not necessarily salubriously).

Rehmat Ali was born in a village in Hoshiarpur district of Punjab in 1895, making him almost 20 years younger than Iqbal and Jinnah. He matriculated from Jullunder and graduated in 1919 from Islamia College, Lahore. About 1931, having "accumulated some money as a legal advisor to a Balochi landlord", he arrived in England and took admission in Emmanuel College, Cambridge.

By way of studies, Rehmat Ali may have passed a set of Part I exams but not perhaps the Part II. There does not seem to be any record of him attending the Inns of Court or of being called to the Bar, though he styled himself "Barrister at Law" in his writings. According to the obituary he received in the Emmanuel College Magazine of 1950-51, "he made Cambridge his home, shifting a little unhappily from lodging to lodging, and using, perhaps rather more than was proper, the College as an accommodation address."

Interviews with his landlady and housekeeper-secretary, conducted by Dr. Taufiq Shelley in 1970-71, yielded that Rehmat Ali was a devout pious Muslim who along with a few compatriots had been secretly and secretively very active as a pamphleteer from England creating and spreading among India's Muslims a radical Islamist ideology for Pakistan, even founding something called the "Pakistan National Liberation Movement".

Rehmat Ali was inspired by Iqbal's 1930 call for a Muslim state in northwest India but felt Iqbal had been too vague and was disappointed that Iqbal had not pressed the issue at the Third Round Table Conference. In 1933, apparently on the top floor of a London bus, Rehmat Ali invented for Iqbal's imagined political entity the name "PAKISTAN", the P standing for his native Punjab, the A for Afghania, K for Kashmir, S for Sind, and the STAN allegedly doubling up for Balochistan.

Rehmat Ali sought a meeting with Jinnah in London, met him and pressed the name 'Pakistan' upon him as a possible nomenclature. "Jinnah disliked Rehmat Ali's ideas and avoided meeting him". Jinnah pointed out to Rehmat Ali he had failed to consider the other Muslim majority province, Bengal, as well as Muslim minority regions.

At this, Rehmat Ali produced a general scheme of Muslim domination all over the subcontinent: there would be "Pakistan" in the northwest including Kashmir, Delhi and Agra; "Bangistan" in Bengal; "Osmanistan" in Hyderabad; "Siddiquistan" in Bundelhand and Malwa; "Faruqistan" in Bihar and Orissa; "Haideristan" in UP; "Muinistan" in Rajasthan; "Maplistan" in Kerala; and even "Safiistan" in "Western Ceylon" and "Nasaristan" in "Eastern Ceylon", etc. The map deriving from such a crank view of history was published by Rehmat Ali in 1934 and came to be widely circulated in his pamphleteering among Indian Muslims at the time.

Rehmat Ali was vituperative in his bigotry against Hindus, referring to the Indian nationalist movement as a "British-Banya alliance" presumably in reference to MK Gandhi's caste. He even declined to refer to an "India" as having ever existed at all and instead personally renamed the entire subcontinent as "Dinia", and the oceans and the seas around India as the "Pakian Sea", the "Osmanian Sea" etc. He urged Sikhs to rise up against the Hindus in a "Sikhistan" (and might have interacted with Master Tara Singh), and indeed urged all of India's peoples who were not Hindus to rise up in war against Hindus. Given the obscurity of the facts of his life before his arrival at Emmanuel College, what experiences may have led him to such extreme bigotry towards Hindus are not known.

When in 1947 a new but "motheaten" country had come to be named with the word he had coined on a London bus more than a dozen years earlier, and was a country which had two "wings" after a partition — the more populous "East Pakistan" and the more arrogant "West Pakistan" — Rehmat Ali turned his wrath from England upon its new government. He condemned Jinnah as being treacherous, and then newly re-interpreted his letters P, A, K, I, S, T, A, N to now refer to Punjab, Afghania, Kashmir, Iran, Sindh, Tukharistan (sic), Afghanistan, and Balochistan.

The word "pak" coincidentally meant pure in Arabic, so Rehmat Ali began to speak of Muslim believers anywhere as being the "Pak" *i.e.* "the pure" people, and of how the national destiny of the new Pakistan should be to liberate "Pak" people everywhere, including the new India, and create a "Pak Commonwealth of Nations" stretching from Arabia to the Indies. The map he now drew placed the word "Punjab" over Jammu & Kashmir. Thus as of 1947 or so, Rehmat Ali's crank view of history led to an Asia dominated by a "Pak" empire: However, when Rehmat Ali landed in the new country whose name had been invented by him, he was apparently placed under arrest and deported back to England immediately. In a previous visit to Sikander Hyat's Punjab, he had been apparently assaulted. He had not been invited to the promulgation of the Lahore Resolution, which, even though it did not refer to his name Pakistan, came to be called the Pakistan Resolution.

Shunned by the officialdom of the new country which now carried the name he had invented, Rehmat Ali died in poverty and obscurity in England during an influenza epidemic in 1951; the Master of Emmanuel College paid for his funeral and was later reimbursed for this by the Government of Pakistan.

In recent years Rehmat Ali has been undergoing a restoration, and his grave at Cambridge has become a site of pilgrimage today for Pakistan's Islamist ideologues, while his maps, writings and rantings have been reprinted in, *e.g.*, *The Nation* newspaper in Pakistan as recently as February 2005.

At best, Rehmat Ali may be described as a pious and devout Muslim who was a sincere and ardent Islamist ideologue. At worst he was a deeply bigoted crank and a reactionary Muslim imperialist. His views on Hindus are not far in the level of their depravity from the views of the author of *Mein Kampf* on the Jews — and ironically the author of *Mein Kampf* had been a model for a few Hindu authors at the time who wrote with equal bigotry about the Muslims of India.

Indeed Rehmat Ali's views against Hindus may be classified with those of other bigoted views at the time such as those against Jews or against Muslims, which may all well have been examples or models or counterfoils for one another in the crank fringes of rival ideological movements at the time.

The anti-Hindu bigotry of Rehmat Ali's views would explain why they were anathema to Jinnah, the secular-minded constitutionalist. Like other Muslim nationalists of his time such as Attaturk, Nasser, Mossadeq or even Saud himself, Jinnah would have been embarrassed to be promoting a reactionary Islamic imperialism in that modernising era that was the middle of the 20th century.

Dr. Roy along with WE James created the book *Foundations of Pakistan's Political Economy: Towards an Agenda for the 1990s* (Sage, Delhi, OUP, Karachi 1992). His most recent book is one edited with John Clarke, *Margaret*

India

The Muslim quarter of India's population became increasingly wary of the Congress's promises and restive in the wake of the collapse of the Khilafat movement, which occurred after Kemal Atatürk announced his modernist Turkish reforms in 1923 and disavowed the very title of caliph the following year.

Hindu-Muslim riots in Malabar claimed hundreds of lives in 1924, and similar religious rioting spread to every major city in northern India, wherever rumours of Muslim "cow slaughter," the polluting appearance of a dead pig's carcass in a mosque, or other clashing doctrinal fears ignited the tinder of distrust ever lurking in the poorer sections of India's towns and villages.

At each stage of reform, as the prospects of real devolution of political power by the British seemed more imminent, separate-electorate formulas and leaders of various parties stirred hopes, which proved almost as dangerous in triggering violence as did fears. The older, more conservative leadership of the pre-World War I Congress found Gandhian satyagraha too radical—moreover, far too revolutionary—to support, and liberals like Sir Tej Bahadur Sapru (1875–1949) organized their own party (eventually to become the National Liberal Federation), while others, like Jinnah, dropped out of political life entirely.

Jinnah, alienated by Gandhi and his illiterate mass of devoutly Hindu disciples, instead devoted himself to his lucrative Bombay law practice, but his energy and ambition lured him back to the leadership of the Muslim League, which he revitalized in the 1930s. Jinnah, who was also instrumental in urging Viceroy Lord Irwin (later, 1st Earl Halifax; governed 1926–31) and Prime Minister MacDonald to convene the Round Table Conference in London, was urged by many Muslim compatriots, including Liaquat Ali Khan (1895–1951), to become the permanent president of the Muslim League.

By 1930 a number of Indian Muslims had begun to think in terms of separate statehood for their minority community, whose population dominated the northwestern provinces of British India and the eastern half of Bengal, as well as important pockets of the United Provinces and the great princely state of Kashmir.

(The princely state of Hyderabad was ruled by a Muslim dynasty but was mostly Hindu.) One of Punjab's greatest Urdu poets, Sir Muhammad Iqbal (1877–1938), while presiding over the Muslim League's annual meeting in Allahabad in 1930, proposed that "the final destiny" of India's Muslims should be to consolidate a "North-West Indian Muslim state."

Although he did not name it Pakistan, his proposal included what became the major provinces of modern Pakistan—Punjab, Sind, the North-West Frontier Province, and Balochistan. Jinnah, the Aga Khan, and other important Muslim leaders were at the time in London attending the Round Table Conference, which still envisaged a single federation of all Indian provinces and princely states as the best possible constitutional solution for India in the aftermath of a future British withdrawal.

Separate electorate seats, as well as special guarantees of Muslim "autonomy" or "veto powers" in dealing with sensitive religious issues, were hoped to be sufficient to avert civil war or any need for actual partition.

As long as the British raj remained in control, such formulas and schemes appeared to suffice, for the British army could always be hurled into the communal fray at the brink of extreme danger, and the army had as yet remained apolitical and—since its post-mutiny reorganization—untainted by communal religious passions.

In 1933 a group of Muslim students at Cambridge, led by Choudhary Rehmat Ali, proposed that the only acceptable solution to Muslim India's internal conflicts and problems would be the birth of a Muslim "fatherland," to be called Pakistan (Persian: "Land of the Pure"), out of the Muslim-majority northwestern and northeastern provinces.

The Muslim League and its president, Jinnah, did not join in the Pakistan demand until after the league's famous Lahore meeting in March 1940, as Jinnah, a secular constitutionalist by predilection and training, continued to hope for a reconciliation with the Congress. Such hopes virtually disappeared, however, when Nehru refused to permit the league to form coalition ministries with the Congress majority in the United Provinces and elsewhere after the 1937 elections.

The Congress had initially entered the elections with the hope of wrecking the act of 1935, but—after it had won so impressive a victory in most provinces and the league had done so poorly, mostly because it had inadequately organized itself for nationwide elections—Nehru agreed to participate in the government and insisted there were but "two parties" in India, the Congress and the British raj.

Jinnah soon proved to Nehru that the Muslims were indeed a formidable "third" party. The years from 1937 to 1939, when the Congress actually ran most of British India's provincial governments, became the seed period for the Muslim League's growth in popularity and power within the entire Muslim community, for many Muslims soon viewed the new "Hindu raj" as biased and tyrannical and the Hindu-led Congress ministries and their helpers as insensitive to Muslim demands or appeals for jobs, as well as to their redress of grievances.

The Congress's partiality toward its own members, prejudice toward its majority community, and jobbery for its leadership's friends and relations all conspired to convince many Muslims that they had become second-class citizens in a land that, while perhaps on the verge of achieving "freedom" for some Indians, would be run by "infidels" and "enemies" to the Muslim minority. The league made the most of the Congress's errors of judgment in governance; by documenting as many reports as it could gather in papers published during 1939, it hoped to prove how wretched a Muslim's life would be under any "Hindu raj."

The Congress's high command insisted, of course, that it was a "secular and national" party, not a sectarian Hindu organization, but Jinnah and the Muslim League responded that they alone could speak for and defend the rights of India's Muslims. Thus, the lines of battle were drawn by the eve of World War II, which served only to intensify and accelerate the process of communal conflict and irreversible political division that would split British India.

8

The Partition of India

14 August, 1947, saw the birth of the new Islamic Republic of Pakistan. At midnight the next day India won its freedom from colonial rule, ending nearly 350 years of British presence in India. During the struggle for freedom, Gandhi had written an appeal "To Every Briton" to free their possessions in Asia and Africa, especially India (Philips and Wainwright, 567). The British left India divided in two. The two countries were founded on the basis of religion, with Pakistan as an Islamic state and India as a secular one.

Whether the partition of these countries was wise and whether it was done too soon is still under debate. Even the imposition of an official boundary has not stopped conflict between them. Boundary issues, left unresolved by the British, have caused two wars and continuing strife between India and Pakistan.

The partition of India and its freedom from colonial rule set a precedent for nations such as Israel, which demanded a separate homeland because of the irreconcilable differences between the Arabs and the Jews. The British left Israel in May 1948, handing the question of division over to the UN. Un-enforced UN Resolutions to map out boundaries between Israel and Palestine has led to several Arab-Israeli wars and the conflict still continues.

REASONS FOR PARTITION

By the end of the 19th century several nationalistic movements had started in India. Indian nationalism had grown largely since British policies of education and the advances made by the British in India in the fields of transportation and communication. However, their complete insensitivity to and distance from the peoples of India and their customs created such disillusionment with them in their subjects that the end of British rule became necessary and inevitable.

However, while the Indian National Congress was calling for Britain to Quit India, the Muslim League, in 1943, passed a resolution for them to Divide and Quit. There were several reasons for the birth of a separate Muslim homeland in the subcontinent, and all three parties-the British, the Congress and the Muslim League-were responsible.

The British had followed a divide-and-rule policy in India. Even in the census they categorised people according to religion and viewed and treated them as separate from each other. They had based their knowledge of the peoples of India on the basic religious texts and the intrinsic differences they found in them instead of on the way they coexisted in the present. The British were also still fearful of the potential threat from the Muslims, who were the former rulers of the subcontinent, ruling India for over 300 years under the Mughal Empire. In order to win them over to their side, the British helped establish the M.A.O. College at Aligarh and supported the All-India Muslim Conference, both of which were institutions from which leaders of the Muslim League and the ideology of Pakistan emerged. As soon as the League was formed, they were placed on a separate electorate. Thus the idea of the separateness of Muslims in India was built into the electoral process of India.

There was also an ideological divide between the Muslims and the Hindus of India. While there were strong feelings of nationalism in India, by the late 19th century there were also communal conflicts and movements in the country that were based on religious communities rather than class or regional ones. Some people felt that the very nature of Islam called for a communal Muslim society. Added to this were the memories of power over the Indian subcontinent that the Muslims held on to, especially those in the old centres of Mughal rule. These memories might have made it exceptionally difficult for Muslims to accept the imposition of colonial power and culture. They refused to learn English and to associate with the British. This was a severe drawback for them as they found that the Hindus were now in better positions in government than they were and thus felt that the British favoured Hindus. The social reformer and educator, Sir Syed Ahmed Khan, who founded M.A.O. College, taught the Muslims that education and cooperation with the British was vital for their survival in the society. Tied to all the movements of Muslim revival was the opposition to assimilation and submergence in Hindu society. Sir Syed Ahmed Khan was also the first to conceive of a separate Muslim homeland.

Hindu revivalists also deepened the chasm between the two nations. They resented the Muslims for their former rule over India. Hindu revivalists rallied for a ban on the slaughter of cows, a cheap source of meat for the Muslims. They also wanted to change the official script form the Persian to the Hindu Devanagri script, effectively making Hindi rather than Urdu the main candidate for the national language.

Congress made several mistakes in their policies which further convinced the League that it was impossible to live in a undivided India after freedom from colonial rule because their interests would be completely suppressed. One such policy was the institution of the "Bande Matram," a national anthem which expressed anti-Muslim sentiments, in the schools of India where Muslim children were forced to sing it.

The Muslim League gained power also due to the Congress. The Congress banned any support for the British during the Second World War. However the Muslim League pledged its full support, which found favour form them from the British, who also needed the help of the largely Muslim army. The Civil Disobedience Movement and the consequent withdrawal of the Congress party from politics also helped the league gain power, as they formed strong ministries in the provinces that had large Muslim populations. At the same time, the League actively campaigned to gain more support from the Muslims in India, especially under the guidance of dynamic leaders like Jinnah.

There had been some hope of an undivided India, with a government consisting of three tiers along basically the same lines as the borders of India and Pakistan at the time of Partition. However, Congress' rejection of the interim government set up under this Cabinet Mission Plan in 1942 convinced the leaders of the Muslim League that compromise was impossible and partition was the only course to take.

IMPACT AND AFTERMATH OF PARTITION

> *"Leave India to God. If that is too much, then leave her to anarchy."—Gandhi, May 1942*

The partition of India left both India and Pakistan devastated. The process of partition had claimed many lives in the riots. Many others were raped and looted. Women, especially, were used as instruments of power by the Hindus and the Muslims; "ghost trains" full of severed breasts of women would arrive in each of the newly-born countries from across the borders.

15 million refugees poured across the borders to regions completely foreign to them, for though they were Hindu or Muslim, their identity had been embedded in the regions where there ancestors were from. Not only was the country divided, but so were the provinces of Punjab and Bengal, divisions which caused catastrophic riots and claimed the lives of Hindus, Muslims and Sikhs alike.

Many years after the partition, the two nations are still trying to heal the wounds left behind by this incision to once-whole body of India. Many are still in search of an identity and a history left behind beyond an impenetrable boundary. The two countries started of with ruined economies and lands and without an established, experienced system of government. They lost many of their most dynamic leaders, such as Gandhi, Jinnah and Allama Iqbal, soon after the partition. Pakistan had to face the separation of Bangladesh in 1971. India and Pakistan have been to war twice since the partition and they are still deadlocked over the issue of possession of Kashmir. The same issues of boundaries and divisions, Hindu and Muslim majorities and differences, still persist in Kashmir.

PARTITION OF PUNJAB

Scholarly works on the partition of India are legion, but those focusing on the partition of the Punjab are very few. Ian Talbot and Kirpal Singh indeed have pioneering works on the Punjab partition to their credit, but much more research needs to be done to shed light on the dynamics of that cataclysmal event. After all the greatest forced migration in history with its gory tales of massacres, looting, arson, rape, abduction of women and children and other acts of savagery were essentially facets of a Punjabi tragedy.

Why and how this happened will be elaborated in my forthcoming book. On the 60th anniversary of the partition of the Punjab it is appropriate that a sketch of the main events is shared with the public. I shall in a series of articles trace the main events that culminated in the bloody division of that province.

Although ideas of partitioning Punjab had existed since at least the beginning of the twentieth century it was only in the wake of the March 23, 1940 Lahore Resolution adopted by the Muslim League that the Sikhs began to demand that the Punjab should also be partitioned on a religious basis.

Sikh religion, culture and history were inextricably linked to the Punjab—the founder of the Sikh faith, Baba Guru Nanak (1469-1539) and his spiritual successors were Punjabis, the only great kingdom ruled a Sikh, the Kingdom of Lahore under Maharaja Ranjit Singh (1799-1839), was essentially a Punjabi state, most of the holy shrines of the Sikhs and the vast majority of their community were based in the Punjab. Therefore the Sikhs demanding partition appears to be a contradiction in terms. But they did and the question is: why? Certainly the clues are not to be found in their demographic complexion.

Unlike the Muslims who were in majority in the northwestern and northeastern zones of the subcontinent, the Sikh were not in a majority anywhere in the Punjab, not even in the central districts where they were mainly located or in their holy city of Amritsar. According to the 1941 census their overall proportion of the total Punjab population was 13.2 per cent in the British-administered areas and it increased to 14. 9 per cent if the Sikh states were also included. The Muslims had an overwhelming majority of 57.1 per cent in the British areas, which decreased to 53.2 per cent if the Sikh states were included. The Hindu population was 29.1 per cent in British districts and it declined to 26.6 if the Sikh states were included. The Sikhs were not in a majority in any of the major Sikh states either.

The Sikh argument was that India should not be partitioned, but if it became inevitable then the Punjab should be divided and the borders between a predominantly Muslim Punjab in the West and a Hindu-Sikh majority East Punjab should be drawn on the Chenab, so that East Punjab would include their holy places as well as the majority of the community. The Sikh leadership feared persecution in a predominantly Muslim Pakistan, just as the Muslim leadership argued that permanent Hindu Raj based on caste prejudices will be established if India remained united.

On February 20, 1947 Prime Minister Clement Attlee announced that His Majesty's Government intended to transfer power to Indian hands, in a united or partitioned India, by June 1948. The Sikhs reacted angrily to that declaration because no mention of a Sikh right to a separate homeland was included in it.

In the meantime, the Muslim League had launched on January 24 1947 direct action in the Punjab against the coalition government headed by Sir Khizr Hayat Tiwana, which it alleged was not representative of the Muslims of Punjab. The main supporters of Punjab Unionist Party, the Muslim landlords, had decamped and were now members of the Punjab Muslim League. The Muslim League won 75 out of the 83 seats fixed for Muslims. Two Unionists crossed the floor and joined it but it was still short of a majority by 10 seats in a house of 175.

On the other hand, the Unionist Party led by Tiwana was routed in the election. It won only 18 seats. Tiwana managed to put together a coalition government, which included the Akalis and other Panthic Sikhs who won 23 seats and the Congress which did very well by winning 50 general seats. The coalition government also included some scheduled caste members of the Punjab

Assembly. Direct action or a civil disobedience movement as the Muslim League preferred to call it lasted from January 24 to February 26. Its mass character multiplied every day and the jails were filled with leaders and cadres who defied Section 144 and were arrested. Although it remained peaceful, each day the slogans the crowds shouted became more and more menacing and threatening, striking fear and terror in the hearts of the non-Muslims.

Slogans such as, 'Pakistan ka nara kiya? La illahah illillah (what is the slogan of Pakistan? It is, there is no God but Allah), 'Assey lein gey Pakistan jaisey liya tha Hindustan' (we will take Pakistan the way we took India) were raised all over the Punjab. Some slogans directly insulted the Punjab premier in a most abusive and shallow manner. Towards the end of the agitation the demonstrators began to harass Hindus and Sikhs and made them fly the Muslim League flag on their cars and shops.

The government and the Muslim League, however, reached an agreement on February 26 according to which the agitation was called off and the Muslim League leaders and cadres were released. But those several weeks of mass agitation provoked a determined reaction from the Hindu and Sikh leaders in the Punjab who vowed not to let a Muslim League minority government come to power. On March 2 Khizr resigned. He had been badly shaken and demoralised by the abuse directed at him and by the fact that the landlords had abandoned him. The Punjab Governor, Sir Evan Jenkins, invited the Muslim League leader Nawab Iftikhar Hussain Khan Mamdot to prove that he had a majority in the house. Although he claimed that he could muster a majority with the help of some scheduled castes members of the Punjab Assembly Mamdot failed to do so. That created a political impasse. Governor Jenkins therefore imposed governor rule on March 5 under Section 93 of the India Act of 1935. Punjab continued to remain under governor's rule until partition in mid-August 1947.

British Rule and Muslim League

The British ruled the Indian subcontinent for nearly 200 years-from 1756 to 1947. After the Indian Mutiny of 1857, the British government abolished the powers of the British East India Company, which had ruled the subcontinent on behalf of the British Crown, and took on direct powers of governance. Political reforms were initiated, allowing the formation of political parties. The Indian National Congress, representing the overwhelming majority of Hindus, was created in 1885. The Muslim League was formed in 1906 to represent and protect the position of the Muslim minority. When the British introduced constitutional reforms in 1909, the Muslims demanded and acquired separate electoral rolls. This guaranteed Muslims representation in the provincial as well as national legislatures until the dawn of independence in 1947. The idea of a separate Muslim state in south Asia was raised in 1930 by the poet and philosopher Sir Muhammad Iqbal.

He suggested that the northwestern provinces of British India and the native state of Jammu and Kashmir should be joined into such a state. The name "Pakistan", which came to be used to describe this grouping, is thought to have originated as a compound abbreviation made up of letters of the names of the provinces involved, as follows: Punjab, Afghania (North West Frontier Province), Kashmir, Indus-Sindh, and Balochistan. An alternative explanation says the name means "Land of the Pure". By the end of the 1930s, Muhammad Ali Jinnah, leader of the Muslim League and considered the founding father of Pakistan, had also decided that the only way to preserve Indian Muslims from Hindu domination was to establish a separate Muslim state.

KASHMIR AND PARTITION OF INDIA

India under the British was divided into two distinct entities, British Provinces and Princely States. Princely States under the Government of India Act 1935 were defined as including any territory, whether described as a state, an estate, a jagir or otherwise. They were under the suzeranity of His Majesty and not a part of the British India. The code of conduct governing the relations of the princely states with the British Government was, therefore, different from that which governed the relations between provinces and the British Government. In the case of the provinces, the authority of the British Government was direct. It was exercised through the British Parliament, the Secretary of State for India, Governor General in Council or Provincial Governors. In the case of the princely states, the authority was indirectly exercised by various treaties, engagements and sanads, supplemented by usage and sufferances.

In 1945, Churchill's coalition government was voted out and Clement Attlee's Labour Party came to power in London. British Prime Minister Clement Attlee announced in the House of Commons, in February 1946, that a Parliamentary delegation would visit India with a view to meeting the national leaders and discuss various problems connected with self government in India. The Cabinet Mission, consisting of Lord Pethic Lawrence, Sir Stafford Cripps, and Mr. L. V. Alexander, all members of the British Government, arrived in India on 23rd March, 1946, and held conferences with four representatives, two each of the Congress and the Muslim League. But the conference failed to devise and agreed formula and the Mission announced their own proposals in the State Paper of May 16,1946.

Their plan rejected the Muslim League's demand for Pakistan and proposed a federal union of India including British India and Indian Princely States. It provided for the establishment of a Constitutional Assembly to frame the future Constitution of India, which was to be based on the principle that the centre would control only three subjects, viz, Foreign Affairs, Defence and Communications, all other subjects were to be administered by autonomous provinces and states.

It was proclaimed by the Secretary of State for India that paramountcy was to lapse after India had achieved independence and that the future relationship of the states with the rest of India was to be decided by the parties themselves through consultations and negotiations. In the meantime, 200 delegates of All India State People's Conference from all over India, met to discuss the Cabinet Mission Plan, on 8-11 June, 1946. During his speech in the meeting Pandit Jawahar Lal Nehru insisted on democratisation of the states to bring them at par with the rest of India. He said," Rulers alone can't decide the fate of nearly 100 million people."

The Cabinet Mission Plan was accepted by the princes, but they wanted to make some proposals during interim period. All these proposals were not at all concerned with people of the states. The situation however changed when the Muslim League, after joining the Interim Government, refused to join the Constitutional Assembly and continued to insist on its demand for Pakistan. It was felt all over the country and in England that events in India were leading towards a dangerous impasse. In order to face the situation more effectively, the British Government appointed Lord Viscount Mountbatten in place of Lord Wavell as Governor-General of India.

Lord Mountbatten, plunged himself in the negotiations with the leaders of different political parties and announced that long before June 1948, the Dominions of India and Pakistan would be established and that the question of Indian states would be dealt with in the light of the Cabinet Mission's memorandum of May 12,1946 .To approve the British plan, a conference between Mountbatten and several Indian leaders was held on June 2, 1947. It was approved on June 3,1947. The plan stated; "while paramountcy will lapse, according to His Majesty's Governments declaration of May 12, and May 16,1946, His Majesty's Government will not enter into military or any other agreement with the Indian states."

Most of the states were under the impression that the lapse of paramountcy meant independent status for the states and they could either join the Constitution Assembly or remain independent. Seeing the attitude of the rulers in taking decision, Pandit Nehru said on June 15,1947, in the All India Congress Committee: Owe will not recognise the independence of the states in India and any recognition of such independence by any foreign power will be considered as unfriendly act ". Mr. Jinnah contested the views of Pandit Nehru. On June 17,1947, he said," Constitutionally and legally the Indian states will be independent sovereign states on the termination of paramountcy and they will be free to decide for themselves and adopt any course they like; it is open to them to join the Hindustan Constitutional Assembly or decide to remain independent. In case they opt for independence they would enter into such agreements or relationships with Hindustan or Pakistan as they may choose."

Throughout the negotiations on the Cabinet Mission proposals as well as the subsequent schemes of partition and transfer of power, the question of states and State People's right was kept in the foreground by the Congress and assurances were extracted from the British Government that on the lapse of paramountcy the princes would not become sovereign rulers .... "Sovereignty must reside in the people and not in any individual. The State people's claim to represent for themselves is justified and will see to it that they are heard. And certainly their rulers cannot speak for them," said Nehru on June 8,1947 before the delegates of State People's conference.

Whereas the Congress supported the cause of the people of the states to determine their relations with the Dominions, Muslim League's attitude towards them was antipathetic. The League's policy of not estranging the princes had become apparent when Mr. Jinnah made the following observations as far back as 1940: The only important states which matter are not in the Eastern but in the North-Western one. They are Kashmir, Bahawalpur, Patiala etc. If these states willingly agree to come into the federation of the Muslim Homeland, we shall be glad to come to a reasonable and honourable settlement with them. We, however, have no desire to force them or coerce them in any way.

With the passing of Indian Independence Act 1947, all the states were released from their obligations to the Crown. They became free to align their future with either of two Dominoins. All the negotations that had already been held on Cabinet Mission proposal of 1946 and the transfer of power and Independence Act of 1947, made it evident that if Indian states became separate independent entities, it would create a serious vacuum between the Central Government and the States; this would effect not only political relations but also economic and other relations between the two. Taking into consideration these problems, Heartley Showcross, the under secretary of States for India in a speech emphatically maintained that the British Government would not recognise any state as a separate international entity, and Prime

Minister Atlee speaking on Independence Bill, hoped that no irrevocable decision to stay out prematurely will be taken. State Department was set up on 27 June, 1947, to deal with matters concerning states. It was divided into two sections; one to be headed by a Congress leader and the other by a Muslim League leader. Sardar Patel and Abdur Rab Nishtar headed these sections. Sardar Patel issued agenda for the conference of rulers of princely states to be held on 25 July, 1947. It included (i) Acession of the states on defence, external affairs, and communications, (ii) Standstill Agreement. It was enthusiastically welcomed by states. The same was repeated by Lord Mountbatten in his capacity as Crown Representative, when the special session of Chamber Princes was held on 25 July, 1947. He assured the princes that their accession on these three subjects would involve no financial liability and that in other matters there would be no encroachment on their sovereignty. Finally he appealed to them to join any one of the two dominions before 15 August, 1947.

In order to expedite work, the Negotiating Committee of Chamber of Princes prepared the draft of Instrument of Accession and Standstill Agreement which were approved by the General Conference of the Chamber of Princes on August 1, 1947. Some of the rulers were inclined to execute Standstill Agreements but wait as the Instrument of Accession was concerned. It was, however, made clear to such rulers in the conference that the Government of India had decided to execute Standstill agreement with only those who had already signed the Instrument of Accession Therefore the only bases which constituted the basis of relationship between the Indian states and the successor government in British India were the Instrument of Accession and the Standstill Agreement.

Thus before 15th August, 1947, all the states except Hyderabad, Junagarh and Kashmir had acceded either to India or Pakistan. In Hyderabad the public opinion was divided; while the majority who were Hindus favoured accession with Indian Union, a strong minority under the leadership of Kasim Rizvi wanted to remain independent as the Muslim state of Hyderabad, and was aggressively hostile to Indian Union. The Government of

Hyderabad failed to check the frequent raids of Muslim razakars and the militant communists of Telegana into the territory of Indian Union. These hostile designs were overcome by police action, before the Nizam consented to accede to the Indian Union.

Junagarh had a Muslim ruling family and 85% Hindu majority population. It had stated it would go along with the policy of other 279 Kathiawar states, many encircling it, all of which acceded to India. It was not contiguous at any point with Pakistan, and its railways, posts and telegraph were an integral part of the Indian communication system. There was a coup de tat on August 10, 1947, by a group of Sindhi Muslims (pro-Pakistan) under the leadership of Bhutto, took over the government and the Nawab became a virtual prisioner in his palace. On September 15, 1947, he eventually acceded to Pakistan. On November 9, 1947, India occupied the state at the invitation of the Prime Minister. On February 24, 1948, a plebiscite was held resulting in an overwhelming vote for accession to India. Finally, in January 1949, Junagarh was merged with Saurashtra, a union of princely states of Kathiawar. Jammu and Kashmir was the only state whose Maharaja delayed the accession of the state to India.

BENGAL PARTITION

The Muslim League

In 1906, as Bengal was divided, Dutch Christians overtook beautiful Bali after the Puputan massacres in which they murdered the Hindu Balinese royal families. Bengal was divided by Lord Curzon, an arrogant British viceroy, to control the rebellious province. (An important building in the University of Dhaka shamefully bears Curzon's name.) This division was an outrage for the people of Bangla but the landlords gave their support to the British. The British were eventually forced to undo the division in 1911 under popular pressure.

The same year, one of the worst things of Indian history happened. This was the formation of the All-India Muslim League. The party was formed in Dhaka (presently capital of Bangladesh) in 1906. It was founded by the rich Muslim landlords. It was indeed a dark day in Bangla when the movement for independence was betrayed.

The Muslim League declared allegiance to the British and sought to draw Muslims away from the independence movement. In their first resolution on December 30, 1906 in Dhaka, the very first thing they declared was, "To promote, among the Musalmans of India, feelings of loyalty to the British Government, and to remove any misconception that may arise as to the intention of Government with regard to any of its measures." This was moved by Nawab Salimullah, whose name is also borne by a student hall in the University of Dhaka. (SHAME).

In 1913, on their 6th session, at Lucknow on March 22-23rd, 1913, there was an ammendment to their constitution. The first objective of Muslim League was then: "According to the revised Constitution, the first object of the League is `to maintain and promote among the people of this country feelings of loyalty towards the British Crown'... It is the British Crown alone which is the permanent and ever-abiding symbol of Empire. It is not to this Government or to that we acknowledge allegiance: it is to the British Crown itself that we owe unswerving and abiding loyalty... It is the paramount duty of every loyal subject of the King Emperor to abstain from doing anything calculated to impair the permanence and stability of British rule in India."—Mian Muhammad Shafi (Leader of Punjab Muslim League and Chairman of session.). The betrayal continued. There were allegations that the Muslim League was a stooge for the British and were financed and supported by them. By their history the Muslim League validates and confirms the allegations.

Muslim League and many Hindu upper caste members fuelled the differences among Hindus and Muslims. Relations further worsened as Muslim League convinced many educated Muslims that there was a Hindu conspiracy against the Muslims. Since then many educated Muslims saw the Hindus encroaching on their rights and saw the Muslim League as championing the rights of Muslims. The Muslim League was in reality trying to create panic among Muslims.

However, Muslim League initially was not very popular. Their leaders had hoped that the Muslims, seeing the name of their party would flock to them out of religious faith. However, initially that did not happen. Their pro-British stance did not help their popularity. But gradually, however, their propaganda paid off. The Muslims started abandoning the national movement to join the sectarian Muslim League. However, not all were swayed by the propaganda and many remained in the Congress. But they were considered to be "Hindu minded".

Hindu Muslim Riots

Some rich Hindus are also to blame for the Hindu-Muslim rift. They treated the Muslims as inferiors. Many Hindu moneylenders were extremely tyrannical and also caused Muslims to distrust Hindus. Hindus also did not condone the killing of cows by Muslims, since it is sacred to them. The Muslims took that as an attack on their faith. Many realities and the myth of a conspiracy gradually drew a seizable portion of the Muslims away from the united independence movement. However, many Muslims stayed on in the fight. And among them of course, was Maulana A. K. Azad, one of the great Indian leaders.

The Hindu Muslim division further grew with the Muslim League's defeat in the 1937 elections. When Muhammad Ali Jinnah took over the Muslim League in 1930s, hatred seeped in gradually leading to terrible violence. Muslim league resorted to violence against the Congress and the young Congress members fought back. This was used then by the Muslim League as evidence that the Hindus were attacking the Muslims and further agitated their supporters.

In the light of these results (1937 elections), the leader of the Muslim League, Mohammed Ali Jinnah decided that "... the League should strengthen its attraction to Muslim voters by an appeal to Islamic anxieties". (Denis Judd: ibid.; p. 27). As India slowly slipped out of British control, the British concentrated their efforts to divide India along religious lines. In 1939, Muhammad Ali Jinnah proclaimed the doom of united India. He called for a separate Muslim land. Muslim League cadres adopted terror tactics all over India. Hindu Muslim riots marred the decade of 1940 through out India.

This part is from an eyewitness: August 16, 1946 was an ominous day. It was declared as the Direct Action Day. Most had thought that it was going to be a day when Muhammad Ali Jinnah was going to give a national address at Gorer (Garh, Gaur, Gaud) Math, in Baliganj, Calcutta. However, many Hindus were fearful of anti-Hindu violence. At the very start of the day, there was much rumours of violence. Processions of Muslim League supporters chanting *Arabic* slogans were picketed by their opponents. This got out of hand as the sun climbed the sky. Non-Bengali Muslims (possibly Biharis) armed themselves and other Muslims with sticks (about 5 ft). Some were armed with hockey sticks and iron bars. Knives and other sharp objects were also wielded.

Thus began the '46 riots in Bengal with heavy casualties on both sides. It was apparent that the Muslim League, pawns of the British had succeeded in dividing the Indian people in the name of Islam. Their violent tactics worked to drive a wedge between the people of India.

The Partition

In February 1947, the new Labour Prime Minister, Clement Attlee, "...announced in the House of Commons that the British would withdraw from India not later than June 1948". (Denis Judd: ibid.; p 49).

After the second world war, the British were severely weakened. India on the other hand had also become too rebellious to control. Besides India was no longer a golden egg laying goose for the British. It had become more of a liability. They were weary and finally decided to give up India. However, they played one last nasty trick of "divide and rule" before leaving. They divided India on religious grounds.

And in March 1947 Lord Mountbatten was sworn in as the last Viceroy of India, charged with bringing about "... a transfer of power". (Denis Judd: ibid.; p. 50). to "... 'responsible' hands". ('New Encyclopaedia Britannica', Volume 21; p. 109). (britneo)

They dealt with reformist moderate leaders like Gandhi and Nehru who were not wholly nationalist and had more faith in western systems and the British than on India and her glorious past. The British knew they would be easier to handle In May 1947 Mountbatten showed Nehru a 'secret' British plan, called significantly 'Plan Balkan', which "... devolved power to the provinces, including the princely states". (Denis Judd: ibid.; p. 52).

Nehru denounced the plan as producing "... fragmentation and conflict and disorder". (Jawaharlal Nehru: Letter to Mountbatten, May 1947, in: Denis Judd: ibid.; p.52). (britneo)

As the riots accelerated out of control, Gandhi, and the other leaders of the nation called for an end to the violence. The Congress fought a half hearted battle to save the unity of the nation. The Muslim League armed its separatist cadres and the Congress watched reluctant to take action, as that would be against their pacifism.

Muhammad Ali Jinnah under the tacit support of the British blackmailed the nation causing it to be divided in what I consider a heinous crime against the people. Jinnah was bent on becoming the Prime Minister. He said that he would give up the division of India, and end the violence if he were made the first Prime Minister. But that was not to be.

After much ado, finally Gandhi gave in, much to the disbelief of many of the freedom leaders, and accepted the formation of two separate states, the creation of Pakistan and India. A great tragedy. (Gandhi really had no real authority to make this call in my opinion. One man with a few others did not have that authority to decide to mutilate a nation).

Mass migration that followed was a nightmare, with tremendous suffering. Gandhi's passive resistance led to a passive ethnic cleansing. 600, 000 died and 14 million were displaced in this unfortunate event. It cemented the hatred between Hindus and Muslims. Whatever unity was there was destroyed... may be permanently.

People think of Gandhi brought great success to India. But in reality he was a failure, despite his great popularity. He caused the birth of a nation out of hatred. The division of India was a curse that caused great suffering to millions who were displaced by this ill decision of Gandhi and the treachery of Jinnah. The curse still haunts the people of the subcontinent, by causing many more wars and much more hatred. The only excuse Gandhi may have had was that he made an honest mistake and had no idea of the great tragedy of his decision. For Jinnah, the British puppet, there is perhaps no excuse.

In 1947, India had a bittersweet celebration... India was independent but had lost 27% of her territory which became Pakistan. (Many claim that the partition was by popular demand. There was an election but it was farcical and will be discussed here next.)

Mahatma Gandhi (one of the greatest men despite the division of India) was killed on January 7th by Nathuram Godse, a 25 year old editor and publisher of a Hindu Mahasabha weekly in Poona for conceding the division of the country. Many believe that since most of the Muslim upper class were descendants of foreign occupiers of India just as the British were, they could live in India if they chose to be Indians but Gandhi had no right to give up 27 % of the country to them. It was seen as an act no less than treason by some.

Fate of Bangla

During the partition of India, Bangla was redivided (was first divided in 1906) into two with the western half given to India and the eastern half to Pakistan. East Bengal became the eastern province of Pakistan, called East Pakistan after 1956. The new state of Pakistan consisted of West Pakistan (now Pakistan) on the Arab Sea and East Pakistan (now Bangladesh) on the Bay of Bengal, separated in the middle by 1100 miles of the vast expanse of India. This was an unnatural division since the Bengalis of East Pakistan and the different ethnic peoples of West Pakistanis spoke different languages and followed different customs and had different history and culture. It also divided many Bengali families. The only thing that was common between the two peoples was their religion. Both nations were predominantly Islamic. Of course, the degree of fanaticism varied. In Bangla, many Muslims did not even go to the mosque (now they do).

Other States

To further aggravate the situation, a number of states were left with their fate undecided. The British did not decide whether they should join India or Pakistan. This was a big problem. One of these states was KASHMIR, the beautiful mountain state. The British left the decision to the King of Kashmir. The big problem with Kashmir was that it was a Muslim majority region under the rule of a Hindu king. Pakistan decided arbitrarily, since much of the division was done according to religious distribution, that Kashmir should belong to them. And no sooner had they decided, they sent in tribal warriors and soldiers into Kashmir. Unfortunately for them, the King of Kashmir decided to join India. He officially joined India and India rushed its fledgling troops to Kashmir but Pakistan had already taken much of Kashmir. That was the first war. It ended in the UN. India decided to hold a referendum to allow the people of Kashmir to decide their fate. The UN also said that Pakistan must withdraw its forces as a precondition for India to hold the referendum. Pakistan never withdrew and no referendum was held. That was just the beginning of the Kashmir problem!

INDIAN NATIONAL CONGRESS AND PARTITION OF INDIA

In 1937 elections to Central and Provincial assemblies under the 1935 Act were held and the Congress won majorities of seats in six provinces. In N.W.F.P it constituted the largest single group with 19 members out of 50-member assembly. A similar situation existed in Assam where 33 out of 108 belonged to the Congress party. The Congress High command committed one of those political mistakes which cost the nation dear when it decided that the Congress would form ministries only in those provinces where it had an absolute majority in the assembly, and would not join hands with any other party.

In Bengal when the governor John Herbert invited Sarat Chandra Bose as the leader of the single largest party to discuss the formation of a ministry, he declined the offer. Fazlul Haq, the leader of the Krishak Praja Party, requested Kiran Shankar Roy, the leader of the Congress assembly party to join him to form a coalition government under his leadership. Sarat Chandra Bose who led an unofficial Congress group was inclined to agree and requested Abul Kalam Azad, the Congress President for permission to join hands with Haq taking into account the special situation in Bengal. This ides was said to have the support of Subhash Chandra Bose. But the Congress High command turned it down despite repeated requests. Haq turned to Muslim League, which promptly seized the initiative when it agreed to join the coalition under Haq's leadership. (Nitish Sengupta, History of the Bengali speaking people, p.422) It is said that Gandhiji was unduly influenced by G.D. Birla and Nalini Rangan Sarkar, both representing Indian business interests. Birla as leader of the Marwari business interest strongly felt that a political unity between the Muslims and Hindus in Bengal would threaten Marwari domination over the trade and economy of Calcutta. According to a letter written by Subhash Chandra Bose to Gandhiji dated 21-12-1938 even in the case of Assam, Maulana Azad opposed Subhash's proposal for a coalition ministry and if Sardar Patel had not come forward to support Subhash, Gandhiji would not have accepted his (Subhash) views and no coalition ministry would have been formed in Assam. Azad was against a coalition in Sindh too while Subhash and other members of the Congress working committee were in its favour. According to Maulana Azad Muslim ministries should be accepted where Muslims are in a majority even though those ministries are blatantly communal. (Nitish Sengupta, pp.423-424)

Resignation of Congress Ministries

The Congress committed a big blunder by resigning from the ministries in 1939 on flimsy grounds. Its main grouse was that the government had not taken it into confidence before involving India in the Second World War. By this act, the Congress not only lost power, but also gave way for Muslim League to form ministries in Assam and N.W.F.P. After the resignation of the Congress ministry in Assam, Sir Sadulla formed a League ministry there after succeeding in the game of intense horse-trading with the members of the legislature. He was able to strengthen the roots of the League deep in Assam by his policy of allowing the Muslim migrants of East Bengal to settle indiscriminately in the province. In N.W.F.P. after the Congress ministry went out, Sardar Aurangzeb Khan headed a Muslim League ministry with the support of a few independent Hindu and Sikh legislators. Gradually the League started gaining ground in the Frontier Province, which was evident from its success in four by-elections that followed soon after. (Sailesh Kumar, Muhammad Ali Jinnah and the creation of Pakistan, pp.227-22

The Quit India Movement

But the biggest blunder committed by the Congress was to launch the Quit India movement at a time when Britain was in the brink of the Second World War. Though the Cripps proposal conceded the right of Indians after the cessation of the war to frame a new constitution on dominion status with the right to secede from the empire, the Congress insisted upon immediate establishment of a cabinet form of government at the Centre, with almost all departments of administration transferred to the representatives of the Indian parties and with the Viceroy as a mere figurehead, shorn of all powers. (Tara Chand,.Vol. IV.pp.344,452-453.) As the government did not agree to the Congress demands, on July 14th 1942 the Congress approved a resolution that if the British did not withdraw its rule from India it would launch a nonviolent struggle. On August 8th the Congress met at Bombay and in a resolution decided to launch a mass nonviolent struggle. (Tara Chand,pp.373,375) The movement was not only violent but also did not achieve the desired goal. The British never forgave the Congress for putting them in grave jeopardy by launching the Quit India movement when the going for them in the war was tough. This grudge was further deepened by the war reducing England to a second rate European power that was in no position to hold on to their Indian empire, the loss of which they realized would further weaken their international standing. (H.N.Bali, India's Wounded Polity, p.99)

Anti-Congress Forces Rally

The government decided to rally anti-Congress parties, particularly the League with a view to weaken the Congress. The governors of the Muslim majority provinces obliged Jinnah by contriving the installation of Muslim League ministries and the removal or dismissal of the non-League governments. In Bengal governor John Herbert forced Fazlul Haq to resign and appointed Nazimuddin of the Muslim League as Premier on April 24, 1943. In Sindh Allah Bakhsh, a non-Leaguer expressed disapproval of the repressive policy of government. The governor under Section 51 of the 1935 Act dismissed him and Ghulam Husain Hidayatullah of the Muslim League was asked to assume office in October 1942. (Tara Chand,.Vol. IV pp.388-390). After his return from London in September 1945 Viceroy Wavell announced elections to the Provincial assemblies with a view to convene a constitution making body.

The Congress leadership's demand for freedom assumed distinctly strident notes as Nehru and others plunged in electioneering, touring the country frantically. Nehru's speech in Lahore set the tone and tenor that was qualitatively different from the Pre-Quit India days. "India is on the brink of mighty revolution. Therefore, to vote for the Congress is to vote for the freedom that is coming soon. By your vote you have to declare whether you stand for freedom or slavery. The elections will decide the fate of the Red fort and the Vice regal lodge. Those who try to go against the great gushing torrent of Indian nationalism will be swept ashore lifeless as a log of wood." As Wavell's secret dispatches show, the government didn't take kindly to what was regarded as arousal of masses for violent action. Those whose responsibility it was to maintain law and order read into the speeches of the Congress leaders (particularly Nehru) something far more than election speech. It is most likely that finding the Congress stand hardening by the day as the 1945 elections approached, the British government finalized their plans for the division of the subcontinent to sow the seeds of permanent discord with a view to teaching, as it were, a bitter lesson to India's freedom fighters. (H.N.Bali, p.70).

INDIAN INDEPENDENCE: TRANSFER OF POWER

The postwar Labour government in Britain was committed to independence for India. A second mission was sent to India by Prime Minister Attlee in 1946 for the preparation of independence. On 16 May this Cabinet Mission published a plan for transferring power to a united India, but over subsequent months it became clear that this plan would fail. The British Government therefore began to draw up alternative plans. It also appointed a new Viceroy Lord Mountbatten to take over from Lord Wavell who had failed to get the Indian parties to agree on any plan. In June 1947, Mountbatten announced that Independence would come at Midnight on 14 August 1947.

1946 CABINET MISSION TO INDIA

The British Cabinet Mission of 1946 to India aimed to discuss and plan for the transfer of power from the British Raj to Indian leadership, providing India with independence under Dominion status in the Commonwealth of Nations. Formulated at the initiative of Clement Attlee, the Prime Minister of the United Kingdom, the mission consisted of Lord Pethick-Lawrence, the Secretary of State for India, Sir Stafford Cripps, President of the Board of Trade, and A. V. Alexander, the First Lord of the Admiralty. It was also not supplemented by Lord Wavell, the Viceroy of India at the time.

Purpose and Proposals

The Mission purpose was:

1. Hold preparatory discussions with elected representatives of British India and the Indian states in order to secure agreement as to the method of framing the constitution.
2. Setting up of a constitution body.
3. Setting up an Executive Council with the support of the main Indian parties.

The Mission held talks with the representatives of the Indian National Congress and the All India Muslim League, the two largest political parties in the Constituent Assembly of India. The two parties had planned on coming to terms of power-sharing between Hindus and Muslims to prevent a communal fall-out as well as to determine British India would be better-off unified or divided. The Congress party under Gandhi-Nehru nexus wanted to obtain *absolute* power for their party, having the discretion to deal with Muslim League and Muslims in general at their discretion after the British departed.

The All India Muslim League under Jinnah, wanted to keep India united but with political safeguards provided to Muslims such as 'guarantee' of 'parity' in the legislatures. This stance of the League was backed up by the wide belief of Muslims that the British Raj was simply going to be turned in to a 'Hindu Raj' once the British departed; and since the Muslim League was the sole spokesman party of Indian Muslims, it was incumbent up on it to take the matter up with the Crown. After initial dialogue, the Mission proposed its plan over the composition of the new government on May 16th, 1946:

Plan of May 16

Promulgated on 16 May 1946, the plan to create a united dominion of India as a loose confederation of provinces came to be known by the date of its announcement:

1. A united Dominion of India would be given independence.
2. Muslim-majority provinces would be grouped-Baluchistan, Sindh, Punjab and North-West Frontier Province would form one group, and Bengal and Assam would form another.
3. Hindu-majority provinces in central and southern India would form another group.
4. The Central government would be empowered to run foreign affairs, defence and communications, while the rest of powers and responsibility would belong to the provinces, coordinated by groups.

Plan of June 16

The plan of May 16, 1946 had envisaged a united India in line with Congress and Muslim League aspirations. But that was where the consensus between the two parties ended since Congress abhorred the idea of having groupings of Muslim majority provinces and that of Hindu majority provinces with the intention of 'balancing' each other at the Central Legislature. The Muslim League could not accept any changes to this plan since the same 'balance' or 'parity' that Congress was loathe to accept formed the basis of Muslim demands of 'political safeguards' built in to post-British Indian laws so as to prevent absolute rule of Hindus over Muslims.

Reaching an impasse, the British proposed a second, alternative plan on June 16, 1946. This plan sought to arrange for India to be divided into Hindu-majority India and a Muslim-majority Pakistan, since Congress had vehemently rejected 'parity' at the Centre. A list of princely states of India that would be permitted to accede to either dominion or attain independence was also drawn up.

The Cabinet Mission arrived in India on March 23, 1946 and in Delhi on April 2, 1946. The announcement of the Plan on May 16, 1946 was preceded by the Simla Conference of 1946 in the first week of May.

Reactions and Acceptance

The approval of the plans would determine the composition of the new government. The Congress Working Committee had initially approved the plan. However, on 10 July, Jawaharlal Nehru, who later became the first prime minister of India, held a press conference in Bombay declaring that the Congress had agreed only to participate in the Constituent Assembly and "regards itself free to change or modify the Cabinet Mission Plan as it thought best." The Congress ruled out the June 16 plan, seeing it as the division of India into small states. Moreover,the Congress was a Centralist party. Intellectuals like Kanji Dawarkadas criticized the Cabinet Plan. Congress was against decentralization and it had been under pressure from Indian capitalists who wanted a strong Centre. The plan's strongest opponent was the principal Indian leader Mohandas Gandhi, due to the reason that the territories had been grouped together on the basis of religion.

The Muslim League gave its approval to the plan. There was an impression that the Congress also had accepted the scheme and the Plan would be the basis of the future constitution of India. Jinnah, in his speech to the League Council, clearly stated that he recommended acceptance only because nothing better could be obtained.

However, on declaration from the Congress President that the Congress could change the scheme through its majority in the Constituent Assembly, this meant that the minorities would be placed at the mercy of the majority. The Muslim League Council met at Bombay on 27 July. "Mr. Jinnah in his opening speech reiterated the demand for Pakistan as the only course left open to the Muslim League. After three days' discussion, the Council passed a resolution rejecting the Cabinet Mission Plan. It also decided to resort to direct action for the achievement of Pakistan."

However, the plan had its advocates. Maulana Azad, a nationalist Muslim leader, said that while the groupings were a major concession to the theme of religious separatism, it would also force the League to accept a framework for a united India. While assuring minority rights and participation, an independent India would be free to do away eventually with the groupings arrangement. Gandhi criticized the Maulana's views for ignoring practical considerations and League ambitions.

Formation of a Government

The Viceroy began organizing the transfer of power to a Congress-League coalition. But League president Muhammad Ali Jinnah denounced the hesitant and conditional approval of the Congress and rescinded League approval of both plans. Thus Congress leaders entered the newly styled Viceroy's Executive Council: Jawaharlal Nehru became the head-vice president in title, but possessing the executive authority. Vallabhbhai Patel became the Home member-responsible for internal security and government agencies. Congress-led governments were formed in most provinces-including in the NWFP, in Punjab (a coalition with the Shiromani Akali Dal and the Unionist Muslim League). The League led governments in Bengal and Sindh. The Constituent Assembly was instructed to begin work to write a new constitution for India.

Coalition and Breakdown

Jinnah and the League condemned the new government, and vowed to agitate for Pakistan by any means possible. Disorder arose in Punjab and Bengal, including the cities of Delhi, Bombay and Calcutta. On the League-organized Direct Action Day, over 5,000 people were killed across India, and Hindu, Sikh and Muslim mobs began clashing routinely. Viceroy Wavell stalled the Central government's efforts to stop the disorder, and the provinces were instructed to leave this to the governors, who did not undertake any major action. To end the disorder and rising bloodshed, Wavell encouraged Nehru to ask the League to enter the government. While Patel and most Congress leaders were opposed to conceding to a party that was organizing disorder, Nehru conceded in hope of preserving communal peace.

League leaders entered the council under the leadership of Liaquat Ali Khan, the future first Prime Minister of Pakistan who became the finance minister. But the council did not function in harmony-separate meetings were not held by League ministers, and both parties vetoed the major initiatives proposed by the other, highlighting their ideological differences and political antagonism. At the arrival of the new (and proclaimed as the last) viceroy, Lord Mountbatten of Burma in early 1947, Congress leaders expressed the view that the coalition was unworkable. This led to the eventual proposal, and acceptance of the partition of India

LOUIS MOUNTBATTEN, 1ST EARL MOUNTBATTEN OF BURMA

Admiral of the Fleet Louis Francis Albert Victor Nicholas George Mountbatten, 1st Earl Mountbatten of Burma KG, GCB, OM, GCSI, GCIE, GCVO, DSO, PC, FRS, né Prince Louis of Battenberg (25 June 1900 – 27 August 1979) was a British admiral and statesman of German descent, and an uncle of Prince Philip, Duke of Edinburgh. He was the last Viceroy of the British Indian Empire (1947) and the first Governor-General of the independent Union of India (1947–48), from which the modern Republic of India would emerge in 1950. From 1954 until 1959 he was the First Sea Lord, a position that had been held by his father, Prince Louis of Battenberg, some forty years earlier. In 1979 Mountbatten was assassinated by the Provisional Irish Republican Army (IRA), who planted a bomb in his boat at Mullaghmore, County Sligo in the Republic of Ireland.

Ancestry

Mountbatten was born as *His Serene Highness Prince Louis of Battenberg*, although his German styles and titles were dropped in 1917. He was the youngest child and the second son of Prince Louis of Battenberg and his wife Princess Victoria of Hesse and by Rhine. His maternal grandparents were Ludwig IV, Grand Duke of Hesse and by Rhine and Princess Alice of the United Kingdom, who was a daughter of Queen Victoria and Prince Albert of Saxe-Coburg and Gotha. His paternal grandparents were Prince Alexander of Hesse and Princess Julia of Battenberg. His paternal grandparents' marriage was morganatic, because his grandmother was not of royal lineage; as a result, he and his father were styled "Serene Highness" rather than "Royal Highness," were not eligible to be titled Princes of Hesse and were given the less desirable Battenberg title. His siblings were Princess Andrew of Greece and Denmark (mother of Prince Philip, Duke of Edinburgh), Queen Louise of Sweden, and George Mountbatten, 2nd Marquess of Milford Haven.

His father's forty-five year career reached its pinnacle in 1912 when he was appointed as First Sea Lord in the Admiralty. However, two years later in 1914, due to the growing anti German sentiments that swept across Europe during the first few months of World War I and a series of lost battles at sea, Prince Louis felt it was his duty to step down from the position. In 1917, when the Royal Family stopped using their German names and titles, Prince Louis of Battenberg became Louis Mountbatten, and was created Marquess of Milford Haven. His second son acquired the courtesy style *Lord Louis Mountbatten* and was known as *Lord Louis* informally until his death notwithstanding his being granted a viscountcy in recognition of his wartime service in the Far East and an earldom for his role in the transition of India from British dependency to sovereign state.

Early Life

Mountbatten was home schooled for the first ten years of his life. He was then sent to Lockers Park Prep School and finally he followed his older brother to the Naval Cadet School. In childhood he visited the Imperial Court of Russia at St. Petersburg and became intimate with the doomed Russian Imperial Family; in later life he was called upon authoritatively to rebut claims by pretenders to be the supposedly surviving Grand Duchess Anastasia. As a young man he had romantic feelings towards Anastasia's sister, the Grand Duchess Maria, and until the end of his life he kept her photograph at his bedside. After his nephew's change of name and engagement to the future Queen, he is alleged to have referred to the United Kingdom's dynasty as the future "House of Mountbatten", whereupon the Dowager Queen Mary reportedly refused to have anything to do with "that Battenberg nonsense", and the name of the Royal house remains Windsor by subsequent Royal decree — this can, however, be changed on the Monarch's wishes. After the marriage of Elizabeth II and Prince Philip, it was decreed that their non-royal descendants were to bear the (maiden) surname "Mountbatten-Windsor". Career

Early Career

Lord Mountbatten served in the Royal Navy as a midshipman during World War I. After his service, he attended Christ's College, Cambridge for two terms where he studied engineering in a program that was specially designed for ex-servicemen. During his time at Cambridge, Mountbatten had to balance his studies with the robust social life he enjoyed as a member of Christ's College. In 1922, Mountbatten accompanied Edward, Prince of Wales, on a royal tour of India. It was during this trip that he met and proposed to his wife-to-be Edwina Ashley. They wed on 18 July 1922. Edward and Mountbatten formed a close friendship during the trip but their bond deteriorated during the Abdication Crisis. Mountbatten's loyalties between the wider Royal Family and the throne, on the one hand, and the then-King, on the other, were tested. Mountbatten came down firmly on the side of Prince Albert, the Duke of York, who was to assume the throne as George VI in his brother's place.

Pursuing his interests in technological development and gadgetry, Mountbatten joined the Portsmouth Signal School in 1924 and then went on to briefly study electronics at Greenwich before returning to military service. Mountbatten was a Member of the Institute of Electrical Engineers (IEE), and the successor organisation, the IET, annually awards the Mountbatten Medal for an outstanding contribution, or contributions over a period, to the promotion of electronics or information technology and their application.

In 1926, Mountbatten was appointed to Assistant Fleet Wireless and Signals Officer of the Mediterranean Fleet under the command of Admiral Sir Roger Keyes. Lord Mountbatten returned to the Signal School in 1929 as Senior Wireless Instructor. In 1931, he was again called back to military service when he was appointed Fleet Wireless Officer to the Mediterranean Fleet. It was during this time that he founded a Signal School in Malta and became acquainted with all the radio operators in the fleet.

In 1934, Mountbatten was appointed to his first command. His ship was a new destroyer which he was to sail to Singapore and exchange for an older ship. He successfully brought the older ship back to port in Malta. By 1936, Mountbatten had been appointed to the Admiralty at Whitehall as a member of the Fleet Air Arm.

Patent

In the late 1930s Mountbatten was issued his 2nd Patent (UK Number 508,956) for a system for maintaining a warship in a fixed position relatively to another ship.

Second World War

When war broke out in 1939, Mountbatten was moved to active service as commander of the 5th Destroyer Flotilla from aboard his ship the HMS Kelly, which was famous for its many daring exploits. In early May 1940, Mountbatten led a British convoy in through the fog to evacuate the Allied forces participating in the Namsos Campaign. It was also in 1940 that he invented the Mountbatten Pink naval camouflage pigment. His ship was sunk in May 1941 during the Battle of Crete.

In August 1941 Mountbatten was appointed captain of HMS *Illustrious* which lay in Norfolk, Virginia for repairs following action at Malta in the Mediterranean in January. During this period of relative inactivity he paid a flying visit to Pearl Harbor, where he was not impressed with the poor state of readiness and a general lack of cooperation between the US Navy and US Army, including the absence of a joint HQ.

Mountbatten was a favourite of Winston Churchill (although after 1948 Churchill never spoke to him again since he was famously annoyed with Mountbatten's later role in the independence of India and Pakistan), and on 27 October 1941 Mountbatten replaced Roger Keyes as Chief of Combined Operations. His duties in this role consisted of planning commando raids across the English Channel and inventing new technical aids to assist with opposed landings. Mountbatten was in large part responsible for the planning and organization of The Raid at St. Nazaire in mid 1942: an operation resulting in the putting into disuse of one of the most heavily defended docks in Nazi-occupied France until well after war's end, the ramifications of which greatly contributed to allied supremacy in the Battle of the Atlantic. He personally pushed through the disastrous Dieppe Raid of 19 August 1942 (which certain elements of the Allied military, notably Field Marshal Montgomery, felt was ill-conceived from the start).

The raid on Dieppe was widely considered to be a disaster, with casualties (including those wounded and/or taken prisoner) numbering in the thousands, the great majority of them Canadians. Historian Brian Loring Villa concluded that Mountbatten conducted the raid without authority, but that his intention to do so was known to several of his superiors, who took no action to stop him.

Three noteworthy technical achievements of Mountbatten and his staff include:

(1) the construction of an underwater oil pipeline from the English coast to Normandy,
(2) an artificial harbor constructed of concrete caissons and sunken ships, and
(3) the development of amphibious Tank-Landing Ships.

Another project that Mountbatten proposed to Churchill was Project Habakkuk. It was to be a massive and impregnable 600 meter aircraft carrier made from reinforced ice or "Pykrete." Habakkuk never was actualised due to its enormous price tag.

Mountbatten claimed that the lessons learned from the Dieppe Raid were necessary for planning the Normandy invasion on D-Day nearly two years later. However, military historians such as former Royal Marine Julian Thompson have written that these lessons should not have needed a debacle such as Dieppe to be recognised. Nevertheless, as a direct result of the failings of the Dieppe raid, The British made several innovations-most notably Hobart's Funnies-innovations which, in the course of the Normandy Landings, undoubtedly saved many lives on those three beach heads upon which commonwealth soldiers were landing (Gold Beach, Juno Beach, and Sword Beach).

As a result of the Dieppe raid, Mountbatten became a controversial figure in Canada, with the Royal Canadian Legion distancing itself from him during his visits there during his later career; his relations with Canadian veterans "remained frosty". Nevertheless, a Royal Canadian Sea Cadet corps (RCSCC #134 Admiral Mountbatten in Sudbury, Ontario) was named after him in 1946.

In October 1943, Churchill appointed Mountbatten the Supreme Allied Commander South East Asia Command. His less practical ideas were sidelined by an experienced planning staff led by Lt-Col. James Allason, though some, such as a proposal to launch an amphibious assault near Rangoon, got as far as Churchill before being quashed. He would hold the post until the South East Asia Command (SEAC) was disbanded in 1946.

During his time as Supreme Allied Commander of the Southeast Asia Theatre, his command oversaw the recapture of Burma from the Japanese by General William Slim. Here, he worked closely with esteemed American general Albert Coady Wedemeyer. His diplomatic handling of General "Vinegar Joe" Stilwell — his deputy and also the officer commanding the American China Burma India Theatre — and Generalissimo Chiang Kai-shek, leader of the Chinese Nationalist forces, was as gifted as that of General

Eisenhower with General Montgomery and Winston Churchill. A personal high point was the reception of the Japanese surrender in Singapore when British troops returned to the island to receive the formal surrender of Japanese forces in the region led by General Itagaki Seishiro on 12 September 1945, codenamed Operation Tiderace.

Last Viceroy

His experience in the region and in particular his perceived Labour sympathies at that time led to Clement Attlee appointing him Viceroy of India after the war, charged with overseeing the transition of British India to independence. Mountbatten's instructions emphasised a united India as a result of the transference of power but authorised him to adapt to a changing situation in order to get Britain out promptly with minimal reputational damage.

These priorities in turn affected the way negotiations took place when independence was discussed, especially between divided parties of Hindus and Muslims.

Mountbatten was fond of Congress leader Nehru and his liberal outlook for the country. He felt differently about the Muslim leader Jinnah, but was aware of his power, stating "If it could be said that any single man held the future of India in the palm of his hand in 1947, that man was Mohammed Ali Jinnah". Mountbatten tried to persuade Jinnah of a united India, citing the difficult task of dividing the mixed states of Punjab and Bengal, but the Muslim leader was unyielding in his goal of establishing a separate Muslim state called Pakistan.

Given the British government's urging to grant independence quickly, Mountbatten concluded that a united India was an unachievable goal and he resigned himself to accept a plan that called for the partitioning of an independent India and Pakistan. Mountbatten insisted on setting a set date for the transfer of power from the British to the Indians, arguing that a fixed timeline would convince Indians of his and the British government's sincerity in working towards a swift and efficient independence, excluding all possibilities of stalling the process.

Among the Indian leaders, Gandhi emphatically insisted on maintaining a united India and for a while successfully rallied people to this goal. However, when Mountbatten's timeline put the prospect of actually attaining independence quickly, sentiments took a different turn. Given Mountbatten's determination and Jinnah's obstinacy, all Indian party leaders (except Gandhi) were coming to accept the stance of Jinnah's plan of dividing India, which in turn eased Mountbatten's task.

Mountbatten also developed a strong relationship with the Indian princes, who ruled those portions of India not directly under British rule. On the basis of his relationship with the British monarchy, he persuaded most of them to accede to the new states of India and Pakistan. Whether or not Mountbatten foresaw this development-and thus deliberately enticed the Indian princes into acceding to their soon-oblivion-remains unclear.

When India and Pakistan attained independence in the night from 14 to 15 August 1947, Mountbatten remained in New Delhi for ten months, serving as India's first governor general until June 1948.

Notwithstanding extremely effective self-promotion during his lifetime as to his own part in Indian independence — notably in the television series "The Life and Times of Admiral of the Fleet Lord Mountbatten of Burma", produced by his son-in-law Lord Brabourne, and Dominique Lapierre and Larry Collins's rather sensationalised *Freedom at Midnight* (as to which he was the main informant) — his record is seen as mixed; one view is that he hastened the independence process unduly, foreseeing vast disruption and loss of life and not wanting this to occur on the British watch, but thereby actually causing it to occur, especially during the partition of the Punjab, but also to a lesser extent, in Bengal.

John Kenneth Galbraith, the Canadian-American Harvard University economist, who advised governments of India during the 1950s, became an intimate of Nehru and served as the American ambassador from 1961–63, was a particularly harsh critic of Mountbatten in this regard. The horrific casualties of the partition of the Punjab are luridly described in Collins' and LaPierre's *Freedom at Midnight*, as to which Mountbatten was the principal informant, and more latterly in Bapsi Sidhwa's novel *Ice Candy Man* (published in the USA as *Cracking India*), made into the film *Earth*.

Career after India and Pakistan

After India, Mountbatten served from 1948–1950 as commander of a cruiser squadron in the Mediterranean Fleet. He then went on to serve as Fourth Sea Lord in the Admiralty from 1950–52 and then returned to the Mediterranean Fleet in 1952 to serve as Naval Commander-in-chief for three years. Mountbatten served his final posting in the Admiralty as First Sea Lord from 1955–59, the position which his father had held some forty years prior. This was the first time in Royal Naval history that a father and son had gained so high a rank.

In his biography of Mountbatten, Philip Ziegler notes on his ambitious character: "His vanity, though child-like, was monstrous, his ambition unbridled. The truth, in his hands, was swiftly converted from what it was, to what it should have been. He sought to rewrite history with cavalier indifference to the facts to magnify his own achievements. There was a time when I became so enraged by what I began to feel was his determination to hoodwink me that I found it necessary to place on my desk a notice saying: Remember, in spite of everything, he was a great man."

While serving as First Sea Lord, his primary concerns dealt with devising plans on how the Royal Navy would keep shipping lanes open in the event that Britain was hit with a nuclear attack. Today this seems of minor importance but at the time few people comprehended the potential limitless destruction nuclear weapons possess and the ongoing dangers posed by the fallout. Military commanders had no need to understand the physics involved in a nuclear explosion. This becomes evident when Mountbatten had to be reassured that the fission reactions from the Bikini Atoll tests would not spread through the oceans and blow up the planet. As Mountbatten became more familiar with this new form of weaponry, he increasingly grew opposed to their use in combat yet at the same time he realised the potential nuclear energy had, especially with regards to submarines. Mountbatten clearly expresses his feelings towards the use of nuclear weapons in combat in his article "A Military Commander Surveys The Nuclear Arms Race," which was published shortly after his death in *International Security* in the winter of 1979–80. After leaving the Admiralty, Lord Mountbatten took the position of Chief of the Defence Staff. He served in this post for six years during which he was able to consolidate the three service departments of the military branch into a single Ministry of Defence.

Mountbatten was Governor of the Isle of Wight from 1969 until 1974 and then appointed the first Lord Lieutenant of the Isle of Wight in 1974. He kept the position until his death. From 1967 until 1978, Mountbatten became president of the United World Colleges Organisation, then represented by a single college: that of Atlantic College in South Wales. Mountbatten supported the United World Colleges and encouraged heads of state, politicians and personalities throughout the world to share his interest. Under Mountbatten's presidency and personal involvement, the United World College of South East Asia was established in Singapore in 1971, followed by the UWC of the Pacific (now known as Pearson College) in Victoria, Canada in 1974. In 1978, Lord Mountbatten of Burma passed the Presidency to his great-nephew, HRH The Prince of Wales.

Alleged Plots against Harold Wilson

Peter Wright, in his book Spycatcher, claimed that in 1967 Mountbatten attended a private meeting with press baron and MI5 agent Cecil King, and the Government's chief scientific adviser, Solly Zuckerman. King and Peter Wright were members of a group of thirty MI5 officers who wanted to stage a coup against the then crisis-stricken Labour Government of Harold Wilson, and King allegedly used the meeting to urge Mountbatten to become the leader of a Government of national salvation. Solly Zuckerman pointed out that it was treason, and the idea came to nothing because of Mountbatten's reluctance to act.

In 2006 the BBC documentary *The Plot Against Harold Wilson* alleged that there had been another plot involving Mountbatten to oust Wilson during his second term in office (1974–76). The period was characterised by high inflation, increasing unemployment and widespread industrial unrest. The alleged plot centred around right-wing former military figures who were supposedly building private armies to counter the perceived threat from trade unions and the Soviet Union. They believed that the Labour Party, which is partly funded by affiliated trade unions, was unable and unwilling to counter these developments and that Wilson was either a Soviet agent or at the very least a Communist sympathiser, claims Wilson strongly denied. The documentary alleged that a coup plot was planned to overthrow Wilson and replace him with Mountbatten using the private armies and sympathisers in the military and MI5. The documentary stated that Mountbatten and other members of the British Royal Family supported the plot and were involved in its planning. Wilson had long believed that there had been an MI5 sponsored plan to overthrow him. This suspicion was heightened in 1974 when the Army occupied Heathrow Airport on the grounds that it was training for a possible IRA terrorist action there. Marcia Falkender, a senior aide and intimate friend of Wilson, asserted that the Prime Minister hadn't been informed of the exercise and that it was ordered as a practice-run for a military takeover. Wilson was also convinced that a small group of right-wing MI5 officers were conducting a smear campaign against him. Such allegations had previously been attributed to Wilson's paranoia, not least because in 1988, Peter Wright admitted that the allegations in his book were "unreliable" and greatly exaggerated. However the BBC documentary interviewed several new witnesses who gave new credibility to the allegations.

Crucially, the first official history of MI5, *The Defence of the Realm* published in 2009, tacitly confirmed that there was a plot against Wilson and that MI5 did have a file on him. Yet it also made clear that the plot was in no way official and that any activity centred around a small group of discontented officers. This much had already been confirmed by former cabinet secretary Lord Hunt, who concluded in a secret inquiry conducted in 1996 that, "There is absolutely no doubt at all that a few, a very few, malcontents in MI5... a lot of them like Peter Wright who were rightwing, malicious and had serious personal grudges – gave vent to these and spread damaging malicious stories about that Labour government." Mountbatten's role in the plotting remains unclear. At the very least he appears to have associated with people who were greatly concerned about the country in the 1970s and were prepared to consider acting against the Government. It also seems certain that he shared their concerns. However, even though the BBC documentary alleged that he had offered his services to the coup plotters, it cannot be confirmed that he actually would have led a coup had it come about. It is notable that any plots that were discussed never actually took place, perhaps because the number of people involved was so small that any chances of success were slim.

Personal Life

Marriage: Mountbatten's nickname among family and friends was "Dickie," notable in that "Richard" was not among his given names. This was because his great-grandmother, Queen Victoria, suggested the nickname of "Nicky", however it got mixed up with the many Nickys of the Russian Imperial Family ("Nicky" was particularly used to refer to Nicholas II, the last Tsar) so they changed it to Dickie.

Mountbatten was married on 18 July 1922 to Edwina Cynthia Annette Ashley, daughter of Wilfred William Ashley, later 1st Baron Mount Temple, himself a grandson of the 7th Earl of Shaftesbury. She was the favourite granddaughter of the Edwardian magnate Sir Ernest Cassel and the principal heir to his fortune. There followed a glamorous honeymoon tour of European courts and America which famously included a visit with Douglas Fairbanks, Mary Pickford, and Charlie Chaplin in Hollywood, Chaplin creating a widely seen home movie "Nice and Easy", featuring the talents of Fairbanks, Pickford, Chaplin, and the Mountbattens. They had two daughters: Patricia Mountbatten, 2nd Countess Mountbatten of Burma (born on 14 February 1924), and Lady Pamela Carmen Louise (Hicks) (born on 19 April 1929).

The couple, in some ways, seemed incompatible from the beginning. Lord Mountbatten's obsession with being organised led him to keep a very close watch on Edwina and he demanded her constant attention. Having no real hobby or passions and living the lifestyle of royalty, Edwina spent most of her time partying with the British and Indian elite, going on cruises and secluding herself at the couple's country house on weekends. Even with growing unhappiness on both their parts, Louis refused to get a divorce fearing that it would hinder his climb up the military command chain.

There were charges of infidelity against both. Edwina's numerous affairs led Louis to pursue a relationship with a French woman named Yola Letellier. From this point forward their marriage disintegrated into constant accusations and suspicions. Throughout the 1930s both readily admitted to numerous affairs. World War II gave Edwina the opportunity to focus on something other than Louis' infidelity. She joined the St. John's Ambulance Brigade as an administrator. This role gave Edwina the legacy of being a heroine of the Partition Period because of her efforts to ease the pain and suffering of the people in the Punjab.

It has been well documented that Edwina and India's first PM Jawaharlal Nehru became intimate friends after Indian Independence. During the summers, she would frequent the PM's house so she could lounge about on his veranda during the hot Delhi days. Personal correspondence between the two reveals a satisfying yet frustrating relationship. Edwina states in one of her letters "Nothing that we did or felt would ever be allowed to come between you and your work or me and mine — because that would spoil everything." Despite this, it is still debated whether or not their relationship became physical. Both Mountbatten daughters have candidly acknowledged that their mother had a fiery temperament and was not always supportive of her husband when jealousy of his high profile overbore a sense of their having common cause. Lady Mountbatten died on 21 February 1960 at the age of 58 while in North Borneo inspecting medical facilities. Her death is thought to have been caused by a heart condition.

Until his assassination in 1979, Mountbatten kept a photograph of his cousin Grand Duchess Maria Nikolaevna of Russia, beside his bed in memory of the crush he once had upon her.

Daughter as Heir

Since Mountbatten had no sons, when he was created Viscount on 23 August 1946, then Earl and Baron on 28 October 1947, the Letters Patent were drafted such that the titles would pass to the female line and its male issue. This was at his firm insistence: his relationship with his elder daughter had always been particularly close and it was his special wish that she succeed to the title in her own right. There was longstanding precedent for such remainders for military commanders: past examples included the 1st Viscount Nelson and the 1st Earl Roberts.

Leisure Interests

Like many members of the royal family, Mountbatten was an aficionado of polo, and received U.S. patent 1,993,334 in 1931 for a polo stick.

Mentorship of Prince of Wales

Mountbatten was a strong influence in the upbringing of his great-nephew, The Prince of Wales, and later as a mentor—"Honorary Grandfather" and "Honorary Grandson", they fondly called each other according to the Jonathan Dimbleby biography of the Prince—though according to both the Ziegler biography of Mountbatten and the Dimbleby biography of the Prince the results may have been mixed. He from time to time strongly upbraided the Prince for showing tendencies towards the idle pleasure-seeking dilettantism of his predecessor as Prince of Wales, King Edward VIII, later known as the Duke of Windsor, whom Mountbatten had known well in their youth. Yet he also encouraged the Prince to enjoy the bachelor life while he could and then to marry a young and inexperienced girl so as to ensure a stable married life.

Mountbatten's qualification for offering advice to this particular heir to the throne was unique; it was he who had arranged the visit of George VI and Queen Elizabeth to Dartmouth Royal Naval College on 22 July 1939, taking care to include the young Princesses Elizabeth and Margaret in the invitation, but assigning his nephew, Cadet Prince Philip of Greece, to keep them amused while their parents toured the facility. This was the first recorded meeting of

Charles's future parents. But a few months later, Mountbatten's efforts nearly came to naught when he received a letter from his sister Alice in Athens informing him that Philip was visiting her and had agreed to permanently repatriate to Greece. Within days, Philip received a command from his cousin and sovereign, King George II of the Hellenes, to resume his naval career in Britain which, though given without explanation, the young prince obeyed.

In 1974 Mountbatten began corresponding with Charles about a potential marriage to his granddaughter, Hon. Amanda Knatchbull. It was about this time he also recommended that the 25-year-old prince get on with sowing some wild oats. Charles dutifully wrote to Amanda's mother (who was also his godmother), Lady Brabourne, about his interest. Her answer was supportive, but advised him that she thought her daughter still rather young to be courted. Four years later Mountbatten secured an invitation for himself and Amanda to accompany Charles on his planned 1980 tour of India. Their fathers promptly objected. Prince Philip thought that the Indian public's reception would more likely reflect response to the uncle than to the nephew. Lord Brabourne counselled that the intense scrutiny of the press would be more likely to drive Mountbatten's godson and granddaughter apart than together.

Charles was re-scheduled to tour India alone, but Mountbatten did not live to the planned date of departure. When Charles finally did propose marriage to Amanda, later in 1979, the circumstances were tragically changed, and she refused him.

Death

Mountbatten usually holidayed at his summer home in Mullaghmore, County Sligo, a small seaside village between Bundoran, County Donegal and Sligo, County Sligo, on the northwest coast of Ireland. Bundoran was a popular holiday destination for volunteers of the IRA, many of whom were aware of Mountbatten's presence and movements in Mullaghmore. Despite security advice and warnings from the Garda Síochána, on 27 August 1979, Mountbatten went lobster-potting and tuna fishing in a thirty-foot (10 m) wooden boat, the *Shadow V*, which had been moored in the harbour at Mullaghmore. An IRA member named Thomas McMahon had slipped on to the unguarded boat that night and attached a radio-controlled fifty-pound (23 kg) bomb. When Mountbatten was on the boat en route to Donegal Bay, an unknown person detonated the bomb from shore. McMahon had been arrested earlier at a Garda checkpoint between Longford and Granard. Mountbatten, then aged 79, was seriously wounded and died soon after the blast by drowning while unconscious in the bay. Others killed in the blast were Nicholas Knatchbull, his elder daughter's 14-year-old son; Paul Maxwell, a 15-year-old youth from County Fermanagh who was working as a crew member; and Baroness Brabourne, his elder daughter's 83-year-old mother-in-law who was seriously injured in the explosion, and died from her injuries the following day. Nicholas Knatchbull's mother and father, along with his twin brother Timothy, survived the explosion but were seriously injured.

McMahon was sentenced to life imprisonment for murder on 23 November 1979. Sinn Féin vice-president Gerry Adams said of Mountbatten's death: The IRA gave clear reasons for the execution. I think it is unfortunate that anyone has to be killed, but the furor created by Mountbatten's death showed up the hypocritical attitude of the media establishment. As a member of the House of Lords, Mountbatten was an emotional figure in both British and Irish politics. What the IRA did to him is what Mountbatten had been doing all his life to other people; and with his war record I don't think he could have objected to dying in what was clearly a war situation. He knew the danger involved in coming to this country. In my opinion, the IRA achieved its objective: people started paying attention to what was happening in Ireland.

On the same day Mountbatten was assassinated, the IRA also ambushed and killed eighteen British Army soldiers, sixteen of them from the Parachute Regiment at Warrenpoint, County Down, in what became known as the Warrenpoint ambush.

Prince Charles took Mountbatten's death particularly hard, remarking to friends that things were never the same after losing his mentor. It has recently been revealed that Mountbatten had been favourable towards the eventual reunification of Ireland.

9

Partition and Independence of India

In 1900, India was part of the British Empire; but by the end of 1947, India had achieved independence. For most of the Nineteenth Century, India was ruled by the British. India was considered the jewel in the crown of the British Empire. Queen Victoria had been made Empress of India and the British had a major military presence in India. Indian nationals had no say in central government and even at a local level, their influence on policy and decision making was minimal. In 1885, educated middle class nationals had founded the Indian National Conference (INC). Their aim was to get a much greater say in the way India was governed. In response to this development, the Morley-Minto reforms were introduced in 1909. Morley was the Secretary of State for India and Lord Morley was Viceroy of India. Their reforms lead to each province in India having its own governor and Indian nationals were allowed to sit on the councils which advised these governors. After 1918, nationalism within India intensified. This was probably due to 2 reasons:

1. Many educated nationals in India were far from satisfied with the Morley-Minto reforms. White Englishmen still dominated India and there had been no real decrease in their power or increase in national power. The INC (Indian National Council) wanted a lot more.
2. Woodrow Wilson had stimulated the minds of many people with his belief in national self-determination – i.e. that

> people from a country had a right to govern themselves. The whole concept of national self-determination undermined the basic idea of the British Empire – that the British governed this empire (or people appointed by the British to do the same). For national self-determination to fully work, India would have to be governed by the Indians living there.

As early as 1917, Britain had toyed with the idea of giving India a measure of self-government: "the gradual development of self-governing institutions with a view to the progressive realisation of responsible government in India as an integral part of the British Empire".

In 1919, the Government of India Act was introduced. This introduced a national parliament with two houses for India. About 5 million of the wealthiest Indians were given the right to vote (a very small percentage of the total population) Within the provincial governments, ministers of education, health and public works could now be Indian nationals A commission would be held in 1929, to see if India was ready for more concessions/reforms. However, the British controlled all central government and within the provincial governments, the British kept control of the key posts of tax and law and order.

Many Tory MP's in Britain were against the whole idea of giving anything whatsoever to India in terms of self-government.

They had two complaints about the whole idea:

1. If you gave India some form of self-rule, where would it end?
2. Would it start the process that would lead to the break-up of the British Empire?

The reforms were introduced very slowly and their spread throughout such a large country was equally as slow. This angered many as there was a general belief that the British were deliberately stalling on introducing these reforms to ensure their continued supremacy in India.

Riots did break out and the most infamous was at Amritsar in the Punjab where 379 unarmed protesters were shot dead by

British soldiers based there. 1200 were injured. This incident shocked many in India but what caused equal outrage was the British reaction to Amritsar – the officer commanding British troops at Amritsar, General Dyer, was simply allowed to resign his commission after an inquiry criticised his leadership during the riot. Many national Indians felt that he, and others in the army, had got away very lightly. The more radical Indians felt that the British government had all but sanctioned murder.

As a result of Amritsar, many Indians rushed to join the INC and it very quickly became the party of the masses. The most vocal opponent of the idea of some form of self-rule for India was Lord Birkenhead whole was Secretary of State for India from 1924 to 1928. With such an opponent, any move to self-rule was very difficult at best, and probably impossible in reality.

In India, the 1920's saw the emergence of three men who were to have a huge impact on the future of India:

- Jawaharlal Nehru
- Mahatma Gandhi
- Muhammed Jinnah.

Gandhi persuaded many of his followers to use nonviolent protests. They had sit-down strikes, they refused to work, they refused to pay their taxes etc. If the British reacted in a heavy-handed manner, it only made the British look worse; essentially, the British would come across as bullies enforcing their rule on the bullied. However, there were those in India who wanted to use more extreme measures.

Part of the 1919 Government of India Act stated that a commission would be established after 10 years to assess whether India could/should have more self-rule. This first met in 1928 – the Simon Commission. This commission reported in 1930. There were no Indians on the commission. It proposed self-government for the provinces but nothing else. This was unacceptable for the INC, which wanted dominion status, granted immediately.

During the time the Simon Commission reported, Gandhi started his second civil disobedience campaign. This included Gandhi deliberately breaking the law. The law in India stated that only the government could manufacture salt. After a 250-mile march to the sea, Gandhi started to produce his own salt. This produced a violent clash with the British authorities and Gandhi was arrested.

At this time, a sympathetic Viceroy to India had been appointed – Lord Irwin. He believed that India should have dominion status – and he publicly expressed this idea. Irwin pushed for the issue to be discussed. He organised two Round Table conferences in 1930 and 1931. They were both held in London.

The first conference failed as no INC members were present. Most were in Indian prisons. Irwin pushed for their release and he persuaded Gandhi to travel to Britain to take part in the second conference. Despite this development, the conference achieved little as it broke down over an issue that was to haunt India in future years – religion. Those present at the second conference, argued and failed to agree over what the representation of Muslims would be in an independent Indian parliament. In 1935, the Government of India Act was introduced. Britain, at this time, had a National Government and progress was made over India purely because Stanley Baldwin, the Tory leader, and Ramsey-MacDonald, the Labour leader, agreed on a joint course of action. Winston Churchill was bitterly opposed to it. The Act introduced:

An elected Indian assembly to have a say in everything in India except defence and foreign affairs. The eleven provincial assemblies were to have effective full control over local affairs. The nationalists in India were not satisfied with this as the act did not introduce dominion status and white dominions were allowed to control their own defence and foreign policies. Also the princes who still ruled areas of India still refused to co-operate with the provincial assemblies so the second strand of the Act would have been meaningless. The act's major failing was that it ignored the religious rivalry between the Muslims and Hindus. Nearly two-thirds of India's population were Hindus and the Muslims feared that in an independent and democratic India they would be treated unfairly. In the 1937 provincial elections, the Hindus, who dominated the Congress Party under Nehru, won eight out of the eleven provinces.

The Muslim League under Jinnah demanded a separate state of their own to be called Pakistan. Both Gandhi and the Congress Party were determined to preserve Indian unity. Such a rivalry between the Hindus and Muslims could only bode ill for the future of India. World War Two shelved the Indian issue – albeit temporarily. The Indians provided valuable military help in the fight against Japan especially in the campaign in Burma. The British promised dominion status for India once the war had ended.

In 1945, the newly elected Labour government headed by Clement Attlee wanted to push ahead with solving what was seen as the "Indian Problem". However, the religious rivalry in India was coming to a head and made any potential solution very complex.

Attempts to draw up a compromise constitution that was acceptable to both Muslims and Hindus failed. The British plan was to allow the provincial governments extensive powers whilst central government would only have limited powers. The Labour government put its faith in the hope that most Muslims lived in one or two provinces and that the governments in these provinces would reflect this in their decision making. If this plan worked, the need for a separate Muslim state would not be needed. The plan was accepted in principle but the details for it were not.

The Governor-General of India, Lord Wavell, invited Nehru to form an interim government in August 1946. Wavell hoped that the details of such a government could be sorted out later– but he hoped that the creation of an actual government headed by Indian nationals would be supported by all. The Hindu Nehru included two Muslims in his cabinet but this did not succeed in stopping violence. Jinnah became convinced that Nehru could not be trusted and he called on Muslims to take "direct action" to get an independent Muslim state. Violence spread and over 5000 people were killed in Calcutta. India descended into civil war.

Early in 1947, Atlee announced that Britain would leave India no later than June 1948. A new Viceroy was appointed– Lord Mountbatten – and he concluded that peace could only be achieved if partition was introduced. The Hindu Congress agreed with him.

Mountbatten became convinced that any delay would increase violence and he pushed forward the date for Britain leaving India to August 1947. In August 1947, the Indian Independence Act was signed. This separated the Muslim majority areas (in the northwest and northeast regions of India) from India to create the independent state of Pakistan. This new state was split in two, the two parts being 1000 miles apart. The act was not easy to put into action.

Some people found themselves on the wrong side of frontiers especially in the mixed provinces of the Punjab and Bengal. Millions moved to the new frontiers – Hindus in what was to be the new Pakistan moved to India while Muslims in India moved to Pakistan. Where the two moving groups met, violence occurred especially in the volatile Punjab province where it is though 250,000 people were murdered in religious clashes. By the end of 1947, it seemed as if the violence was on the wane but in January 1948, a Hindu assassinated Gandhi. In a gesture that summed up the whole problem of India, the Hindu detested Gandhi's tolerance towards Muslims. However, the murder of Gandhi shocked so many people, that ironically it ushered in a period of stability.

MOUNTBATTEN'S PLAN OF PARTITION

After difficult negotiations a federal solution was proposed. Despite initial agreement, both sides eventually rejected the plan. An interim government with representatives of all the Indian parties was proposed and implemented. However, it soon collapsed through lack of agreement. While the Muslim League consented to join the interim government the Indian National Congress refused.

By the end of 1946 communal violence was escalating and the British began to fear that India would descend into civil war. The British government's representative, Lord Wavell, put forward a breakdown plan as a safeguard in the event of political deadlock. Wavell, however, believed that once the disadvantages of the Pakistan scheme were exposed, Jinnah would see the advantages of working for the best possible terms inside a united India. He wrote: 'Unfortunately the fact that Pakistan, when soberly and realistically examined, is found to be a very unattractive proposition, will place the Moslems in a very disadvantageous position for making satisfactory terms with India for a Federal Union.' This view was based on a report, which claimed that a future Pakistan would have no manufacturing or industrial areas of importance: no ports, except Karachi, or rail centres. It was also argued that the connection between East and West Pakistan would be difficult to defend and maintain. The report concluded:

'It is hard to resist the conclusion that taking all considerations into account the splitting up of India will be the reverse of beneficial as far as the livelihood of its people is concerned'. Lord Mountbatten replaced Lord Wavell as Viceroy of India in 1947.

Mountbatten's first proposed solution for the Indian subcontinent, known as the 'May Plan', was rejected by Congress leader Jawaharlal Nehru on the grounds it would cause the 'balkanisation of India'. The following month the 'May Plan' was substituted for the 'June Plan', in which provinces would have to choose between India and Pakistan. Bengal and Punjab both voted for partition.

On 3 June 1947, Lord Mountbatten announced his plan. The salient features were:-

1. Mountbatten's formula was to divide India but retain maximum unity. The country would be partitioned but so would Punjab and Bengal, so that the limited Pakistan that emerged would meet both the Congress and League's position to some extent. The League's position on Pakistan was conceded to the extent that it would be created, but the Congress position on unity would be taken into account to make Pakistan as small as possible. Whether it was ruling out independence for the princes or unity for Bengal or Hyderabad's joining up with Pakistan instead of India, Mountbatten firmly supported Congress on these issues.
2. The Mountbatten Plan sought to effect an early transfer of power on the basis of Dominion status to two successor states, India and Pakistan. For Britain, Dominion Status offered a chance of keeping India in the commonwealth for India's economic strength and defence potential were

deemed sounder and Britain had a greater value of trade and investment there.

3. The rationale for the early date for transfer of power was securing Congress agreement to Dominion status. The additional benefit was that the British could escape responsibility for the rapidly deteriorating communal situation.
4. A referendum was to be held in NWEP to ascertain whether the people in the area wanted to join India or not. The princely states would have the option of joining either of the two dominions or to remain independent. The Provinces of Assam, Punjab and Bengal were also to be divided. A boundary commission was to be set up to determine the boundaries of these states.

Reasons for the Acceptance of "Partition" by the Congress

By accepting the Mountbatten Plan/Partition, the Congress was only accepting what had become inevitable because of the long-term failure of the Congress to draw in the Muslim masses into the national movement and stem the surging waves of Muslim communalism, which, especially since 1937, had been beating with increasing fury.

The Congress leaders felt by June, 1947 that only an immediate transfer of power could forestall the spread of Direct Action and communal disturbances. Sardar Patel rightly said, "a united India even if it was smaller in size was better than a disorganised and troubled and weak bigger India."

TRUE HISTORY OF INDEPENDENCE AND PARTITION OF INDIA

Common impression in India and the world is that Atlee and Labour Party were good and wanted to give independence to India after WW II, but due to differences among Indian leaders, they had to divide the country. This belief is based on British version and is totally false. History books written in Britain, US, and even in India are based on this version. The truth is England did NOT want their raj to end in India. Atlee, Cripps, Labour Party and Churchill wanted British raj to continue in India. The British propagated this version to hide their guilt. One million Indians were killed and 12 million were forced to migrate leaving their homes where they had lived for centuries due to British plan to partition India. This false version of Indian history is very injurious to India. It is high time that we learn our true history, so that we can defend ourselves and will not repeat old mistakes. Independence was not due to good will of England but due to balance of military force.

To understand the history of 1946-1948 period, it is necessary to know a few ideas. Mao said that political power comes from the barrel of a gun. This has been always true in the past, is true even now and will remain so in future. Idealism has no place in politics, which concerns with power-how to get it and how to use it after getting it. An imperial power rules by the policy of "divide and rule". Previously an imperial power ruled the subject country directly and exploited it. As this became unpopular, imperialism changed its form into neo-imperialism. Divide and rule became "divide and dominate." The imperial power does not rule directly but through appointed ruler and exploits the subject country. The US developed this method of neo-imperialism in the 19th century in South America. The South American countries were politically and internationally free. The invisible empire was economic. It exploited and dominated. The invisible empire is not resented, as people do not see it, as is the case with political domination.

Gandhiji used to describe the British policy of divide and rule as monkey justice from an Aesop's fable. This fable is about two cats, which were fighting for the just division of a loaf of bread and went to a monkey to divide it justly between them. The monkey deliberately divided the bread into two unequal pieces. When the cat with smaller piece objected, the monkey took a big bite from the bigger piece, so that it became smaller. The other cat objected now and the monkey kept on taking bites from the bigger piece, till the cats found that the monkey had eaten all the bread while pretending to divide it equally.

When Viceroy Linlithgow's replacement was considered in 1943, Prime Minister Churchill wanted his trusted lieutenant, Eden as Viceroy. Churchill told Eden on April 21, 1943 that "what a calamity it would be to win the war and lose India." Eden opposed the idea because he felt once he was out in India; he could not be considered Churchill's successor. Churchill agreed with Eden on this point and after lot of arguments dropped the idea. Churchill selected General Wavell in stead in June 1943 to hold the status quo in India till war end. Then Wavell was Commander-in Chief of British Indian Army. This shows the British had no intention of leaving India. Labour Minister in Labour government wanted Libya for Britain in the discussion of disposal of Italian colonies in the meeting of big powers, even though the British government had declared earlier that Britain did not want any new colony after the war,

When Viceroy Wavell went to London, he met Bevin and Alexander on December 21, 1945. He writes that Bevin like everyone else hated the idea of leaving India, but Bevin had no alternative to suggest. Bevin said that America was very much worried about India and did not want England to leave India. Wavell replied that US had changed its policy, now they could hardly expect British to face another Palestine in India, because it suited American commercial interest that Britain should remain in India. All this proves that the British and even US did not want the raj to end in India.

There were many reasons put together why Britain had to give India independence. Gandhiji's Satyagrah movements in 1920s and 1930s, the widespread Quit India movement in 1942, formation of Indian National Army by Subhas Chandra Bose in South East Asia, trial of I.N.A officers, then mutiny of Indian navy and air force, sending of Indian army to Indo-China and Indonesia to take surrender for Japan, expansion of Indian army to 2.5 lacs to fight expected Japanese invasion of India made Wavell realize that he could not trust the loyalty of Indian army and England could not rule India militarily. To control India militarily, British policy had been to have one British soldier to two Indians in the Indian Army. This changed due to wartime expansion from 210,000 troops to 2.5 million, making Indian Army preponderantly Hindu with number of British troops remaining at 70,000. Moreover England had become very weak economically and militarily after war end. Only one year after it's declaration of war against Germany in September 1939, it found it had spent most of its gold and dollar reserves. It had to depend on the US for money and arms to carry on the war. Britain's worldwide empire was based on naval supremacy. After the war the British Navy was not the strongest. Atom bomb appeared as a weapon of war, but Britain had no atom bombs. Naval ships could be destroyed by aeroplanes.

Hence Wavell made a blue print of Pakistan in December 1945 and sent it to Secretary of State for India in a most secret letter. This letter has been now made public. The letter reveals that partition was necessary to protect British interests in Asia and NOT Muslim interests as believed in India and Pakistan. Aim was to protect Near East from Soviet expansion to Indian Ocean and oil wells there. The English had been working on creation of Pakistan since 1888.

The Cabinet Delegation was sent to India in March 1946 ostensibly to help Indians to become free but really to make Indians agree to Partition. To further this aim, the English made Jinnah start communal riots to prove that Hindus and Muslims cannot live together and the country had to be divided. One million lives were lost in communal riots during 1946-1947. Though the British were powerless to control India, they had enough power to create trouble before leaving. Indian navy was much weaker than Royal Navy, which could blockade India and prevent import of many necessary items. To defeat Congress demand for a free united India, they threatened that if Congress did not agree to partition they would leave India in more than 500 pieces. Sardar Patel had become in charge of Home in the provisional government in September 1946. He read all secret government papers and found how the British were intriguing to make India very weak before departure. He decided that it was better to accept India in two parts rather than in more than 500. In December 1946, he made V.P. Menon make a blue print of partition, which was different from Wavell's partition plan. It was this plan, which was ultimately adopted in August 1947. Patel talked to Nehru about his idea, but Nehru said that Gandhiji would never agree to this plan. Gandhiji had realized the harm to India from partition and declared that partition would take place over his dead body. Gandhiji was willing to have a civil war to prevent partition. Patel told Nehru that he would make Gandhiji agree to his plan. Both went to Gandhiji and told him about Patel's idea. Gandhiji asked them if they had become afraid due to loss of lives in raging communal riots in India. Both Patel and Nehru replied that they were not scared, but facts had to be faced. And that it would be better to accept partition. Gandhiji agreed to partition on condition that it would be a partition between two brothers. The wily English defeated Gandhiji's wish by creating Kashmir problem so that the two nations would keep fighting. Patel explained later in November 1947 the logic for acceptance of partition. He said that with Partition 80 % of India would be free. India will develop economically and militarily and then take the other 20%.

Partition took place on August 14 and 15, 1947. All top civil and military officers were British in Pakistan. They made a plan for Pakistan to attack Kashmir, which had not decided which Dominion to accede, with some tribesmen and Pakistan Army men in mufti to invade Kashmir on October 20. This made Maharaja and National Conference of Shiekh Abdullah ask for India's help. After accepting accession, Indian army was sent to prevent the Pak invaders from occupation of Kashmir. As the fighting was going on, Mountbatten asked Congress leaders not to attack Pakistan but to complain to UN. Gandhiji, Nehru and Patel were against Mountbatten's suggestion, but Nehru had to agree as Britain reduced supply of arms and petrol to India to put pressure to agree to go to UN. As expected, UN, dominated by US and England did not declare Pakistan as an aggressor, but appointed a mediator (i.e. justice monkey). Pakistan was never declared an aggressor and it continues to occupy parts of Kashmir.

To say that Jinnah created Pakistan is a joke. Jinnah had no gun to get political power. Jinnah was ignorant and he allowed the British to use him as a stooge to divide the country. Later Jinnah himself realized his mistake and wanted India and Pakistan to unite just before his death. Jinnah may be called second Mir Jafar.

PARTITION OF INDIA 1947

The systematic exploration that the partition of the Indian subcontinent demands vis-à-vis it's planning and implementation has largely escaped the attention of writers and scholars of Indian history. Political accounts of official policies and procedures that precipitated partition have generally formed the core of major studies made on the subject. The human dimension constituting the violent aftermath of partition and resulting from a hasty planning and an even more ill-conceived implementation has also not been catalogued in detail and density that its scale and historical importance might warrant. It is indeed true that issues relating to the historic event that produced two new nation-states on the subcontinent in 1947 have received comparatively greater importance in the recent years and a kind of 'partition industry' seems to have been set in motion.

Nevertheless, most works still concentrate on the political or rather official aspect of it. Some social and cultural studies highlighting the 'human dimension' have surfaced in the last decade or so, but the overtones ascribe a rather melancholy if not an altogether macabre touch to the division of India as if its happening was indeed a misdeed. Some scholars of Modern South Asia have even begun to use the term 'holocaust' for the tumultuous episode of the partition either in a direct context or by assumption.

Works of Ritu Menon, Kamla Bhasin, Gyanendra Pandey, Urvashi Butalia and most recently Madhav Godbole are some instances. Such studies having emerged in the last two decades and mainly falling in the realm of social history have attempted to change the mind set in which partition was so far understood. Literary efforts had always been there to capture through drama the agony of millions who crossed over from one land to another or lost their lives. But society becoming an academic subject of post partition milieu is a recent and fast developing phenomenon highlighting human sufferings in all their agonising details.

There is no denying the fact that partition was a painful event in the light of the violence and dislocation it brought in its wake with thousands killed and millions displaced, yet not a 'tragedy' as some prefer to regard it and for which catharsis has not yet come about. Moreover, partition must also be considered synonymous to a nationalist struggle that culminated in independence and freedom for a great multitude of souls held in bondage for over a century. The history of this struggle needs an authentic and objective analysis not only of the course that it followed or the humanistic perspective that it developed but the sheer manner in which it was planned by the departing authorities.

It was not the act but the way it was performed that has brought a whole aura of negativism to be associated with such a historic episode leading many to state and believe that it was a mistake. Partition needs to be salvaged from such a myopic approach to be redefined as the most significant event in the evolution of South Asia as a socio-political unit.7

The Indian subcontinent was partitioned on the forceful demand of the Muslims represented by Jinnah and the Muslim League. It was neither the desire of the British nor the dream of the Hindu led Congress to see India divided and separate states emerging out of a single and united entity. The fact that Pakistan was, nonetheless, created speaks volumes of a leader's perseverance and a nation's will to sacrifice for the cause of independence. The British could not reconcile to the ending of a Raj they had come to regard as their most prized possession and the Hindus could hardly accept their motherland breaking up and the Muslims gaining a land of their own. The plan to bring about such a partition that did not enjoy the willing acceptance of two out of three major parties involved, therefore, offers an interesting study for therein lie most of the troubles that the nascent state of Pakistan had to encounter soon after independence.

The question as to 'Why' India was divided has been debated upon from almost all conceivable angles and in almost all the studies that have been conducted on the subject. It is the essential theme on which revolves the political writings of Modern South Asia. It is the issue of 'How' India was partitioned that has received much less of any serious attention. More than sixty years have elapsed since, the occurrence and that definitely gives sufficient historical period to reflect upon its ramifications. In other words most of the studies conducted so far on partition revolve around factual details and the analysis of the outcome of this historic deed.

Very few have deliberated upon it as an act in its own right with direct emphasis upon its planning and execution. Though many would find no benefit in repeating old and worn out arguments of apportioning blame for the communal frenzy that accompanied the execution of Partition Plan, it nevertheless, remains a reality which has for long suffered unfortunate scholarly neglect and unwarranted academic evasiveness. The onus of partition has to be appropriately delegated to the rightful doer, as it entails matters of intense and very sensitive nature. The British having reluctantly accepted partition found themselves in a tight niche; the desire to appease the Congress on the one hand and to fulfill the Muslim League demand for Pakistan, on the other required a level of impartiality and administrative acumen, the combination of which was no minor task.

A subcontinent was being divided with a great chunk of its population and assets. The planning to execute and implement this was indeed a job that needed sufficient time and efforts of a high calibre. The framework that was ultimately approved to work out the modalities of the division of India, by authorities in London, compromised on both with the result that partition became synonymous to a colossal tragedy. Some writers of partition history hold the view that the Indian leaders, mostly tired old men, sacrificed the national cause by seising the first opportunity to grasp power and thus hastily accepted partition of India.

It is, however, the definition of this 'national cause' and its interpretation that has largely made this argument controversial and debatable. Indian destiny might have been in the hands of these, as some tend to believe, worn out men who were only jockeying for power, and not actually fighting a freedom struggle, but the goal orientation of individual leaders varied and made all the difference in the final analysis. For some it was nothing more than preserving the unity of India and for others nothing less than partition and a separate homeland. This was the difference in the Congress and the Muslim League perspectives.

Independence from the British, however, remained a common ideal with both and it was towards this end and on this ideal that all efforts were concentrated. Moreover, the whims and idiosyncrasies of individuals do not alone create nations; the conjunction of forces and circumstances do. In case of India, however, leadership remained a crucial factor all along that played its role forcefully and very effectively. The British considered partition to be a natural consequence of the communal divide, a very normal sequel to the age old Hindu-Muslim enmity, something that they failed to acknowledge was of their own doing. The policies of the colonial government and its representatives, so central to the evolution of 'separatist politics' in India, however, speak an altogether different jargon, that does not either lift the burden of responsibility from their shoulders nor exonerate them of the gruesome errors committed in executing the deed of partitioning India.

In the decade preceding the divide all attempts made at the official level to resolve the communal deadlock aimed at preserving the unity of India one way or the other. As late as August 1945 Churchill was advising the then Indian Viceroy Lord Wavell "to keep a bit of India" and the last constitutional effort that came in the form of Cabinet Mission in 1946 was essentially for a union of India and reluctant to accept the idea of partition straightaway. Then there were occasions that the British could have acted positively to heal the growing rift between Muslims and Hindus as in the fateful days of 1937 Congress Ministries. But they preferred to watch the developments with mild complacency and woke up to the fearful consequences when even the most desperate efforts could not avert them.

It was, however, the last act of the drama ‑ the partition of India; its planning and implementation ‑ that exposed and revealed the policies of the Raj, its intentions, motives and limitations, like no other prior episode had done. The holocaust that accompanied partition was undoubtedly the end result of human errors and not the culmination of long term trends in the Indian polity. Never before had South Asian history witnessed so few deciding the future and the fate of so many. The political negotiations of the last ten years of British rule in India seem to have been made up of a policy of delaying tactics so obviously conspicuous in the picture from 1940 onwards.

Finally, when it appeared impossible to sit on the political fence indefinitely until the two parties resolved their major disputes, partition remained the only option to avoid outright civil war and anarchy, and the only way to conduct a graceful retreat. However, with thousands raped and massacred, and millions uprooted and displaced, it could hardly be termed graceful. Moreover, as far as the British were concerned the constitutional change that they so magnanimously brought about in the form of partition was not designed to destroy but preserve and develop an important relationship. Prime Minister Attlee's historic reading of the Indian Independence Bill on 4th July 1947 in the House of Commons that "this Bill brings to an end one chapter in the long connection between Britain and India, but it opens another," clearly influenced the way in which the British were conducting their part of the negotiations for a complete transfer of power.

The role of individual leaders who by their acts of omission or commission made partition a *fait accompli* offers interesting insight into the making of a plan for dividing India. Lord Mountbatten as the last Viceroy of united India assumes the most controversial place in the vast gallery of leaders in the final phase of India's freedom movement. Appointed by Attlee to replace Lord Wavell at one of the most sensitive times in South Asian history when the subcontinent was on the brink of a major change, Mountbatten arrived with a prepared agenda, extraordinary powers, special instructions and a selected staff.

This change in Viceroyalty has remained a contentious issue not only because Wavell was removed so unceremoniously long before the completion of his term but also because India of 1947 could not afford a replacement of such a massive scale given the economic, political and communal crisis. But Mountbatten as was soon revealed was a man given the task of averting partition if not independence to which the British had already committed themselves in Attlee speech of February 1947. To establish his credibility he carried with him the precise date ‾ 30th June 1948, by which the British intended to make a peaceful transfer of power to Indian hands.

At least British withdrawal was in sight even if partition still remained a subject to contend with, largely because it jeopardised British interests of keeping a united India in the commonwealth. June 1948 gave to the British authorities a mere fifteen months to wrap up an empire whose political, administrative and constitutional decisions were far too tricky to be resolved in such a short period. The issues were many and needed not only concentrated attention but essentially a lot more time that was finally made available. There was the question of law and order which loomed large particularly in the Punjab given the hold of the

Sikhs who were apprehensive and extremely jittery about the division of the province. The Princely States posed yet another sensitive issue that demanded careful handling, which unfortunately it did not receive and opened up a new chapter of tension and turmoil in South Asian history. Kashmir stands even to the present day as a bitter legacy of mishandling the partition process. Then there was the crucial matter of the division of the Indian armed forces along with its so many allied subjects. Mountbatten's abilities might have been varied as believed by those who chose him for the task. Attlee's belief was that only a new man could find a new way, for in his view the Indian situation demanded a different style and a fresh handling, but Mountbatten's approach towards resolving practical problems of the day remained overshadowed by an imperialist thinking pattern and ill-conceived Congress links.

His personal charm and charisma could have carried the opinion of many in his favour but the ground realities of dividing an empire needed more solid credentials than that. Apart from the fact that his administration was the last British government of India, he brought few new ideas. It was above all the 'antedating' of partition by Mountbatten from June 1948 to August 1947 that resulted in one of the greatest upheavals in recorded human history. At the most conservative estimate 200,000 people had been killed and five million made homeless. Figures may vary but their staggering nature remains in tact. The justifications extended for this early transfer of power

To project an image of victory in retreat, they put a lot at stake in India, throwing to the winds their responsibility of ensuring a smooth transfer of power to the successor states. It was the 'manner and method'of partition that resulted in a high cost of human lives and brought untold misery to millions.This 'hurried scuttle'have been numerous given by all shades of British historians but the real fact of the matter was none other than a desire for pressing on to glory in the annals of future history by achieving a fast handover of formal authority.

The capacity of the government to control the situation or the parties was fast diminishing and it was essential to transfer power before nothing was left to transfer. Moreover, it was the price paid to the Congress for consenting to stay within the commonwealth and for this one benefit the British were prepared to go to any extremes, even at the cost of severely threatening the interests of the other party, *i.e.*, the Muslim League. Mountbatten realised the gravity of the situation and forwarded his plan of 3 June 1947, after hasty negotiations and talks with Indian leaders led to partition as the only logical conclusion of the problem. The British Cabinet urged by him to make haste also approved of the plan within a week, virtually unaltered. All this surely gives a lucid insight into British policy at this precise moment in Indian history, for only a couple of weeks earlier they had been seeking the new Viceroy to work for a united India. Could have been avoided only if the British had considered their obligation to the India they so proudly ruled over

Mountbatten's role holds verdict to not only hasty and flawed planning of one of the greatest events of history but also to the farce of impartiality that he conveniently and boastfully adhered to but could not honour in the entire partition proceedings. He had a reasonably good idea of the colossal administrative difficulties involved in the transfer of power, had been in knowledge of what was happening particularly in the Punjab through his Governor Evan Jenkins, but still preferred to mess up the entire situation with his ill-placed sense of urgency and speed. For Pakistan it amounted to nothing but a calculated attempt to bring about a complete breakdown of political, administrative and economic structures.

For a person who comes to India as a Viceroy with a mandate of rendering the subcontinent independent and for supervising British withdrawal, with intentions and instructions to the effect that Indian union can still be preserved, but under the compulsion of circumstances, is forced to draw a plan for partition for which he has just seventy two days, could not be expected to do justice either to his role or to his task.

Time became a matter of the most crucial importance. Nations that take thousands of years to be built deserve at least some reasonable time to go through the process of reorganisation and re-demarcation if such a need arises, given the complex nature of their administrative and constitutional systems. The division of India was one such case that put to test the abilities of those who had once ruled over an extensive empire but unfortunately could not live up to the tradition of that 'glorious' past in working out a smooth transfer of power to two successor states. The issues were varied and each demanded separate and individual attention for which not only expertise but time was required. It was a commodity the importance of which was neglected altogether leading to a speedy and scuttled transfer with extraordinary misfortune attending upon the populace caught in the turmoil.

The demarcation of boundaries resulted in a movement of people which has been described as the largest migration of its kind in world history. The planning to set India free had started with Prime Minister Attlee's announcement of February 20, 1947, both in India and Great Britain and its culmination was the Radcliffe Award of August 1947 that initiated the process of chalking out the boundaries of the new states. It was the result of prolonged deliberations to meet the deadline of a hasty decision and the outcome of this decision proved to be one of the most fateful in the history of South Asia.

The two Boundary Commissions that were constituted by June 30 1947, had members both from the Congress and the Muslim League. Sir Cyril Radcliffe chaired both the commissions, for the division of the Punjab and Bengal, that were evenly divided between pro-India and pro-Pakistan members with the chairman holding the all important power of the deciding veto. When he was initially approached to act as the chairman of the commission, the date of granting independence was June 1948, which was later brought back to August 15, 1947 as announced in the Mountbatten Plan of June 3, 1947. Herein lay not only Radcliffe's difficulties but this acceleration of the process of independence with the Award of the Boundary Commission creating the most serious of all crisis, consequently also effected the new states, in particular Pakistan, largely because of its vulnerability that was left inherent in its roots at inception.

Radcliff Award has been critically analysed from various standpoints; that it was an arbitrary and biased Award far from the judicious document that it was supposed or acclaimed to be; that Radcliffe had virtually no idea of the Indian terrain that he was assigned to dissect being only at the mercy of maps and that the Award came two days after independence causing not only confusion and chaos but huge loss of precious human lives. But still the need to review it remains pressing, for its rulings were at the core of all the injustices that were done to Pakistan in the early days of its birth. Despite all British proclamations, Mountbatten was tacitly kept informed about the proceedings of the Boundary Commissions and the details of not only their findings but also decisions. Kashmir dispute that has crippled the relations of the two states for all the years of their existence, was not merely a legacy of partition but more specifically of the Radcliffe Award.

Then the lines demarcated on the map ran through villages and deserts, along rivers and canal banks and at some points across waterways, railways and roads. The demarcation of such complex boundaries of which Radcliffe had only a cursory knowledge added to the misery of the inhabitants of a nascent state. Such circumstances were bound to give rise to boundary disputes of serious magnitude. Finally, the delay in the announcement of the Award served as the proverbial last nail in the coffin.

Here again Radcliffe acted on the behest of Lord Mountbatten who did not wish to tarnish the grandeur and glamour of independence celebrations by letting people know of the fate that lay in store for them and thereby unleashing a chain of violent communal strife. Not only that but it was also an impulsive attempt to avoid turning a day of rejoicing into one of mourning over disappointed territorial hopes. The Award came on August 17, two days after freedom had dawned on the subcontinent horizon with the people rejoicing the birth of a new era but unaware of the true nature of their identity and forced to embark upon unplanned migrations under extremely unguarded and dangerous circumstances.

A job that required months of grueling paperwork and hectic ground activity was completed in thirty six days, and by the time it was made public, its chief architect Sir Cyril Radcliffe had left India, unable and unwilling to face the consequences of his deed. The implementation of the Partition Plan entered its final phase as the two nations began a frenzied move to divide the assets of a united India into two halves. It entailed a very sensitive aspect since, the two states were technically equal inheritors to the departing authority of the British government.

The assets of the Government of India consisted of almost everything ranging from the armed forces, waterways and railway networks down to printing presses, chairs and typewriters, and offered a challenge of no less magnitude than the division of the subcontinent itself. It was further aggravated by the heavy influx of refugees on both sides that Gyanendra Pandey chooses to call the 'third partition'. For the state of Pakistan these issues once again spelled disaster as

Hindustan was taken to be the actual successor of former India and Pakistan was just cutting itself off from India. In all the assets Pakistan's share remained cut to the minimum; in cash payments, arms and ammunition, railways, industries, secretarial staff and structure or canal and water distribution the Congress/British liaison remained strong and over bearing.

The question of the division of army posed the most serious of all problems. It was on this score that the new governments faced a big challenge given the very sensitive composition of the British Indian Army. On Jinnah's insistence it was decided that the armed forces were to be split up on communal lines, dividing Hindu and Muslim regiments respectively. No other decision could have suited the nature of the defence requirements of the two nations more adequately in the existing scenario that was charged with a heightened level of communal tension and strife.

However, the whole idea of dividing the Indian Armed Forces remained abhorrent to the British till the very end even when partition had been accepted in principle and reality by all parties concerned. Mountbatten had carried with him specific instructions "to avoid a break in the continuity of the Indian Army." Field Marshal Sir Claude Auchinleck the Commander-in-Chief of the British Indian Army also refused to hear of any such plan that would split up an institution they had built up so proudly and with so much devotion and skill. The delay in such a sensitive matter of national importance suited the Congress designs well, as it would inherit the capital at New Delhi along with its civil and military administration, including control over the armed forces.

The result of yet another mismanaged affair was obvious. Pakistan ended up with its share of military stores withheld, with not even a single ordnance factory, with shortages in technical arms and trained personnel and with only one school of instruction at Quetta. The decision regarding the fate of Princely States was no small issue when preparations for implementing the Partition Plan actually began. Junagardh, Kashmir and Hyderabad had not come to any agreement with regard to their future course of action at the time of independence in August 1947. Had the British conduct been more impartial and had the Congress adhered to the generally accepted and jointly agreed upon principles of geographical contiguity and notional representation as laid down in the Partition Plan, Indo-Pak history might have not been blemished by so much strife and turmoil as in the early years of freedom.

Nehru's passionate attachment to Kashmir swayed the balance in favour of India and the last act of the drama saw the Maharaja signing the instrument of accession for India resulting in the speedy landing of Indian troops to forcibly occupy the state. Among the scars of partition it is the one still profusely bleeding. The amicable structures that the two states are now struggling to build could have been established decades ago, only if the last Viceroyalty in its connivance with the Congress had not failed so miserably in this respect. Its performance was undoubtedly flawed in the most important matters concerning the partition of the Indian subcontinent.

INDEPENDENCE DAY (INDIA)

India's Independence Day is celebrated on 15 August to commemorate its independence from British rule and its birth as a sovereign nation on that day in 1947. The day is a national holiday in India. All over the country, flag-hoisting ceremonies are conducted by the local administration in attendance. The main event takes place in New Delhi, where the Prime Minister hoists the National Flag at the Red Fort and delivers a nationally televised speech from its ramparts. In his speech, he highlights the achievements of his government during the past year, raises important issues and gives a call for further development. The Prime Minister also pays his tribute to leaders of the freedom struggle. A colourful pageant showcasing India's cultural diversity, symbolic depictions of the country's advances in science and technology, and a joint display of India's military capabilities by the armed forces are an essential part of the Independence Day celebrations.

Road to Independence

Main articles: History of Independent India, Political Integration of India, and Partition of India

On 3 June 1947, Viscount Lord Mountbatten of Burma, the last British Governor-General of India, announced the partitioning of the British Indian Empire into India and Pakistan, under the provisions of the Indian Independence Act 1947. At the stroke of midnight, on 14 August 1947, India became an independent nation. This was preceded by Pandit Jawaharlal Nehru's famous speech titled Tryst with Destiny.

"At the stroke of the midnight hour, when the world sleeps, India will awake to life and freedom. A moment comes, which comes but rarely in history, when we step out from the old to the new, when an age ends, and when the soul of a nation, long suppressed, finds utterance..... We end today a period of ill fortune, and India discovers herself again."

Celebrations

Prime Minister of India hoists the Indian flag on the ramparts of the this historical site, Red Fort, Delhi, On August 15. 15 August is a national holiday in India.

Government Offices are lit up. Flag hoisting ceremonies and cultural programs take place in all the state capitals. In the cities around the country the national flag is hoisted by politicians in their respective constituencies.

In various private organisations the flag hoisting is carried out by a senior official of that organisation. Schools and colleges around the country organise flag hoisting ceremonies and various cultural events within their premises, where younger children in costume do impersonations of their favourite characters of the Independence era. Families and friends get together for lunch or dinner, or for an outing. Housing colonies, cultural centres, clubs and societies hold entertainment programmes and competitions, usually based on the Independence Day theme. Most national and regional television channels screen old and new film classics with patriotic themes on Independence Day

INDEPENDENCE DAY IN INDIA

About Independence Day

"A moment comes, which comes but rarely in history, when we step out from the old to the new...India discovers herself again."-J.L.Nehru

On the eve of India's independence, Pandit Jawaharlal Nehru famous speech "Tryst with Destiny" marked the beginning of a free India with words symbolizing hope and triumph. India got its independence from the clutches of British rule on 15th August

1947. It was this day when India's tricolor flag was unfolded by Pandit Nehru on the barricades of the Red Fort at Delhi. Each and every patriotic soul watched with excitement and paid tribute to thousands of martyrs who sacrificed their lives for India's freedom.

The Independence Day of India is a moment of delight and grandeur but to achieve it the nation had to put up a long battle for over two centuries against the British Empire. At last on 3rd June 1947, the last British Viceroy of India, Lord Mountbatten of Burma, declared the separation of the British Empire in India into India and Pakistan. The announcement was made under the terms of the Indian Independence Act 1947.

Significance of Independence Day

The significance of the Independence Day in the existence of a nation is of greater value. The day is much more than merely celebrating the anniversary of India's free statehood. On this day India attained a major part of Asian subcontinent's 562 extensively spread territories besides British owned states.

15th August 1947 symbolizes the victory of Indian patriotism which the nation got after uncertain yet brutal struggle from the repression of the British colonialism. The British, who oppressed India for centuries had primarily arrived to initiate business but steadily captured the entire government of the nation. They educated the Indians and in the process generated enthusiasts who weren't hesitant in helping them expanding their regime.

Men and women from all over India joined hands and fought for India's freedom. Many were acclaimed while others contribution went unnoticed. However, praise wasn't what they desired for. It was the dream of free and autonomous India which motivated them to walk the path of struggle unselfishly. Neither did they battle for their region nor for their natives, but for India and Indians.

At the time of growing communal and caste conflicts, it becomes significant to remind us that the people who laid the foundation of free India has always dreamt of an integrated nation. Hence, it is our duty to live and sustain their dreams, the sole reason for which Independence Day in India is observed.

It is a day to pay a mark of respect to our saviors because of whom we are breathing an air of freedom which does not have the elements of exploitation and repression.

Independence Day Celebrations in India

Independence Day is considered as a national holiday in India. The arrangement begins a month before the D-day and the roads are embellished with ribbons and Indian flags.

Flag-hoisting ceremonies are executed all over India by state governments. However, the chief event is conducted in the capital city of India, New Delhi where the Prime Minister of India unfurls the tricolor at the barricades of Red Fort which receives a salutation of 21 guns, and addresses the nation with his speech.

The Prime Minister's speech holds major importance as it pays tribute to the great souls who sacrificed their lives for nation's independence and reveals the achievements of the nation during the past year beside discussing significant issues and proposing steps for further growth.

A vibrant parade exhibiting India's cultural multiplicity, emblematic portrayals of the nation's developments in science and technology, a collaborative parade of India's armed competencies by the three forces and patriotic skits and dramas by school children are an integral part of the Independence Day festivities.

On this day the skyline of the capital city gets sprinkled with innumerable multicolored kites. People indulge in kite flying competitions and children cheer aloud elevating the spirit of the day.

India Political Impasse and Independence

The Congress neither acknowledged the Muslim League's performance, albeit poor, in the elections nor deigned to form a coalition government with the League, a situation that led to the collapse of negotiations and mutual trust between the leaders. Mohammad Ali Jinnah, a Western-educated Muslim lawyer, took over the presidency of the moribund Muslim League and galvanized it into a national force under the battle cry of "Islam in danger." Jinnah doubted the motives of Gandhi and Nehru and accused them of practicing Hindu chauvinism. He relentlessly attacked the Congress-led ministries, accusing them of casteism, corruption, and nepotism.

Skillfully, he succeeded in unifying various regional Islamic organizations and factions in Punjab and Bengal under the umbrella of the Muslim League.

Electoral gains by the Congress in 1937 were rendered ephemeral as its leaders ordered provincial ministries to resign in November 1939, when the viceroy (Victor Alexander John Hope, Marquis of Linlithgow—1936-43) declared India's entrance into World War II without consulting Indian leaders. Jinnah and the Muslim League welcomed the Congress withdrawal from government as a timely opportunity and observed a day of thanksgiving on December 22, 1939. Jinnah persuaded the participants at the annual Muslim League session in Lahore in 1940 to adopt what later came to be known as the Pakistan Resolution, demanding the division of India into two separate sovereign states, one Muslim, the other Hindu. Although the idea of Pakistan had been introduced as early as 1930 at Allahabad, very few had responded to it. However, the volatile political climate, the personal hostilities between the leaders, and the opportunism of Jinnah transformed the idea of Pakistan into a popular demand.

Independence of India

Between 1940 and 1942, the Congress launched two abortive agitations against the British, and 60,000 Congress members were arrested, including Gandhi and Nehru. Unlike the uncooperative and belligerent Congress, the Muslim League supported the British during World War II. Belated but perhaps sincere British attempts to accommodate the demands of the two rival parties, while preserving the unitary state in India, seemed unacceptable to both as they alternately rejected whatever proposal was put forward during the war years. As a result, a three-way impasse settled in: the Congress and the Muslim League doubted British motives in handing over power to Indians, while the British struggled to retain some hold on India while offering to give greater autonomy.

The Congress wasted precious time denouncing the British rather than allaying Muslim fears during the highly charged election campaign of 1946. Even the more mature Congress leaders, especially Gandhi and Nehru, failed to see how genuinely afraid the Muslims were and how exhausted and weak the British had become in the aftermath of the war. When it appeared that the Congress had no desire to share power with the Muslim League at the centre, Jinnah declared August 16, 1946, Direct Action Day, which brought communal rioting and massacre in many places in the north. Partition seemed preferable to civil war. On June 3, 1947, Viscount Louis Mountbatten, the viceroy (1947) and governor-general (1947-48), announced plans for partition of the British Indian Empire into the nations of India and Pakistan, which itself was divided into east and west wings on either side of India. At midnight, on August 15, 1947, India strode to freedom amidst ecstatic shouting of *"Jai Hind"* (roughly, Long Live India), when Nehru delivered a memorable and moving speech on India's "tryst with destiny." Independence of India-*Data 1995*. Courtesy Library of Congress.

Bibliography

Ahmad, Razi: *Iqbal's Letters to Quaid-i-Azam*, Lahore, Friends Educational Service, 1976.

Ahmed, Waheed: *Quaid-I-Azam Muhammed Ali Jinnah : Speeches Indian Legislative Assembly 1935-1947*, Quaid-i-Azam Accademy, 1991.

Akbar S.: *Jinnah, Pakistan, and Islamic Identity: The Search for Saladin*, 1997.

Ammu Menon: *Social Welfare in India; Mahatma Gandhi's Contributions*, Asia Pub. House, London, 1964.

Anand, Som: *Lahore: Portrait of a Lost City*. Lahore: Vanguard Books, 1998.

Ansari, Sarah: *Life after Partition: Migration, Community and Strife in Sindh: 1947—1962*. Oxford, UK: Oxford University Press, 2005.

Balan, K. : *Mahatma Gandhi and Jawaharlal Nehru : The Two Stalwarts Who Shaped India*, Delhi, Authorspress, 2002.

Bhattarcharjea, Ajit: *Countdown to Partition: The Final Days*. New Delhi: HarperCollins, 1998.

Brahm Datt: *Gandhi and Gandhism Unmasked: Was Gandhi a Traitor?*, India: Erabooks, New Delhi, 1992.

Campbell-Johnson, Alan: *Mission with Mountbatten*. London: Hale, 1982.

Chathanatt, S.J. John : *Gandhi and Gutierrez : Two Paradigms of Liberative Transformation*, New Delhi, Decent Books, 2004.

Chatterji, Joya: *Bengal Divided: Hindu Communalism and Partition, 1932—1947*. Cambridge and New York: Cambridge University Press, 2002.

Chaudhary, M.: *Partition and the Curse of Rehabilitation*. Calcutta: Bengal Rehabilitation Organization, 1964.

Chopra, P. N.: *Towards Freedom: Documents on the Movement for Independence in India, 1937*. Delhi: Oxford UP, 1986.

Das, Dipty Moyee : *Gandhi's Doctrine of Truth and Non-Violence : A Critical Study*, New Delhi, Dominant Pub., 2008.

Dhawan, S.K. : *Discovery of Indira Gandhi : A Select Chronology*, Wave Pub., Delhi, 1986.

Dominique Lapierre: *Freedom at Midnight*. London: Collins, 1975.

Erik H.: *Gandhi's Truth: On the Origins of Militant Nonviolence*, W. W. Norton, New York, 1969.

Gandhi, Sita : *In the Shadow of Mahatma : A Grand-Daughter Remembers*, New Delhi, Sampark, 2005.

Gaur, Mahendra : *Indian Political Parties Annual*, Delhi, Kalpaz Pub., 2006.

Gossman, Partricia: *Riots and Victims: Violence and the Construction of Communal Identity Among Bengali Muslims, 1905-1947*. Westview Press, 1999.

Gupta, P. S.: *Towards Freedom: Documents on the Movement for Independence in India, 1942-1944*. Delhi: Oxford UP, 1997.

Hodson, H. V.: *The Great Divide: Britain-India-Pakistan*, Karachi, Oxford UP, 1993.

Ikram, S. M.: *Indian Muslims and Partition of India*. Delhi: Atlantic, 1995.

Jafar, Malik Muhammad: *Jinnah as a Parliamentarian*, Lahore, Afzar Publications, 1977.

Johari, J.C. : *Indian Political System : A Critical Study of the Constitutional Structure and the Emerging Trends of Indian Politics*, 1996.

Khan, Yasmin: *The Great Partition: The Making of India and Pakistan*, New Haven and London: Yale University Press, 2007.

Lumby, E. W. R.; and Moon, Penderel: *India: The Transfer of Power 1942-1947*, London, 1983.

Memon, M. U.: *An Epic Unwritten: The Penguin Book of Partition Stories*. New Delhi: Penguin, 1998.

Mohini Gupta : *Cross-Currents of Indian History and Culture : The Gandhian Era*, New Delhi, Radha, 2007.

Mukhtar, Zaman: *Students' Role in the Pakistan Movement*. Karachi, Quaid-iAzam Academy, 1978.

Nevile, P.: *Lahore: A Sentimental Journey*. New Delhi: Penguin, 1993.

Pandey, B. N.: *The Break-up of British India*. London: Macmillan, 1969.

Sherwani, L. A.: *The Partition of India and Mountbatten*, Karachi, Council for Pakistan Studies, 1986.

Tinker, Hugh: *Experiment with Freedom, India and Pakistan 1947*. London: Oxford UP, 1967.

Wolpert, Stanley A. : *Tilak and Gokhale: Revolution and Reform in the Making of Modern India*, Berkeley, 1962.

Index

□□□